ALFRED HITCHCOCK'S AMERICA

America Through the Lens
Martin Scorsese's America, Ellis Cashmore
Alfred Hitchcock's America, Murray Pomerance
Spike Lee's America, David Sterritt
Steven Spielberg's America, Frederick Wasser

ALFRED HITCHCOCK'S AMERICA

MURRAY POMERANCE

polity

Copyright © Murray Pomerance 2013

The right of Murray Pomerance to be identified as Author of this Work has been asserted in accordance with the UK Copyright, Designs and Patents Act 1988.

First published in 2013 by Polity Press

Polity Press
65 Bridge Street
Cambridge CB2 1UR, UK

Polity Press
350 Main Street
Malden, MA 02148, USA

All rights reserved. Except for the quotation of short passages for the purpose of criticism and review, no part of this publication may be reproduced, stored in a retrieval system, or transmitted, in any form or by any means, electronic, mechanical, photocopying, recording or otherwise, without the prior permission of the publisher.

ISBN-13: 978-0-7456-5302-0
ISBN-13: 978-0-7456-5303-7 (pb)

A catalogue record for this book is available from the British Library.

Typeset in 10.75 on 14 pt Adobe Janson
by Toppan Best-set Premedia Limited
Printed and bound in Great Britain by the MPG Books Group

The publisher has used its best endeavours to ensure that the URLs for external websites referred to in this book are correct and active at the time of going to press. However, the publisher has no responsibility for the websites and can make no guarantee that a site will remain live or that the content is or will remain appropriate.

Every effort has been made to trace all copyright holders, but if any have been inadvertently overlooked the publisher will be pleased to include any necessary credits in any subsequent reprint or edition.

For further information on Polity, visit our website: www.politybooks.com

3 1327 00575 2548

to Andrew Hunter

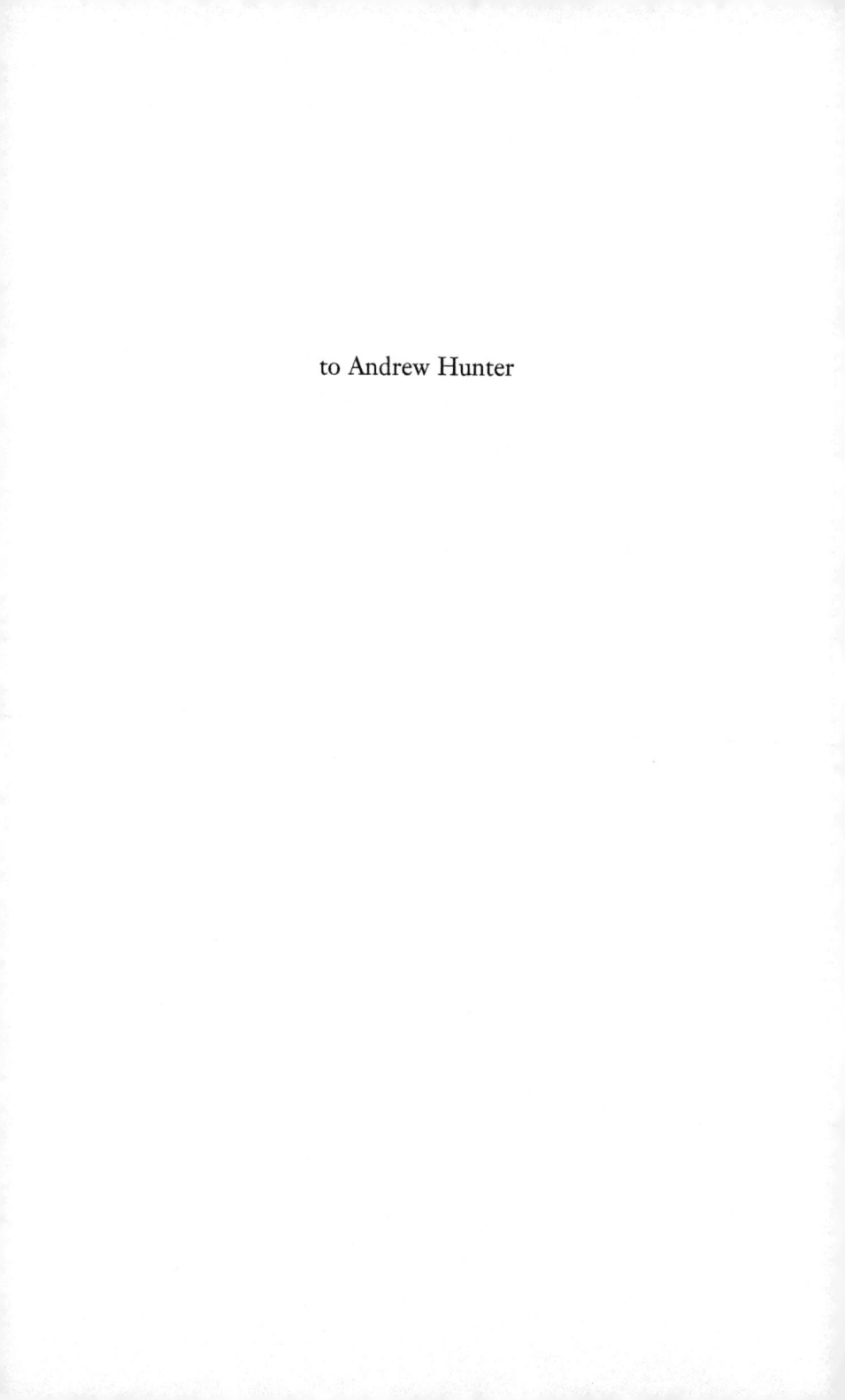

CONTENTS

Acknowledgments   ix

   Introduction: Alfred Hitchcock in America   1
1   Hitchcock's American Scapes   18
2   Hitchcock's American Personalities   71
3   Hitchcock and American Values   123
4   Hitchcock and American Social Form   176
5   Hitchcock and the American Marriage   225

Works Cited and Consulted   284
Index   305

If you want to understand my films, you have to see the landscapes of my America.

Stéphane Delorme paraphrasing Abel Ferrara,
Cahiers du cinéma (October 2011)

*

All of us who worked learned a great deal from Hitch. . . . He became fascinated with America. . . . He became very interested in America and he became a very staunch supporter of America and American ideals.

Robert Boyle

ACKNOWLEDGMENTS

I would like to express my sincere gratitude to a number of individuals without whose gracious assistance I would not have been able to complete this volume: Mark Pane and Judith Wolfe, Amagansett Free Library; Anastasia Kerameos, Library of the British Film Institute; Allie Berntsen, Sue Guldin, Barbara Hall, Kristine Krueger, Linda Harris Mehr, Jenny Romero, Faye Thompson, and the staff of the Margaret Herrick Library, Academy of Motion Picture Arts and Sciences, Beverly Hills; Sandra Joy Lee Aguilar and Jonathon Auxier, Warner Bros. Archive, Library of the University of Southern California; as well as to Janet Lum, Associate Dean, Research and Graduate Studies, Faculty of Arts, Ryerson University. For support in acquiring a number of the images included here I thank Philip Coppack and Wade Pickren, Ryerson University. And I am indebted for their kind assistance and generous help to Kate Barrett (Greensboro) and Linda Barrett (New York); Daniel Browne (Toronto); Terry Dale (Los Angeles); Mark Kermode

(Southampton); Bill Krohn (Los Angeles); Jerry Mosher (Long Beach); William Rothman (Miami), Nick White (Toronto), and Linda Ruth Williams (Southampton). My colleagues at Polity Press, Susan Beer, Neil de Cort, Andrea Drugan, Lauren Mulholland, and Vanessa Parker, have made this work a constant pleasure. Thanks also to Ian Mottashed and Eric Schramm. And my family partners, Nellie Perret and Ariel Pomerance, have been insightful, patient, and an energizing inspiration.

INTRODUCTION: ALFRED HITCHCOCK IN AMERICA

At seven o'clock in the evening of Monday, June 6, 1938, about an hour and twenty minutes before sunset, the Queen Mary docked at West Fiftieth Street and Twelfth Avenue, New York, and within the hour Alfred Hitchcock, his wife Alma, and their daughter Patricia stepped into the United States. Alfred and Alma would soon turn thirty-eight; Patricia would soon turn ten. Hitchcock had in fact been charmed by things American, especially the American city, since as a boy he memorized train and trolley schedules from printed pamphlets that had become his treasure. One of his biographers, Patrick McGilligan, suggests that "early in life he learned from Americans and practiced American strategies" and quotes Hitchcock's self-estimation as an "Americophile" ("Dreams" 1). Now, under the stewardship of Kay Brown (1905–1992), David O. Selznick's New York representative, and without much further ado, the Hitchcocks were bustled off to California for meetings with Selznick before their return to England. Within a year they would be back, this time for good, landing in New York in early March 1939 and, by way of Palm Beach, reaching California by the end of the month (Spoto 214). As is evidenced by photographs taken on board the Queen Mary on that sailing, especially one of the three Hitchcocks marching merrily, side by side, and in lock-step along the sunny deck, the voyage was an unqualified delight and the prospect of living in America nothing less than a dream coming true (Païni and Cogeval 440).

In the summer of 1937 they had sailed over for a quick preliminary visit (arriving August 22 at 8 A.M., with the breakup of an intense heat wave) and had a taste of American style with Brown's hospitality. "Their life in England, after all, was quite luxurious," writes Donald Spoto. "As undisputed prince of the British directors, he had more control than any other filmmaker in his country's history. He was also in great social demand, and his Surrey home never wanted for grateful guests" (185). Brown saw to it that he would be fêted at "21," where he gobbled filets, vanilla ice cream, and brandy to his heart's content; then visit Saratoga Springs, to see "rocking chairs. Actual rocking chairs, with people rocking in them. If we have rocking chairs in England it is only as curiosities. But here you have them in real life as well as in the movies" (Hitchcock qtd. in Spoto 188) and "carefully [place it] all under the bell jar of his prodigious memory" (188); and Washington, D.C. For Hitchcock America looked the green pasture. The Hitchcocks as a family took warmly to Brown. She and her husband, the lawyer James Barrett, lived in a duplex on East Eighty-Sixth Street with their two daughters, Laurinda and Kate, young enough to be playmates for Patricia Hitchcock but never particular friends of hers. Early that first summer, the Hitchcocks were invited for a weekend in the Hamptons, at the Barretts' summer rental, Windmill

Cottage, Amagansett.[1] Nearby, on low wooden fences, blankets of primroses would have been in bloom. Laurinda, who became an actor and worked later for Hitchcock,[2] recollects bonfire picnics at "our beach," which would have been Indian Wells Beach, about half a mile down a narrow straight tree-lined road dotted with clapboard houses and ending in a vast stretch of lush dunes. "Hitchcock was such a cook," she recollects. "I learned from him that the only way to cook corn is to leave it in the husk, soak it in salt water, and put it in the coals of the fire." Barrett told me of a later visit to the Hitchcock home in Los Angeles while he was making *The Wrong Man*:

> *I was invited to dinner, and while I was there – I can't remember if Pat was there or not – but Alma was there. He decided he would show me the kitchen because it was pretty fancy. I remember him showing me a drawer with great pride. Instead of pulling it out squarely, you pull the drawer down so you have slots in it. He kept fourteen fry pans. He started to show me the refrigerator; it was a walk-in refrigerator. I was much taller than he was. He opens the door and goes in, and points to the cow that he had all cut up in various steaks and chops, all bundled and tied. "Well, Hitch, where's the meat hook?" He was standing behind me. I felt this tapping on my right shoulder. I turned around. And there indeed was the meat hook hanging right off to my right-hand side. Just tap tap tap. (Interview)*

On the Amagansett beach, they always had champagne, and an endlessly beautiful vista of surf and sand in both

---

[1] Built by Samuel S. Babcock at the northwest corner of Montauk Highway and Windmill Lane, and operated as a guesthouse between 1880 and 1962. Other guests of the Barretts at the same location, but not at the same time, were Ingrid Bergman and Burgess Meredith (conversation with Laurinda Barrett, July 27, 2012).
[2] In *The Wrong Man*, as one of the false accusers of Manny Balestrero.

directions as far as the eye could see. It was a taste of very old American hospitality that the Hitchcocks were getting on Long Island – the village of Amagansett was founded in 1630, and there were numerous early nineteenth-century structures, and even earlier ones, to be seen in addition to long swaths of old, quite enormous trees. Brown had been working out the deal her boss so fiercely desired, to have the celebrated Hitchcock working at Selznick International, fixed on his payroll and, as he would fantasize it, under his creative control. In the spring of 1939, newly arrived in Los Angeles, Hitchcock was assigned to direct *Rebecca* (Leff 39).

The translation to film of this very popular Daphne du Maurier novel was a signal undertaking for Selznick, who at the time was just finishing postproduction on *Gone with the Wind*. But it was not a thoroughgoing American project. Fundamentally an English story set in (constructed) British and French locales, *Rebecca* contained only one somewhat contracted reference to America or Americans, the character of Mrs. Van Hopper (Florence Bates). This wealthy widowed harridan, whose central preoccupations are the subjugation of a charming English girl and the obsequious admiration of an aristocratic English widower, shows off a particularly fawning and anxious side of the American character. Lost in the upper climes of the American middle class, and having no true European aristocracy upon which to model herself, Mrs. Van Hopper perfectly exemplifies a kind of desperation about self-image and social control that Hitchcock was eminently equipped to diagnose, detail, and replicate (since it is virtually impossible to come of age in the United Kingdom without gaining an articulate perspective on social class). In filming *Foreign Correspondent* immediately afterward, on loan-out to Walter Wanger, he was able to effect a more developed reprise, posting his central

American hero to war-torn Europe, an Old World that could now be made to seem quaintly puzzling even as it charmed the all-business reporter who was all enthusiasm, get-go, and make-do.[3]

Not all of the films Hitchcock made from 1940 onward in America can be said to be "American" in terms of their content, although they were all consistently produced through the agency of American studio practice. *Suspicion* (1941, with the American actor Joan Fontaine leading), *The Paradine Case* (1947, starring Gregory Peck as a London advocate), *Under Capricorn* (1949, starring Ingrid Bergman as a tormented Australian wife), *Stage Fright* (1950, starring Richard Todd as a two-faced English chorus boy), and *I Confess* (1953, starring Montgomery Clift as a Canadian priest) are thus excepted from consideration here, as are *Frenzy* (1972, with Barry Foster as a Covent Garden fruit dealer). *Topaz* (1969, an international spy thriller) is not centrally about America, although it has some American characters; and the same is true of *Dial M for Murder* (1953), with one well-meaning but marginal American in it.

Numerous other films show aspects of Hitchcock's depiction of American life: *Foreign Correspondent* (1940), *Saboteur* (1942), *Shadow of a Doubt* (1943), *Lifeboat* (1944), *Spellbound* (1945), *Notorious* (1946), *Rope* (1948), *Strangers on a Train* (1951), *Rear Window* (1954), *To Catch a Thief* (1955), *The Trouble with Harry* (1955), *The Man Who Knew Too Much*

---

[3] "Shortly after the war broke out, a small group of British expatriates in Hollywood began to meet to devise ways to confront American neutrality and promote England's cause," writes Patrick McGilligan. "Hollywood mirrored America with its split between citizens anxious to join the fight against Hitler and those – a peculiar alliance of America Firsters and Communists abiding by the Hitler-Stalin pact – who preached isolationism." The group operated "as a virtual cell of British intelligence" for two years, including among its membership Boris Karloff and others. Hitchcock was brought to meetings (256).

In Topaz *(Universal, 1969), a Cuban delegation to the United Nations headed by Rico Parra has taken up residence at the Hotel Theresa (Seventh Avenue and 125th Street). Here, the bodyguard Hernandez (Carlos Rivas) points out a fleeing man. Fidel Castro had occupied a two-room suite on the ninth floor there when he visited New York for the 1960 opening of the U.N. and the film reconstructs that visit. Courtesy Academy of Motion Picture Arts and Sciences.*

(1956), *The Wrong Man* (1956), *Vertigo* (1958), *North by Northwest* (1959), *Psycho* (1960), *The Birds* (1963), *Marnie* (1964), *Torn Curtain* (1966), and *Family Plot* (1976).

Of these latter, *Lifeboat* merits some special mention. Made at Twentieth Century–Fox, with Hitchcock on loan-out from Selznick International; through the teamwork of Hitchcock, his partner Alma Reville Hitchcock, author John Steinbeck, playwright Jo Swerling, and producer Kenneth Macgowan; and starring Tallulah Bankhead, Henry Hull, John Hodiak,

William Bendix, and Walter Slezak, the film depicts the experience of nine survivors of a U-boat attack in the mid-Atlantic. One of these is a German, as it turns out the captain of the U-boat himself (Slezak). The others suffer through the torments of being lost at sea without a compass, parching thirst and hunger, storms, and the fear that the wily German is leading them surreptitiously to a rendezvous with his own supply ship, on which they will be taken prisoner. A particularly desperate survivor is Gus Smith (né Schmidt (Bendix)), a sailor whose leg has been so severely wounded that gangrene has developed and he must have an amputation at sea,

Lifeboat *(Twentieth Century–Fox, 1944)*: *From left, Canada Lee, John Hodiak, Henry Hull, Mary Anderson (partially obscuring Heather Angel), William Bendix, and Hume Cronyn. The boat rig is set up in front of an eight-foot rear projection screen. Courtesy Academy of Motion Picture Arts and Sciences.*

at the hands of the German captain, no less, a doctor in civilian life. Produced through the great technical expertise of Fred Sersen, with crisp, even alluring cinematography by Glen Macwilliams and design by James Basevi (who had achieved the astonishing storm effects for John Ford's *The Hurricane* [1937]), the film is shot almost exclusively on a rear-projection stage where the seascape plates are seamlessly blended with soundstage photography of the rolling boat. Some of the twilight sequences – such as one in which the ship's steward (Canada Lee) recites the Lord's Prayer at the funeral service of a young woman's deceased infant – are directed and photographed with profound aesthetic force.

Hitchcock's grasp of social class relations and the tiny revealing indices of class membership was more than articulate and precise. He was never unaware of the class implications of his characters' relationships, indeed often architected his films in order to highlight class difference as an explanation for what might otherwise be seen as arbitrary behavioral thrusts. There are two very significant revelations of the class structure of American society in *Lifeboat*. First, we have the sharply drawn portraits of various American characters' attitudes toward, and resentments about, the self-made millionaire C. J. Rittenhouse (Hull), owner of several companies including a shipbuilding concern.[4] Happy to be saved out of the sea and eager to show how chummy he can be in situations as unfortunate as this, Rittenhouse begs his boatmates to call him "Rit." But Kovac (Hodiak), the working-stiff hero from the engine room, and Gus, even in the agonies of his pain, are both notably put off by this false gesture of equanimity. They can see plainly that even though he's the most

---

[4] The shipbuilding magnate will return to Hitchcock in the persona of Gavin Elster in *Vertigo*; and will play an off-camera role in the narrative of *Psycho*.

philosophical and principled person onboard, "Rit" won't take a cigar out of his mouth or stop signaling his wealth and dominance. Accordingly, they use a slight turn of vocalization when uttering his nickname, as if to say, "We call you what you command us to, but not because we feel friendly." The hierarchy that indelibly differentiates Rit from Kovac became palpable early in the film. Coming aboard the boat, Kovac fished some cash out of the water, but meeting Rittenhouse he sighed and pressed the money into the tycoon's hand, a gesture plainer than words: "You are the one with all the money; you will always be the one with all the money; this would seem naturally to belong to you." Kovac is labeled a "fellow traveler" by Connie Porter, an ostensibly cold-hearted journalist/documentarian (Bankhead), mostly because his socialist views are expressed sloppily, one suspects, and she is herself too classy to appreciate his rudeness. Evident in his attitude toward Rittenhouse is a deep-seated Schelerian *ressentience*, a refusal to acknowledge that he himself desires to have what Rittenhouse already possesses. As Kovac and Rit play poker, the betting quickly climbs out of Kovac's range.

A second illumination of class relations occurs in a quiet love scene between Connie and Kovac, in which she reveals to him one of the secrets of her now-glamorous professional life: she was born, like him, on the south side of Chicago – the meat-packing district – and was able to take the up elevator only because she became involved with a wealthy man who bought her a diamond bracelet. With the bracelet as her key to success she soon found her way to the Gold Coast.[5] Connie's sophistication, substantial cultural capital, and social

---

[5] North of Chicago's miracle mile, an extremely elite enclave first developed when Potter Palmer moved there after 1882. In *North by Northwest*, Roger Thornhill will also find his way there (to the Ambassador East Hotel) after a cropduster doesn't manage to kill him.

command are only put-ons, evidence perhaps for the traditional American claim that everybody can make it yet also proof that for many – Connie is not alone – success is all show. Hitchcock knows that the only people who make it without having been there all along are the ones who have been handed directions to a secret passage, in Connie's case the bracelet. She gives it up to the group so that they can use it as bait to catch a fish, and indeed they do, but at the same moment the African American steward Joe sights the German supply ship and in excitement the fishing line is let go and the fish, Connie's bracelet, and the twine all slowly recede into the sea.

The America that Alfred Hitchcock knew as the 1940s became the 1950s was filled with energetic social climbers and dreamers, people convinced they inhabited a classless utopia where success and wealth could be theirs by entitlement. It was in every man's power to transform himself and his world in this society that was rapidly accommodating to the grand shifts of modernity and marshaling its economy for the gear-up to war production and the rationalization of consumerism and advertising that burgeoned in the 1950s. Technical infrastructure was being developed – the interstate highway system and its road culture, for example – while the expansion of the cities into newly developed suburbs, the explosion of media with the growth of television, the social changes accompanying the redomestication of women, and the climate of pervasive fear occasioned by the Cold War all produced tensions, frustrations, and desires hitherto unimagined in a culture that had been stable and agrarian. The population was shifting away from the farm, toward the cities and suburbs, in a trenchant mobility both physical and social; jettisoned as dead weight were the consistencies of Victorian morality. Marital strain, psychoanalysis, space travel – all these were invoked or established by the late 1950s. Not only did this atmosphere of excitement, yearning, optimism, and deep-seated fear inspire Hitchcock's work, but the new country displaced him: if not from his class roots and class consciousness then at least from many of his old working relationships, since the producers, cinematographers, and designers who had collaborated with him in England were unavailable – indeed often considered undesirable – in a Hollywood tightly gripped by unionized American workers. We can see that Hitchcock made the transition with ease because *Rebecca*, as a first American film, is a virtually flawless technical production. But culturally he was still itching. George Perry notes that although "he clearly had a great love for his adopted country and things American, relishing the variety and vastness of the landscape, the diversity and occasional eccentricities of its people," he might "complain about some aspect of American bureaucracy that was irking him. Perhaps his airmail copy of the *London Times* had been held up and was a day late, or Washington had decreed that the succulent Melton Mowbray pork pies he liked to have flown in from Fortnum & Mason no longer complied with the FDA's fierce standards" (37).

Some of the influential cultural events and transformations that Hitchcock would have experienced as a worker in America – just to give a cursory kind of glance at the era, the place, and the temper of the times without paying attention to the Second World War, the Korean War, the Vietnam War, or any dedicated military contest: nylon stockings (1940); the Pentagon (1943); FDR winning a fourth term as president (1944); atomic bomb tests (1946); the creation of the Central Intelligence Agency (1947); the UNIVAC computer (1951); the Cuban Revolution (1953); color television (1953); the civil rights movement (1955); Sputnik (1957); the Barbie doll (1959); the Playboy Club (1960); the failed Bay of Pigs invasion (1961); Bob Dylan's debut (1961); the JFK assassination (1963); the Beatles in the U.S.A. (1964); the National Organization of Women (1966); the synthesis of DNA (1967); Martin Luther King and Robert F. Kennedy assassinated (1968); Neil Armstrong stepping onto the moon (1969); Jeffrey Miller and other students being shot at Kent State University (1970); Nixon in China (1972); the Watergate break-in (1972); the resignation of Richard M. Nixon (1974); the Apple personal computer (1976); the American bicentennial (1976).

In cinema: the three-dimensional camera movement in the animated *Pinocchio* (1940); the controversial *Citizen Kane* (1941); his cherished friend Carole Lombard perishing in a plane crash (1942); the trial of the Hollywood Ten (1947); Twentieth Century–Fox programming for television (1949); James Stewart sharing in film profits, with *Winchester '73* (1950); VistaVision (1954); Joseph Breen replaced as Hollywood censor (1954); a rock sound track for *Blackboard Jungle* (1955); death of Humphrey Bogart (1957); death of Marilyn Monroe (1962); "Star Trek" (1966); the end of the Production Code (1968); the videocassette recorder (1974); *Jaws*, the beginning of blockbuster cinema (1975).

While Hitchcock did not make explicit reference to developments such as these,[6] or to many of the ongoing political machinations that made for daily news; and while he hardly strove to substantiate David Lehman's claim for the overriding theme in Hitchcock's America, that "paranoia is sometimes a reasonable response to events in a world of menace" (29), his films were diligently faithful in their representation of the look and style of American everyday reality and did repeatedly focus on the "uncertainty of appearances" that Marshall Deutelbaum notices in *Saboteur* and elsewhere. His

---

[6] Excepting the Central Intelligence Agency, which moves the story of *North by Northwest* and figures prominently in *Topaz*.

characters are fully sprung from the American crowd, much as though in making them he were some reincarnation of Baudelaire's "painter of modern life," mingling with strangers in the marketplace and quickly seizing their characteristics for his sketches. As a visionary adept at noticing and encapsulating tiny nuances of behavior, attitude, and conviction he was unparalleled in Hollywood. Consider even a small variegated cluster of portraits: the humiliated and snubbing expression with which Mrs. Van Hopper wishes her companion (Joan Fontaine) happiness in her just-announced marriage to Maxim de Winter (Laurence Olivier): the nose upraised, the smile not merely forced but virtually cranked onto the lips, the head thrown back as though confronting an impossible odor:

MRS. VAN HOPPER (with withering sarcasm): Mrs. de Winter.
(with a sour laugh): Good-bye, my dear, and *good luck*.

Or the traditionalist Mr. Kentley (Cedric Hardwicke) in *Rope*, politely declining a glass of champagne but eager to have his hands on a good solid glass of Scotch on the rocks. Again with alcohol (something Hitchcock knew intimately): in *Rear Window*, as Jeff (James Stewart) tries to convince his chum Doyle (Wendell Corey) that something strange is going on in the courtyard, Lisa (Grace Kelly) emerges from the kitchenette with three snifters of brandy, silently hands them around, begins a swirling motion with her wrist. Doyle picks it up like a bright monkey, swirling his wrist, too, as does Jeff. Lisa is all about the "right" way of doing things. Or consider the droning, stupefying voice of the coroner in *Vertigo* (Henry Jones), that echoing singsong phrasing and nasally inflected boredom as, summarizing the sad death of Madeleine Elster, he feels obliged to point to Scottie's "lack of initiative." Or

Rita the cleaner in *Marnie* (Edith Evanson), eager to finish her work so she can go to bed. Or the pathetic East German bodyguard Gromek (Wolfgang Kieling) in *Torn Curtain*, confessing nostalgically to Michael (Paul Newman) and Sarah (Julie Andrews) that he used to live in New York, used to eat at Pete's Pizza, Eighty-Eighth and Eighth. The exorbitant fondness and pristine particularity of Gromek's happy memory, as though dragged up from a dream childhood: he is like Hitchcock, an immigrant so absorbed with American culture that its fragments become embedded as treasures.

It is impossible to claim that this book constitutes a complete analysis, of either American culture or Hitchcockian film, and much could be said, about America and about Hitchcock, beyond what takes shape in these limited pages. The considerations that follow treat Hitchcock's screened America as a locus of land- and cityscapes, personalities, values, social forms, and marriages – arbitrarily chosen features of American experience useful because they permit a certain organization of analysis, a hopefully refreshing reexamination of much-considered films, and a fidelity to the deep structures of American organization, behavior, and design that an astute observer such as Hitchcock would have been likely to notice and take interest in. My intention with this small book is to raise new questions and considerations, challenge viewers to look at Hitchcock's wonderful films yet again, and see in his work an illumination of American form and life that has perhaps not been shown before in this way. Hitchcock's films are seen here only in fragments, such as are necessary for the analyses at hand. I try to make a point of avoiding or at least diminishing conventional, canonical readings of Hitchcock films: for example, *Rear Window* as a murder mystery, but also a metaphor for cinema because of the limited window frames through which we see the action; *Vertigo* as a tale about haunting, love, and masquerade; *The*

Trouble with Harry as a charming little murder comedy; *North by Northwest* as a picaresque adventure about mistaken identity; *Psycho* as a personality study; *Torn Curtain* as a spy story; *Shadow of a Doubt* as a dark melodrama; *Rope* as a study in psychopathology; *Saboteur* as an anti-Nazi war film; *The Birds* as a mystery about man and nature, and so on. Such readings as these, given out as fundamental refreshments, have been so often published and republished, so thirstily imbibed, that it has become difficult to penetrate the froth of theory and repeated observation in order to see and re-experience much of the delicacy, charge, and meaning that is available for us. I want here to work toward grasping how it is that Hitchcock's American stories could not have been set anywhere else.

If I make bold to concentrate on tiny moments, gestures, angles, or other nuances of depiction, the reader should never forget that beyond his penetrating philosophy and arch wit Hitchcock was at heart a designer, who conceived his camera setups in physical terms and his screened images as carefully composed pictorializations. Laurinda Barrett was one of a small army of performers who worked for him, but her recollection of even a tiny engagement in *The Wrong Man* nicely exemplifies the Hitchcock method:

> *I remember the scene: police lineup. I remember offering to move, and being told that I couldn't move a muscle, and do exactly what you're told. I remember him showing me the pictures, and showing a window shade across the street at a certain level, and at a different level in the next shot. The fact that as an actor you didn't have to do anything, you didn't have to offer anything original, even a little breath of anything. I got the impression I wasn't permitted to do it. I thought, "Ooo, I'd better shut up here." He wouldn't allow it at all, but he showed me the shots and he said, "That's what every shot is." He didn't do anything else but what*

he drew on those pieces of paper. They were all followed systematically and to the letter. (Interview)

It may help to remember that for fully seventeen years it was as a British citizen that Alfred Hitchcock lived and worked in the United States. On April 20, 1955, during preproduction of *The Man Who Knew Too Much* (on the day a cable arrived with the news that Niall MacGinnis would probably not be available to play Drayton [Meiklejohn], and at a moment when consideration was being given to the words the dying Frenchman Louis Bernard would whisper into Ben McKenna's ears), Henry Bumstead drove him over to the Los Angeles County Court where he swore the oath and became

Jo McKenna (Doris Day) and her son Hank (Christopher Olsen) singing "Que Sera, Sera" in The Man Who Knew Too Much *(Paramount, 1956). The gown is by Edith Head. The opulent set was designed by Henry Bumstead and built on Paramount's Stage 1. Courtesy Academy of Motion Picture Arts and Sciences.*

an official American (Spoto 388). In a charming way, then, *The Man Who Knew Too Much*, an American family's encounter with the darkest side of European power struggles and a horrid personal misfortune, became Hitchcock's first "true" American film. Ben McKenna's tongue-tied exasperations; Jo Conway's frustrations both as a mother who believes she has lost a child and as a performer who believes she has lost her career; the kidnapped child's wide-eyed astonishment at the nefarious spectacles opening around him – all this brilliantly formalizes Hitchcock's own encounter, both with America and with the possibilities of cinema.

Not only Hitchcock's encounter, I should finally confess. In 1956, when this film came out, I, too, was ten years old, just like Hank (whom I watched at Shea's Buffalo, my parents having driven us across the border just for such an opportunity). If not my very earliest encounter with film as spectacle and marvel, or with America, *The Man Who Knew Too Much* it was that first opened me to film's intensity, its mystery, and its delirious complication, and to the American family as a strangely warped mirror of my own. With gratitude to Alfred Hitchcock in memory, then, I dedicate these thoughts.

1

HITCHCOCK'S AMERICAN SCAPES

When from a strategic promontory in the twenty-first century we look upon the cultural space of America, it seems preponderantly urban and to a significant degree internationalized. The American modern spatial form, largely agglomerated urban development characterized by dense clusters of skyscrapers and vast surrounding tracts of suburban sprawl, is also to be found in Europe, Asia, South America, Australia, and parts of Africa, but in America it somehow seems aboriginal, natural, characteristic, unimposed. While in the United States there are pastoral regions spreading across parts of the south and the Midwest – central Georgia, southern Illinois, New Mexico, Arizona are some – the typical image of the American scene today is neither a pasture nor a tiny village nor a meandering river with paddle-wheelers churning upstream, but instead a seemingly endless interlocking chain of expressways jammed with vehicular traffic and a cityscape remarkably unchanging from Boston to Minneapolis to New Orleans to San Diego, one that features dozens of vertical glass-faced dominoes full of accountants, bankers, brokers, and lawyers shuffling to and from work in identical business garb, aboard a subway or tram system, and whisked to suburban homes each boasting a view of dozens like it. Mobility, instant readiness for communication, gregariousness, brevity of relationship, and self-doubt characterize the American character who inhabits this twenty-first century world.

The America depicted by Hitchcock between the 1940s and the early 1970s was altogether a different kind of place, one that only toward the end of that period was modulating into the vastly more complex social world we recognize today. What Hitchcock saw and understood was an American city still in the relatively early stages of development, with its foundation in a bucolic small town associated with agriculture and long-lasting human relations. Even New York, that American prototype, was a more characteristic environment then than it is today (see, for example, Berman "Too Much"). The view of Phoenix in *Psycho* (1960) is a good example: although real estate is booming (as per the storyline), what we are given to see is a modest, even genteel urban environment (some of it realized onscreen through rear-projection plates made in architecturally unprepossessing sections of Los Angeles). True, in *North by Northwest* (1959) and *Topaz* (1969) Hitchcock's urban scene became at least occasionally caustic and dark, but in many ways *Saboteur* (1942), *Shadow of a Doubt* (1943), *Spellbound* (1945), *Strangers on a Train* (1951), *Rear Window* (1954), and *The Wrong Man* (1956) deploy townscapes and cityscapes still culture-bound to the nineteenth century. These films foreground interpersonal civility, living spaces intermeshed with working environments, evocative topographies, and a discreet sense of settlement and groundedness.

Los Angeles posing as Phoenix for a rear-projection plate to be used in Psycho *(Universal, 1960) as Marion Crane stops her car at an intersection. Courtesy Academy of Motion Picture Arts and Sciences.*

Consider the glitz-free Los Angeles of *Saboteur*.[1] It is first presented by an aircraft factory configured like a giant barn,[2] with relatively little depiction of churning machinery, mechanical grit, or regularized brutal labor; soon afterward by a community of tiny bungalows, each the shell of a warm and tightly knit family. The plot moves quickly to a lonely highway (probably in the Mojave National Preserve) – something relatively new in America in the early 1940s; it would be a decade before the substantial development of the interstate highway system – and here we discover an amiable

---

[1] A Los Angeles interestingly absent any hints of the "irrigated paradise" early observers like Carey McWilliams or later ones like Mike Davis knew how to find there (see Pomerance, *Antonioni* 157–62).
[2] Made, claimed designer Robert Boyle, out of "storage bins on the lot" (Krohn, *Work* 41).

trucker (worker bonded with the road), a territory marked by farms and ranches that bespeak an agrarian economy, and architecture set into the natural forms of the graceful hills and low mountains. Indeed, the dominance of the Californian mountainous form was conceived early on as part of the intrinsic design of this film. One farm in particular Hitchcock graces with a twinkly swimming pool; so this is a view of the West in development, a frontier heading toward a technotopological futurity in which hard physical labor will be replaced by automation, intellectual property production and management, and leisure. Soon later, we discover a dense forest, then the stunning prospect of what was at the time a relatively new marvel of architecture and engineering – the Hoover Dam (dedicated September 30, 1935).[3] When the tale finally moves to New York, it is only an abbreviated and quickly suggestive view that Hitchcock presents there, including a shot taken from a skyscraper window as a help note floats hopelessly down to the street far below. En route to the Brooklyn Navy Yard we catch a swift view (through inserted newsreel footage) of the S. S. Normandie swamped in its riverside berth, but the basic pictorial information is that of a port location with ships in place. For the climax at the Statue of Liberty, Hitchcock uses contrasty, dynamically composed establishing shots that highlight the gigantic figure as a freestanding icon, floating in a kind of patrioticintellectual atmosphere removed from the busy streets of the city (as, indeed, the Statue is). By the time of *North by Northwest*, Hitchcock is revealing a different New York, plunging into those streets to find a bustling businesslike jungle.

[3] And shown by way of an artist's rendering, since the Department of the Interior had issued a wartime ban on photography (to defend against just such characters as Hitchcock emplaced in the nearby vantage point of Soda City). See Krohn, *Work* 42.

What, then, is the America that we discover in Hitchcock, if we look at his landscapes, townscapes, and cityscapes, his ways of picturing place? D. H. Lawrence had written in *Studies in Classic American Literature* that there was a spirit of place, and that the spirit of America was escape. The Pilgrim Fathers "came largely to get *away* – that most simple of motives. To get away. Away from what? In the long run, away from themselves. Away from everything. That's why most people have come to America, and still do come. To get away from everything they are and have been" (9). How, having gotten away himself, did Hitchcock portray that spirit?

Walden in the Woods

Saboteur was Hitchcock's first expressly American film.[4] (In *Rebecca* and *Foreign Correspondent* [both 1940], he had imposed American characters and motifs, but neither film was self-consciously about America as a place.) Not far into it, earnest aircraft worker Barry Kane (Robert Cummings), accused of setting a factory fire that killed his best friend and in flight from the police, wanders desperately into a rain-sogged California forest. This is one of those utterly primeval stands of tall densely packed conifers, a sanctum of silent darkness, eerie foreboding, and rich natural potential.[5] It is the forest primeval, the source of social formations, indeed the untapped wilderness that is one of the great

---

[4] "*Saboteur* was the first picture he was to make in America about America using America as a background," the screenwriter Peter Viertel wrote (qtd. in McGilligan 297).
[5] This setting is a foreshadowing in some ways of the Big Basin Redwood Forest scene in *Vertigo* (1958), where again we have towering vegetation shrinking the human proportion both spatially and temporally (for more on this sequence see Pomerance, *Eye* 234–7; and Turner "Acrophobic Vision").

strengths and beauties of the American dream. It is also the domain of those who did not reach America from Europe: "Last evening," wrote Meriwether Lewis in his journal on June 25, 1806,

> the indians entertained us with seting [sic] the fir trees on fire. they have a great number of dry lims [sic] near their bodies which when set on fire creates a very suddon [sic] and immence [sic] blaze from bottom to top of those tall trees. they are a beatifull [sic] object in this situation at night. this exhibition reminded me of a display of fireworks. the natives told us that their object in seting [sic] those trees on fire was to bring fair weather for our journey. (396)

There is a log cabin – the Lincoln model! – with smoke sweetly twisting from its chimney: habitation, the rudiments of civilization, an abode built by human hands in human proportion and with the enchanting modesty of materials taken straight from nature and used according to principles of natural harmony. This America of the woods is not only rustic but also noble and purposive, forthright and upstanding, an America of principles, signaling the undergirding importance of justice, civility, tolerance, aspiration, and trust. Seen in its best light, according to an "accurate moral compass" (Hark 297), this is the America of the founding fathers; the America that beckoned to immigrant sufferers late in the nineteenth century and early in the twentieth, "Give me your tired, your poor..."; the America that offered not only opportunities for advancement but the promise of fresh air unpolluted by tyranny, class conflict, hatred, or vice. Also, of course, it is an Arcadian space that for Hitchcock may have recalled the green zones and green men of British lore, for all its hazy black-and-white glow nothing less than a greenwood.

At the cabin,[6] Barry meets Phillip Martin (Vaughan Glazer), an aging and blind Thoreau figure, a naturalist-philosopher and "the central spokesperson for true American virtue" (Hark 297), eager to offer this stranger hospitality and warm shelter from the rain outside. If he is not quite an ancestor of the British Henry Hastings, who, we are told by Simon Schama, "made a point of dressing only in green broadcloth" and whose hovel "that had been built for him in the hollow of an oak" was edged with "a carpet of half-gnawed marrowbones, while the evil-smelling chamber itself was filled with an inconceivable number of hunting, pointing, and retrieving dogs" (135), still Martin does have for company a gruffy and gregarious German Shepard and his own independent spirit nurtured by long silences in the awesome shades of this magnificent and uncivilized place. For some minutes, the shivering fugitive Kane has been able to keep the shackles that bind his wrists camouflaged from his unseeing host, but when the old man's niece Pat (Priscilla Lane) arrives – she comes every year from New York to spend a month, after which time she "finds the quiet deafening" – young Barry, surprised by her stunning good looks (stunning in part because he has been seeing her face plastered on roadside billboards as he hitchhikes across the country), much too soon finds himself optically and morally probed. It is true that for all her surface glamour Pat is nothing if not the epitome of the fresh-faced and healthy all-American girl, but she harbors a fearful and anxious personality, a rote (and, in the face of her uncle it may be observed, blind) subservience to the brutalizing forces of order. She is on the point of detecting the handcuffs Barry presumes the blind seer has missed,[7] and of being drawn into fear.

[6] And in a scene written by Dorothy Parker (McGilligan 299).
[7] The characterization is recaptured from a scene in James Whale's *Frankenstein* (1931).

Eagerly, she blurts out that the police are searching for a runaway, a man who is "dangerous." Although Barry is a shining epitome of innocence, she finds it possible to imagine in him a nefarious type who has crept malevolently through the woods. "The police," replies the old man dismissively, "are always on the alarmist side." But, presses she, they said he was *really* dangerous. "I'm sure they did. How could they be heroes if he were harmless?" Now, the manacled wrists cannot but announce themselves, and "he must be the man they're looking for!" cries Pat, panic floundering in her voice. "Yes," says the uncle matter-of-factly, "very probably." The girl with some urgency: You should have given him to the police. "Are you frightened, Pat? Is that what makes you so cruel?" This last, surely an observation not merely of Martin's but also of Hitchcock's, is of great interest and significance, since rather than merely allaying the niece's fears, rather than merely disagreeing with her, the wise old man is making bold to offer a critical, even pedagogical, comment, one that points neither to attitudes nor to rational alignment but to fundamental human nature and the vital necessity of standing upon it. He is offering a conviction and a way of seeing the social world: that to turn people over to the police based on one's fears is an act not only of surrender and injustice but also of cruelty. Further, when Pat chides him about his civic duties, he continues to elevate his thoughts (in a way that no other character in Hitchcock ever manages to do): "It is my duty as an American citizen to believe a man innocent until he's been proved guilty. . . . I have my own ideas about my duties as a citizen. They sometimes involve disregarding the law."

Here is Henry David Thoreau, anticipating by almost ninety years what Hitchcock's Phillip Martin would believe and aver:

"I have my own ideas about my duties as a citizen," says Phillip Martin. Vaughan Glazer (l.) with Robert Cummings in Saboteur (Frank Lloyd Productions/Universal, 1942). On the piano at rear he will proceed to play Frederick Delius's "Summer Night on the River" (1911–12), explaining that he sees with his ears. Courtesy Academy of Motion Picture Arts and Sciences.

It is said that Mirabeau took to highway robbery "to ascertain what degree of resolution was necessary in order to place one's self in formal opposition to the most sacred laws of society." . . . This was manly, as the world goes; and yet it was idle, if not desperate. A saner man would have found himself often enough "in formal opposition" to what are deemed "the most sacred laws of society," through obedience to yet more sacred laws, and so have tested his resolution without going out of his way. It is not for a man to put himself in such an attitude to society, but to maintain himself in whatever attitude he find himself through obedience to the laws of his being, which will never be one of opposition to a just government, if he should chance to meet with such. (371)

How fascinating and revealing, then, that commencing his portraiture of America with *Saboteur*, and riding upon a fondness for that country and its customs cultured from afar, Hitchcock would apotheosize not the tycoon –

> the "Titan," as Dreiser called him; the "Tycoon," as Fortune called him. Where other civilization types have pursued wisdom, beauty, sanctity, military glory, predacity, asceticism, the businessman pursues the magnitudes of profit with a similar single-minded drive.... "The business of America," as Calvin Coolidge put it, "is business." (Lerner 274)

– he who by the early 1940s had come to symbolize all that was energetic and indomitably progressive about the American plan, but instead this solitary and debilitated philosopher withdrawn into the rainy woods, a man stubbornly following the laws of his true self rather than society's shibboleths.

Regardless of the weight and meaning of this scene in the overall plot (at the uncle's insistence Barry and Pat will go off together, and he will cut his chains and eventually struggle hard to persuade her that he is the noble innocent he has been claiming to be), the arrangement of interactions functions to show a lambent vision of American civility and social organization that, whether or not it figured personally for Hitchcock at this time in his life, was distinctively absent from the films noirs and melodramas so profusely turned out by Hollywood studios in the early 1940s. There is a dim aura in Martin of Gregory La Cava's noble and liberty-loving butler (William Powell) in *My Man Godfrey* (1936), but only an aura: Godfrey speaks out of dignity and insouciance, while Martin speaks as a victim and prisoner in a tormenting world that must be overcome and transcended with

One of John De Cuir's numerous sketches anticipating the Statue of Liberty sequence that climaxes Saboteur. *Fry is visible dangling from Lady Liberty's thumb, and Barry Kane is leaning over the railing on the torch. Note how De Cuir artfully suggested wide-angle compositions, many of which would be used even though the action as Hitchcock shot the scene was reconfigured. Courtesy Academy of Motion Picture Arts and Sciences.*

kindness.[8] In this cabin in the woods, secluded, retreated from the pall mall of urbanizing modernity, he bespeaks the values and poise, the rugged assurance and indomitable yearning of a frontier America, exemplifying the dignity that is implicit in the act of treating all men as equals, all men as free, all men as ideal citizens.

---

[8] In *Spellbound* (1945), the sagacious and liberty-loving Dr. Brulov (Michael Chekhov) shares Martin's abhorrence of the police – a standard Hitchcockian trope (see Spoto 7, 14–15) – but not his conviction in transcending kindness.

All around him Thoreau saw "lives of quiet desperation" (see Lerner 561). So, we might surmise, did Hitchcock. As reflected in the film, such lives include those of Pat and surely Fry (Norman Lloyd), the real saboteur and a slimy and valueless punk, and every member of the Nazi coterie for whom Fry works so slavishly and with such carelessness. Even hapless Barry is desperate – and at moments only desperate – to clear his name. By contrast, Phillip Martin, the persona who reposes at the true center of this film, is a paragon of tranquility and faith, signifying and embodying a fundamental American spirit. His cabin in the woods is a bucolic dream of the simple, good, yeoman life. To depict this abode and other locations in this film (his first with designer Robert Boyle), Hitchcock and his team make use of painted backdrops, mattes, and other simulation effects. "Hitchcock," writes Bill Krohn, "seems to have relished the idea of doing a picture so large in scope ... on a modest budget, necessitating ... production ingenuity and camera tricks" (*Work* 41). The finale sequence on the Statue of Liberty, for example, where Fry meets his doom, was shot with stereos made by John Fulton (Turner, "*Saboteur*" 71),[9] foreshadowing a technique Boyle would use later for *North by Northwest* (see Pomerance, *Horse* 67ff.). Many of the desert shots including the circus caravan were also done using rear projection (and some of the caravan shots also used a succession of full-size sets, miniatures, and toys gradually receding from the camera [Turner, "*Saboteur*" 89–90]).[10] Krohn

---

[9] A "stereo" is a still photograph, typically shot with a large-format (4 × 5 or 8 × 10) camera and projected behind soundstage action to achieve a rear-projection composite (for an example, see page 35). A "plate" is a moving image used in the same way.
[10] Involved as well was a careful placement of "midgets" in the background dressed to match their larger colleagues, who were closer to the lens, as well as cut-outs of vehicles (see Krohn, *Work* 46).

specifies how "second-unit cameramen were instructed to shoot plates and scenes with extras – for intercutting with Kane and Pat against a process screen[11] – using telephoto lenses, to give a sense of the vastness of the American landscape" (*Work* 51).

When he learns that his guest has been hitchhiking, Barry's blind host makes a revealing comment: "I have always thought that that was the best way to learn about this country, and the surest test of the American heart." No other Hitchcockian character thinks of the prudence of testing the American heart. There is such a thing, Martin and Hitchcock are saying, and Barry has one. Did the American viewer? More generally, the social landscape invoked by this wise hermit is framed in terms of goodness and vivacity. Given the craven deceit and hungers we will encounter later in the story, as Barry contends with the pack of German spies working darkly to sabotage American culture,[12] this introduction to a vision of the enduring, the enduringly natural, and the naturally civil equips us with a dignified point of view. As Martin puts it, not without the poetic sensibility of Walt Whitman or Emily Dickinson, "It's a pleasant thing to have a guest sharing the fire when the rain is beating on the roof."

The forces of modernity had already made inroads into pastoral culture across the country by the time Hitchcock

---

[11] A rear-projection screen: these had to be made of very specific material so as to permit light to permeate with even strength, both directly and laterally (on the basic principle, see Fielding 272ff.).
[12] David O. Selznick, under whose aegis preparation for the film began, had become obsessed with the German threat, wiring Kay Brown immediately after the Pearl Harbor attack to acquire the rights to *Mein Kampf* for Hitchcock to direct – a project that never saw the light of day. As to *Saboteur*, Selznick was never happy with the scripts and let Hitchcock market the film by himself (for a profit to Selznick on the loan-out of around three hundred percent) (Leff 100–1).

finished making *Rebecca* for Selznick (early March 1940). The 1920 census had "pronounced America a predominantly urban nation for the first time in its history" (Douglas 73), and Los Angeles became the most advertised place in the world (McWilliams 108). Employment was to be found increasingly in the cities. Transportation was almost universally vehicular, so that as it cut through the geographical landscape the highway system, still in its infancy, gained a certain centrality in cultural experience. Even in his isolated cabin, Martin knows what it means – both on the surface and in depth – when Barry explains he's been hitchhiking. The idea of billboards placed end to end and stretching across America with Pat's face on them – one of Martin's little jokes – is by this time hardly esoteric. Small-town social relations are dissipating in the face of urban circulation and the normative encounter with strangers, a phenomenon that for a keen social observer like Hitchcock immediately implies the necessity of etiquette and social form even though those who are caught up in it, like young Pat with her new modeling career, see progress, movement, achievement, and speed as being more pressing needs than courtesy, kindness, and hospitality. Hospitality by the early 1940s is starting to become a widespread business, highly capitalized and modernized, much to the detriment of the polite interactional patterns and obligations of pastoral life, in which opening the door to strangers was an intrinsic sign of civility.[13]

It would be a mistake to underestimate the eagerness with which Hitchcock's rather noble vision of American possibility and dignity was received at Radio City Music Hall when the film opened there on May 7, 1942, notwithstanding some

---

[13] Hitchcock's elegant crofter scene in *The 39 Steps* (1935), a guidebook on hospitality and its implications, shows how civility and friendliness are not necessarily related.

audience confusion[14] and the often equivocal response of critics: "To put it mildly," crowed Bosley Crowther in the *New York Times*, for example, "Mr. Hitchcock and his writers have really let themselves go":

> *Melodramatic action is their forte, but they scoff at speed limits this trip. All the old master's experience at milking thrills has been called upon. As a consequence – and according to Hitchcock custom – "Saboteur" is a swift, high-tension film which throws itself forward so rapidly that it permits slight opportunity for looking back. . . . So fast, indeed, is the action and so abundant the breathless events that one might forget, in the hubbub, that there is no logic in this wild-goose chase.* (May 8, 1942, 27)

Hitchcock himself thought the picture should have been "pruned and tightly edited long before the actual shooting" (Truffaut 151).

Saboteur opened only months after the Pearl Harbor attack that drew American forces to the Pacific front. An attitude of bravura seriousness had penetrated the national psyche. In every corner of the country, as though with a National Purpose, ordinary citizens were scrimping and saving to aid the war effort, collecting scrap metal, opting for cheaper clothing and food, and thinking twice before filling the car, cognizant about the fact that, as a Shell advertisement in the April 20, 1942, issue of *Life* magazine had it, "Oil is ammunition – use it wisely." Oil was all over that magazine – in

---

[14] Even as they sat in it watching, patrons would have found the Music Hall itself depicted onscreen. Universal's Stage 12 was used for rear-projection shots, but even though the chase sequence, in which a man in the audience is accidentally shot by the villain, was not filmed there in actuality, "the management of the Music Hall, where the picture was slated to premier, objected to the sequence, so it had to be severely cut to avoid identification of the theater" (Turner, "*Saboteur*" 91).

gasoline ads, by implication in ads for heavy equipment and transportation – just as in the early days of the Los Angeles boom after 1906 it had been all over the city that turned itself to aircraft manufacture (and thus became the platform for *Saboteur*). "By 1909," writes Carey McWilliams, "the district north of Wilshire and west of Vermont[15] had 160 producing wells in operation and Santa Monica Boulevard had become an oil-workers' shacktown" (130). It was oil, ultimately, that touched off the worst of Hitchcock's diegetic blaze, since unbeknownst to him (thus evidencing his innocence) the extinguisher Barry handed his friend for fighting a little fire had been filled with gasoline.[16]

An examination of the dozens of full-page advertisements in this one issue of *Life* alone reveals an intensive and diffuse preoccupation with the war effort, ranging from galvanizing images of war equipment depicted as progressive and thrusting to stabilizing images of American values drawn to an apotheosis of purity and homeliness, as in the numerous ads for alcoholic beverages that showed the fishing streams and lounge chairs soldiers were fighting to preserve. General Motors Truck and Coach was shown transporting war workers (Barry Kane and his cohort) on their way to the factory and, in a matching shot, troops on their way to the battlefield. A full-color cartoon image for Cliquot Ginger Ale had four little boys playing soldier, holding wooden

---

[15] That is, what became known as Hollywood.
[16] The fire, Hitchcock knew, would be a sufficiently dramatic punctum to begin his film, even in black and white, so he paid no attention to an offer from Gustav Brock, an expert in hand-coloring fire scenes, to touch up the sequence for twenty-five cents a foot and thereby produce a sequence "which will startle the audience and which will make your fire scenes live and be remembered" (Brock to Hitchcock). The fire scene was mostly composed using a painted backing by Robert Boyle, with one "hard-won shot of the real location" (at Lockheed, available only by permission from the Army) (Krohn, *Work* 51).

rifles on a sunny meadow with kitchen pots and safari hats perched on their eager heads: "This army fights on its stomach, too." And under the header, "Women Lose Pockets and Frills to Save Fabrics," the magazine posted one of its numerous reminders that anything and everything could be saved to aid in the battle effort, in this case pleats, pockets, and hem depth. We see precisely this economy in Vera West's designs for Pat's clothing in the film and explicitly not, of course, in the fashionable excesses worn by the Nazi sympathizer Mrs. Sutton (Alma Kruger). Apparently, too, citizens were not to lose their sense of delicacy in their engagement with the brutality of the war: in the magazine's letters column, Mrs. Robert A. Lennen of Kansas City, Kansas, complains archly about a *March of Time* radio broadcast in which "every time you have a character who is supposed to be a soldier, particularly, he has to say 'damn' or 'hell' in almost every sentence" (2).

As for confused but well-meaning Pat, who never says "damn" or "hell" and whose scrubbed face adorns all those billboards – advertising here beauty cream and there a funeral parlor: what was she in her expressive effervescence but a living paradigm of social engagement as performance, of putting on face? And at the same time, of course, a modern girl, a pure American type. Lerner informs us that by the 1840s "de Tocqueville saw and described the democratic structure of the American family, the ease and quality of manners within it, and the *new paths opened up in the education of girls*" (561, my emphasis). Ann Douglas writes at length about the development in America, since the 1920s, of heightened opticality, detection of social nuance, and the search for truth instead of platitude; and of the vast importance of "pure theater," that is, putting on masks and attitudes onstage and off-, riddling one's life with stances, illuminations, gestures, and put-ups: "Constance Rourke, the finest cultural historian of the decade, saw all American culture past and present – politics, religion, advertising, *everything* – as 'theatrical'" (55). As innocent Barry Kane flees for his life, trailed initially by the forces of law and order who believe he has sabotaged the war effort and then by Nazi conspirators, who have sabotaged it in fact and know he is trying to unmask them, beautiful Pat, the face of fresh-hearted American optimism, at first wears nothing but the mask of sanctimonious uprightness. Finally, however, she changes it, when the truth of Barry's innocence dawns upon her, for a mask of daredevil helpfulness and love.

Priscilla Lane and Robert Cummings in a posed publicity shot showing the "mountainous area" where they meet up with the circus band. The cloudy sky is a stereo (see note 9). This photograph has exceptionally skillful lighting on both the actors and the scene (all the boulders and vegetation are soundstage constructions). Courtesy Academy of Motion Picture Arts and Sciences.

Atomic Modernity

If in *Saboteur* Hitchcock had offered inspired but abbreviated sketches of domestic space in America – Barry's chum Ken Mason's mother's tiny bungalow in Los Angeles, its rear kitchen door backing onto that of the busy-body next-door neighbor; Martin's abode in the woods; the villainous Tobin's sprawling ranch territory and cozy poolside retreat; the two-faced Mrs. Sutton's grandiose mansion in the heart of New York – it remained for him to develop a detailed picture of American family and domestic life in films that would render more prolonged and complex visions of the culture. He "had felt that *Saboteur* was not as successful in re-creating the real America he had been discovering on weekends," Dan Auiler suggests (103).

Three films are noteworthy for the details they reveal about the American homescape in the 1940s and 1950s. *Shadow of a Doubt* is set in the bucolic northern California town of Santa Rosa, where the charming and reflective young woman Charlie Newton lives with her parents, siblings, and friends. The action of *Rope* (1948) takes place in fluid "real" time inside the penthouse apartment of two male lovers (and murderers) in Manhattan. And *Rear Window* is narrated through the experience of a recuperating photographer trapped in a full-leg cast and wheelchair in his Greenwich Village bachelor pad and espying all around him the hopeful – and sometimes far from hopeful – lives of his neighbors played out as tiny dramas opened to his engagement.

Virtually all critical studies of *Rear Window* concentrate to some degree on the array of tiny "narratives" displayed in the windows across L. B. "Jeff" Jefferies's courtyard that he can watch with his eager eyes and through the agency of his expensive telephoto lens. Miss Torso (Georgine Darcy) is a modern dancer almost always rehearsing a routine or fending off the advances of older men. Miss Lonelyhearts (Judith Evelyn), a single woman no longer quite young, is eager – perhaps too eager – to have a beau. The composer (Ross Bagdasarian) is slaving over a melody that has obsessed him (and that, soon enough, will obsess us, too). The "Whistlers" (Sara Berner and Frank Cady), a married couple who are sleeping on the fire escape because it is so warm, have a Norwich terrier they lower into the courtyard in a little basket. The "Newlyweds" (Rand Harper and Havis Davenport) have just moved into the apartment on Jeff's left, drawn their blind, and set themselves to newlywed work for almost the entire film. A partially deaf sculptor (Jesslyn Fax) lives under Miss Torso, and once in a while haplessly attempts a conversation with someone or other while remaining a relatively neutral figure, much like the lumps of clay she molds as "art." And Lars Thorwald (Raymond Burr) is a traveling salesman whose apartment is directly across the way – and in Jeff's (James Stewart) direct line of sight.

As the story of Jeff's recuperation progresses (that story is the envelope that contains all the action in the film [see Pomerance "Recuperation"]), he gradually comes to conclude that Thorwald has slain his petulant (and also recuperating) wife, chopped her into pieces, and distributed her around the city. Jeff's stylish girlfriend Lisa Fremont (Grace Kelly), his therapeutic nurse Stella (Thelma Ritter), and his old police-detective buddy Tom Doyle (Wendell Corey) at first suspect his perceptions and motives, then gradually, and in different ways, slide over to his view of things. To find out whether Jeff has been correct in his fragmented observations of Thorwald – or, for that matter, in his readings of any of the other characters "out there" – we must wait until the climax of the film, which leads to a surprise that is at once nasty and invigorating.

Clearly, the overall structure of *Rear Window*, that a photographer laid up after a work accident whiles away his time staring at his neighbors and decoding snippets of their behavior into credible and coherent "tales," permits the filmmaker a delicious reflexivity (a point not lost on scholars who have written about the film's recursion): Jeff is Hitchcock's stand-in, and thus works also as substitute for the viewer who, in working to stitch together these fragments of the narrative quilt, is performing the same sort of calculation, adumbration, and composition as Jeff as he surveils Thorwald, Miss Lonelyhearts, and the others.[17] *Rear Window* having thus become a film about filmmaking, we have no trouble noticing that the windows of the apartments Jeff is staring at are all rectangular, in some ways like the screen on which we are watching this production (on this theme see in particular Krohn, *Work* 146ff.).[18]

To the extent that we bring morality to bear in questioning the probity of a man who peeps into the lives of others,

---

[17] Much of the critical writing that likens the dramas Jeff is watching to films-within-the-film has linked him explicitly to Hitchcock as a seer, image-maker, or director. Spoto mentions the wheelchair as a surrogate of the director's chair, for example (370); and one finds the analogy expounded fully by Curtis, Chion, Wood (101ff.), and White (189ff.). Jeff is not the only spy here. A pair of rooftop sunbathers (Stephanie Griffin and Joy Lansing) are being watched from an intruding helicopter as the film begins.

[18] It is not uninteresting that Paramount's VistaVision process premiered with *White Christmas* on October 14, 1954, ten weeks after *Rear Window* was opened. This process was Paramount's answer to the technical innovation of CinemaScope, proprietary to Twentieth Century–Fox and a significant factor in drawing audiences to theaters in the 1950s. Rather than stretching an image across a wider screen as CinemaScope did, VistaVision worked with a double-sized negative and produced a screen image in the 1.85:1 format, sometimes screened with 70 mm projection to make a truly enormous, and very crisp, picture. Thorwald's sitting-room window and that of Miss Lonelyhearts beneath him are modeled after the 2.55:1 ratio of CinemaScope. See generally Belton *Widescreen Cinema*.

we might also begin to wonder about the kind of realistic filmmaking we see on evidence here: who is any filmmaking artist, after all, to peep into lives and motives in such a way as to show a real world? Is not every filmmaker in some sense doing what Hitchcock is doing here, and having Jeff do along with him? John Belton brings some moral relief when he concludes that Jeff "imposes a logic and meaning on a human activity that ultimately defies understanding. . . . Jeff's vigilance keeps chaos at bay; his voyeurism is an attempt to defeat disturbances out there in the world of 1950s America" ("Introduction" 16). But until she becomes convinced of Thorwald as a murderer, Stella would not be convinced by this argument: she thinks Mr. Jefferies is a Peeping Tom.

Central to Hitchcock's endeavor in producing *Rear Window*, quite beyond the careful casting, scripting, and choreography, was the world of the apartment complex as it would appear to the contemporary viewer. New York's Greenwich Village, Hitchcock well understood, was an enclave of isolated and labyrinthine warrens, angular tiny streets, alleyways, and small apartment buildings set around city blocks in contiguity, so that their rear facades linked together to form closed courtyards of exactly the type we see figured in this film. On the outer perimeter one would find paved streets faced with similar buildings across the way, just such a vision as presents itself at the end of the tiny alley that leads past the sculptress's apartment and "out" of the scene (to the street behind, where Thorwald goes to meet Jeff and where Stella goes looking for a garbage truck that has vanished too quickly). Hitchcock is careful as the film winds on to arrange for bits of "local" action in this street: a milkman with his delivery truck, a passing vehicle here and there, pedestrians stepping along the opposite sidewalk, and, at one point, a street cleaner

Joseph MacMillan Johnson's elaborate apartment complex on Stage 18 at Paramount, as Hitchcock photographed it for Rear Window *(Paramount, 1954). The veranda of Miss Torso's apartment at the top of the wooden staircase (l.) is roughly at the studio's street level, with everything below it constructed in the soundstage's storage tank. The little street at the far end of the alley at left is practical but the facades and skyline beyond are painted. Note how some of the windows opposite simulate widescreen format. Courtesy Academy of Motion Picture Arts and Sciences.*

spraying water with a gaggle of kids merrily splashing about in its wake.[19]

But more dominant in our vision than the little street, more opulent as a construction, and more astonishing as an artistic rendition is Hitchcock's apartment structure itself, poised against the painted backing that shows some buildings

[19] A 1938 photograph by Ben Heller of kids cavorting around an open fire hydrant in the heat of summer and a later hydrant spree with a mother and son by Helen Levitt became iconic images of the Manhattan experience.

in the distance and the New York sky. This complex, rendered on Paramount's Stage 18 by Joseph MacMillan "Mac" Johnson as a copy of typical Greenwich Village low-rises, was at the time of shooting the largest single interior set ever constructed for a Hollywood production.[20] The soundstage, some hundred and eighty-six feet long and forty feet from ground level to rafters, has a storage basement beneath its floor dropping down an additional twenty feet. The entire floor covering was lifted out, and the basement was used for building the courtyard itself, so that Jeff's apartment, from which vantage point we witness virtually everything in the film, was constructed at ground level. Another forty feet of height was available to Johnson for building the apartment complex, a design so efficient that it contained in finished form thirty-one apartments of which twelve were fully practical, fitted with electricity, running hot and cold water, and decoration (by Sam Comer), not to mention a one-way communication system through which Hitchcock could issue commands to the various actors from Jeff's apartment, where along with his protagonist he "resided." Before construction began, Johnson had requested unit production manager "Doc" Erickson to find a rear court in Greenwich Village with a north vista, so that the camera could shoot from the shadow on the south side. "Shoot at least three different courts. Also shoot random color shots of rear courtyards in the Village, for detail of color of buildings, any time of day. I will use these in painting the set" (Johnson memorandum).[21]

[20] Working on the same soundstage in 1961, but using the VistaVision process, Jerry Lewis built a similarly gigantic set for *The Ladies Man*, this one a working "doll's house" with the front sliced off so that the camera – on a crane – could probe into the action in any of the rooms.
[21] Further, Hitchcock wanted 200-foot-long (just over two minutes) tape recordings of typical Greenwich Village sounds, made on small side streets (Erickson to Brown; Coleman to Caffey; Caffey to Innes).

Here, in collaboration with his designers, Hitchcock fashioned a peculiarly American vista. (A look at Murnau's *The Last Laugh* [1924] will reveal the European apartment setting by contrast, much more closed-in and formal.) As we look out in accompaniment with Jeff's curious gaze, we see the variegated urban population, each resident going through the day with an indomitable sense of purpose and placement, each with a distinctive, even flamboyant, personality, whether energetic, compulsive, depressive, or distracted. "The idea here," wrote Claude Chabrol,

> *is to illuminate, justify, and affirm the fundamental conception of the work, its hypothesis: the egocentric structure of the world as it is, a structure in which a faithful image is sought through the thematic relations between the people. The individual is thus the supremely differentiated atom, the couple a molecule, the apartment building a body composed of a number of molecules and set apart itself from the rest of the world.* (42, my translation)

Because as Jeff scouts through the apartment windows for entertainment he must be constantly shifting his concentration – like the hero of Poe's "The Man of the Crowd" (1840), he is recovering from serious debility as he gazes – the action in any one apartment never occupies his attention for very long. Thorwald, an apparent murderer, has the greatest claim. As to the others, their activities are observed, and made intelligible to us, through abrupt and fragmentary pantomimes, these only sometimes accompanied by (usually incomplete or muffled) sound. (When one lives in an apartment complex, the other tenants are partial mirrors of the self.) Like Jeff we must piece together the fragments of action if we are to make fluid dramatic stories, but it is also true that the reduction in action requires of the filmmaking a tremendous concentration of focal energy. The performers must execute their gestures with exact precision and tellingly, at a distance.

Miss Torso is an interesting example. First seen, she is at work on a choreographic routine set to Leonard Bernstein's *Fancy Free*[22] while dressing in her kitchen of a morning. On an evening later on, a number of well-dressed gentlemen have come to court her and she dances around the tiny space, avoiding them one by one, while Lisa, observing along with Jeff, notes the young dancer facing woman's greatest challenge, fighting sharks. This "caption" from Lisa radically enhances an analysis from Jeff's rather chauvinistic masculine point of view. Still later in the film, Miss Torso's true love has come back from afar: a soldier in uniform, notably shorter than she is, bespectacled, clearly what we would now call a nerd, yet the man of her heart. Each of the characters Jeff watches works through a tiny drama of this kind, by way of tableaux and gestures that are instantly readable even in abbreviation.

Seen in this way, *Rear Window* becomes an intriguingly detailed portrait of American life, less a full-fledged landscape and more a set of artist's sketches delicately fleshed out in detail. The apartment structure and its requisite fragmentation testified to America's modernity: people who in the agrarian mode had known one another intimately and over a long time had now shifted into movement, had become urbanized, and were strangers to one another whose contacts were abbreviated, rhythmical, curtailed. Chabrol's observation notwithstanding, New Yorkers are perhaps no more self-centered and isolated in their social feeling than the citizens one could meet in any great modern city: in this way, Hitchcock is making a picture of his time, not only a

---

[22] Choreographed by Jerome Robbins and premiering April 18, 1944. Three sailors on leave vie for a girl's attention.

particular locale. When the Whistlers' pup is murdered in the courtyard, the apartment dwellers scream Chabrol's atomistic formula into the nocturnal space: nobody cares for anyone but himself;[23] yet it is also a fact that this disconnected neutrality is the tenor of communal living in the modern city, a zone of intrepid individualism, rapid continual physical and social mobility, and a circulatory pattern that brings uncountable collisions with strangers. In such a zone, as Georg Simmel once pointed out, one is in visual proximity of people one cannot really hear, and this is confusing, frightening, disturbing ("Visual Interaction"). They are one's neighbors at the same time as they are utterly strange and unknown, all the while remaining comprehensible to the extent that one can read their actions against the implicit (and mediated) script of normalized everyday life.

It is not a psychological but an economic imperative that forces the kind of visible but detached social interaction we can see developed and highlighted in this film. Heightened land value leads to vertical agglomeration and population density; and the character of New York as a trading and communication center (it is a major port and rail hub) draws strangers from all directions who want to establish themselves in the same confined spaces, that is, pushed against one another in complexes like Jeff's. While it is possible here for people to meet and form associations – Jeff certainly finally meets the nefarious Thorwald; and the devoted composer is united with Miss Lonelyhearts once his song is completed and it turns out the melody saved her from

---

[23] This was also a significant hue and cry ten years later, when in the Kew Gardens section of Queens "Kitty" Genovese was brutally murdered on the sidewalk outside her apartment building as neighbors passively watched.

suicide – more broadly it is a combination of emotional and cultural isolation coupled with optical exposure and proximity that characterizes the sort of apartment life one finds epitomized in New York. The windows – eyes themselves, as they seem – are always present and glaring, almost always open to the view of those who can only surmise what they are seeing.

Small Enterprises

Hitchcock's familiarity with the topography and culture of the modern American city was hardly cursory. He proceeded to film only after the most intensive research on all aspects of the story and location. The details of a place, particularly, had always interested him (see for some of the early roots of this McGilligan, *Darkness* 13–15), and it is thus unsurprising that searching through his films one comes across a substantial array of very precise renderings of city life and urban nuance. New York, for example, he was not content to explore only in *Rear Window* – a film that shows a remarkable sensitivity to the routines of daily life in Greenwich Village but includes only passing allusion to Lisa's uptown world. Not long afterward, he returned to detail the midtown area, parts of the Bronx, and Queens in *The Wrong Man*, and at the end of the 1950s he gave expert rendering to the East Side and adjacent Long Island in *North by Northwest* (both films to which I return in this volume). In *Rope* we see a picture of wealthy upper-East Siders, although the urban ambience of this film is constructed almost exclusively through precise characterization and with the use of a painted backing (effected with "buildings, clouds and sunset ... modeled on photographs" [Krohn, *Work* 107]). *Topaz* has important scenes shot in

Harlem and makes reference to other parts of New York and to Washington, D.C.

Washington is central – along with a satellite small town – in *Strangers on a Train* (1951). In *Vertigo* (1958), Hitchcock takes source material (by Pierre Boileau and Thomas Narcejac) originally set in Paris and Marseilles and transports the locale to the city and surrounding region of San Francisco, with a marvelous mise-en-scène that places Scottie Ferguson's search for the elusive Madeleine Elster and the ghost who haunts her, Carlotta Valdes, in such spots as the Palace of the Legion of Honor, the underside of the Golden Gate Bridge at Fort Point, the Mission Dolores, Ernie's restaurant, and the florist Podesta Baldocchi near Union Square, not to mention the Big Basin Redwood Forest and the old Spanish mission at San Juan Bautista (at which considerable footage was shot, some with the inclusion through a matte process of a bell tower important to the narrative). A *Vertigo* preproduction memorandum from Hitchcock's personal assistant listed other "Important Locations," including the Brocklebank Apartments, the McKittrick Hotel, the apartment structure at Lombard and Jones Streets (where Scottie lives), Twin Peaks, and the Empire Hotel (at Sutter and Leavenworth) (Robertson to Goodfreed). Other American cities and rural sites fascinated Hitchcock, too. In *Marnie* (1964) we see Philadelphia and Virginia, in *The Trouble with Harry* (1955) Stowe, Vermont, and in *Psycho* Phoenix, however briefly.

Consistently in Hitchcock's American work the camera's angle of concentration, the exact details of the setting included in the frame, and the relation between the action and its locale are stunningly precise and telling; no one could reasonably conclude Hitchcock was working in the United States with the mentality of a tourist. (We can note, for instance, that in the opening of *North by Northwest* no one is looking up at the skyscrapers: in fact, New Yorkers don't, ever.) He had devoted himself to knowing and appreciating any place he shot, as locals did. To capture Ernie's in San Francisco, with its scarlet-flocked wallpaper and prestigious clientele, in order that Scottie might first encounter Madeleine in a properly "romantic" environment, the filmmaker arranged with the restaurant ownership, Victor and Roland Gotti, that his designer Henry Bumstead should recreate the dining room point for point on a Paramount soundstage. The recreation was undertaken with such diligence and seriousness that Hitchcock arranged for the cast and crew to be (realistically) served a meal from Ernie's while they shot (Kraft and Leventhal 86).[24] Especially characteristic of Hitchcock's work is the detailed and informed sense of San Francisco culture that we get from this scene; or the taste of the city available in the opening twilight shot that depicts the rooftop chase leading to Scottie's horrible acrophobia; or the view from the outside of a sanatorium where Scottie is recuperating after Madeleine's death, with the camera slowly panning over the prospect of the city upon the bay; or his rendering of the art galleries of the Legion of Honor; or the ambience as Scottie and Judy Barton stroll tranquilly beside the Palace of Fine Arts; or the eerie atmosphere of the sadly overgrown garden around the tombs in the Mission Dolores.[25]

---

[24] If for comparison with *Vertigo* one looked at another fiction set on the same streets, say, Peter Yates's exciting action thriller *Bullitt* (1968), one could easily see how in the later film there is only the scantest attention to the city space as an actually lived environment, the story reflecting on San Francisco mostly by way of telling exteriors that emphasize the vertical structure of the city. Notable, for instance, is the use of the steeply falling streets to establish the key car chase scene (a scene that has become famous precisely for its setting).
[25] Hitchcock shared with Truffaut his fondness for centering dramatic action in appropriate places (see Truffaut 256–7).

Less urban topographies interested him as much. The little town of Bodega Bay, north of San Francisco, is exploited from numerous angles to establish the story of *The Birds* (1963), and in some very brief narrative moments there, with a keen attention to the way personality is configured in and through geographic space, Hitchcock offers a sharp and tonally accurate view of American rural culture persisting in the face of urbanization and modernity. Take, for example, the petulant princess Melanie Daniels's ('Tippi' Hedren) introduction to the town by way of a conversation with Brinkmayer (John McGovern), the postmaster and owner of the general store. Brinkmayer has a pointed, nononsense, utterly practical way of speaking that characterizes a pioneer spirit without lapsing into the old-fashioned quaintness that Hitchcock wished to avoid in "village types" (Hitchcock to Hunter). It was even desirable for the filmmaker to find out what sorts of contemporary yummies the Bodega Bay general store offered: would they, for instance, "sell anything like muu muus – and length of same" (Research Note)? The store's distinctly bounteous stock is a telling historical reflection as well as a narrative detail, since the white settlers of California had all immigrated as contestants for the anticipated riches of an undeveloped and rugged territory.

Bodega Bay, further, is a fishing community (such as Hitchcock had explored in *The Manxman* [1929]), where discourse is spare, purposeful, directive, and serious. In *The Birds*, the only central characters who use language metaphorically, playfully, and ironically are Melanie, daughter of the owner of a city newspaper, and her new beau Mitch Brenner, a city lawyer (Rod Taylor). Mitch's old girlfriend and the local schoolteacher, Annie Hayworth (Suzanne Pleshette), knows how to use language artfully but usually doesn't, since she has set herself fully to rural life, a transformation Mitch doesn't quite accomplish through his frequent visits. His mother, Lydia (Jessica Tandy), behaves and speaks like a city person retired to the country. Comfortably, and with directness and simplicity, she runs a little farm on the far side of the bay;[26] and the various denizens of The Tides restaurant, even the educated ornithologist (Ethel Griffies), all use a direct, unpresuming, unadorned sort of speech. If the American city is a nexus for the moving population, filled with ambitious and confused personalities hunting, exploiting, climbing upon, evading, and surveilling one another, the small village is a different enterprise entirely. Here, nobody is planning to "go" anywhere; this isn't a way stop. Not jitteriness, not acquisitiveness, not careerism but Mitch's loyalty to his mother and sister bring him up on weekends; Melanie has been following him.

The American small town particularly fascinated Hitchcock, but even in the early 1940s he didn't want his smalltown characters "too homespun for modern times" (Krohn, *Work* 62) and desired instead to make a picture of rural life inflected by the spirit of modernity. Preparing for *Shadow of a Doubt*, he had been explicit in a May 11, 1942 memorandum entitled "Some Notes about the Small Town Atmosphere":

---

[26] The sequences were shot at the Gaffney ranch, a 432-acre spread two and a half miles from the town (Winokur to Gaffney). "It is fair to assume," states a memorandum regarding set dressing requirements for the film, "... that whatever their business was, the elder Brenners were well off enough to have an apartment in San Francisco and the farm at Bodega Bay as a weekend retreat. We can obviously infer that, after Mr. Brenner's death, the two places were more than sufficient for Mrs. Brenner's needs so she gave up the apartment and came to live permanently at the small farm at Bodega Bay.... One interesting effect of the furnishings might be that the dining chairs came from the apartment in San Francisco but the oval table belonged originally to the farm setting" (Hitchcock memorandum).

If possible I am extremely anxious to avoid the conventional small town American scene. By conventional I mean the stock figures which have been seen in so many films of this type. I would like them to be very modern; in fact, one could almost lay the story in the present day. . . . But by modern I mean that the small town should be influenced by movies, radio, juke boxes, etc.; in other words, as it were, life in a small town lit by neon signs.

As a rural environment Santa Rosa, his setting for *Shadow*, differs considerably from Bodega Bay, which is about thirty kilometers away. It is neither coastal nor an enclave for a predominantly working-class population. A county seat in Sonoma wine country, the town in fact supported significant population growth starting around the time of the film. Further, while *The Birds* plays out an abrasive encounter between urban and rural mentalities, philosophies, and conditions, there is nothing intrinsically urban about *Shadow of a Doubt* – surely not the Newton family, in whose spacious and substantially middle-class home the action is centered; not (the recently urban*ized*) Charles Oakley (Joseph Cotten), who has come on a visit from the East to see his sister again; not even Jack Graham (Macdonald Carey) and Fred Saunders (Wallace Ford), detectives on a national hunt for a serial killer who they think may well have found his way to this charming tree-lined place, this perfect American town and perfect analogue to Thornton Wilder's *Our Town* (Wilder was instrumental in, as he put it, "characteriz[ing] that family and . . . work[ing] with Mr. Hitchcock on the plotting of the dramatic interest" [Wilder wire]). If the town is generally a repository of fundamental American virtues, such as modesty and neighborliness, moderation and thrift, it is also a garden of seclusion in the modern world, hence a perfect place to hide. Not everyone who lived there was happy with the quaint and old-fashioned environment: the bar waitress whom our young protagonist meets (Janet Shaw) is ravenous for another life, something more akin to her dreams and less demeaningly restrictive. As a filmic work, in many ways *Shadow* is colloquial ("as colloquial as apple pie" [Louise Levitas, *PM*, January 13, 1943]), and took its place in a tradition. The visual and topical conceit of the "charming small town" had been tried many times in Hollywood film, a similarly enchanting nook, its streets lined by aged massive spreading trees, its population well meaning and orderly, its social values traditional and egalitarian (it was a holdover from agrarian America before the shocking forces of modernity took it over), having appeared in parts of Sam Wood's *Kings Row* (1942), Orson Welles's *The Magnificent Ambersons* (1942), and again in *The Stranger* (1946); and in an MGM backlot design by Lemuel Ayres, Jack Martin Smith, and Cedric Gibbons for Vincente Minnelli's *Meet Me in St. Louis* (1944). Later the idea would persist in Robert Mulligan's *To Kill a Mockingbird* (1962, here in an elaborate backlot design at Universal by Henry Bumstead) and (shot on the same lot) *Back to the Future* (1985). Two years after America's entry into the Second World War, Hitchcock rendered in *Shadow* an image of a town well settled into – and, its citizens are convinced, well protected by – comfort and stability. We see the staid banker managing his pleasantly shady offices, the virtually empty and scenic railway station – reminiscent, as Uncle Charlie's train pulls in (with its black, black smoke signaling the arrival of the Devil, claimed Hitchcock [Truffaut 154]), of the little *gare* at La Ciotat made famous in early cinema by the brothers Lumière – the ivied edifice of the public library with its resident rule-abiding matriarch (the 1940s and 1950s were a time when a great deal of attention was committed to the beauty of rules and public order, and the necessity of good behavior), and on the immaculate sidewalks breaths of conversation spelling out the essential cordiality and civility, not to say familiarity, that obtained between citizens. In small towns like Santa Rosa, everyone knows everyone else's business. In the British small town depicted at the same diegetic time, say, for example, in Michael Powell and Emeric Pressburger's *A Matter of Life and Death* (1946),[27] the residents are more insular as personalities, the interaction between them considerably less fluid and more limited; England, after all, lacks the vast space in which people may shuffle to get away from one another's insults, while the American identity, even in the smallest and most provincial of towns, posits itself as boundless.

"In so many ways," writes Paula Marantz Cohen, *Shadow* "extols the virtues of small-town family life. The cheerful home, the humorous squabbling siblings, the flighty but lovable mother, the warm-hearted, ineffectual father all capture our sympathy and arouse our protective impulses" (131) – protective impulses, we might imagine, because the virtues of small-town life are already, and broadly, under threat from what Kenneth Burke called "metropolitan bickerings" (272). Cohen goes on to suggest that the film sustains interest and generates suspense because "though it may critique the family in some respects, [it] supports it in countervailing ones," creating a "tension between critique and support, transgression and maintenance." Beyond the filmic structure there is a tension implicit in the very rendering of American character onscreen, at this critical historical moment.

The Newtons, after all, like other small-town citizens in the early 1940s, are caught on the cusp of modernity but still resolutely clinging to traditional ways, hurled into a future

---

[27] And canonized for the popular taste a decade earlier in Agatha Christie's Miss Marple mysteries.

whose principles they have not yet accepted. (Oddly, the *New York Herald Tribune* saw the film as having been "conceived against a background of middle-class placidity" [Howard Barnes, January 13, 1943]). The patriarch, Joe (Henry Travers), until he is gifted one by the visiting Charles Oakley, has never owned a wristwatch (an invention of the First Great War). The mother (Patricia Collinge), hardly liberated by images of vamps and nail polish from the 1920s (as is the crofter's wife in *The 39 Steps* [1935], at least in her imagination), has organized herself around routines – shopping routines, cooking routines, servile routines, maternal routines. She is a woman for whom in virtually all things the eggs don't go into the cake until the butter and sugar have been creamed. Charlie (Teresa Wright),[28] the oldest child and the family member most dramatically poised at the edge of a philosophical threshold, feels enormous sympathy for her mother as a person whose life has been restricted, seems ready to bound out of this town, and is yet the very model of old-fashioned modesty, decorum, and propriety. The younger children are obsessed with the abstract: one is an addicted reader of fiction, the other is mapping the town in footsteps.[29] "There is much honesty of observation here," wrote Archer Winston, "as well as the amusement of recognition rather than that of the joke" ("'Shadow of a Doubt' Opens at the Rivoli Theatre," *New York Post*, January 13, 1943, 46). All these "amusing" folk are contained in a white

---

[28] Before Wright was cast, Hitchcock had asked confidentially whether Joan Fontaine wanted to play the role (Wire).
[29] It is fascinating that Ann (Edna May Wonacott) has plunged into Sir Walter Scott while her brother Roger (Charles Bates) is a wannabe cartographer. Scott's *Waverley* (1814) was a tale of the 1745 Jacobite uprising, an event that ultimately drew to the Highlands – especially for the purpose of mapping transportation routes between forts there in the British attempt to overcome the Jacobites – one David Watson (1704–61), who originated the British Ordnance Survey (see Hewitt).

clapboard house[30] with spacious lawns and tall hedges, where the garage door that sometimes sticks has always sometimes stuck, the kitchen has always been the site of luscious hospitality, the visitor from next door (Hume Cronyn) has seemingly always shown up before dessert to plot hypothetical murders with Joe. In this utterly conventional social space, language is always modest and restrained, feeling held in; money never talked about; tradition always revered above novelty. Searching for their mass killer, the two detectives move like extraterrestrials, prying their way into the family abode by pretending to be carrying out a national survey. For the Newtons, models of typicality and small-town goodness, the very thought of being singled out for scientific questioning is sufficient to ruffle the placid waters of their everyday lives.

The idea of burying dark motives and fears under the pristine surface of small-town life was not merely a dramatic flourish of Hitchcock's. He recognized implicitly that there was a tension in rural life between, as it were, the newly painted exterior and the murderous thoughts at the dinner table inside, as though reflecting Valéry's ironic observation that nothing in man is deeper than the skin. Small-town life was both charming and precarious. Arthur Vidich and Joseph Bensman describe the problem:

> *There is silent recognition among members of the community that facts and ideas which are disturbing to the accepted system of illusions are not to be verbalized except, perhaps, as we have noted, in connection with one's enemies. Instead, the social mores of the small town at every opportunity demand that only those facts and*

---

[30] Some of *Shadow of a Doubt* was filmed on location in Santa Rosa, but many of the shots were done on a soundstage, where a huge replica of the house exterior was built (see Krohn, *Work* 66–7).

ideas which support the dreamwork of everyday life are to be verbalized and selected out for emphasis and repetition. People note other people's successes, comment on them with public congratulations and expect similar recognition for themselves. . . . In this process each individual reinforces the illusions of the other. (303)

If the behavior of characters in *Shadow of a Doubt* seems quintessentially American in the agrarian sense, this surely owes to the rich mythologizing of the agrarian persona – the Andy Hardy films, *Winesburg, Ohio, Our Town*, the paintings of Thomas Hart Benton or the Hudson River School; and to the fact that the American actors knew how to find their characters and the American screenwriters knew how to craft dialogue and situations.[31]

Not yet an American himself, Hitchcock brings to the film two astonishing additional qualities, and these make the cultural features and details of social life radiate onscreen. First, there is a remarkable illumination: dappling the sidewalk, for example, as Charlie and Jack walk home after Sunday church and he informs her about her uncle; wafting out of the window of the 'Til Two bar as Charlie and her uncle go in for a disturbing conversation one night; flooding the railway platform as Uncle Charles arrives and again as he departs; warmly touching the Newton living room at the party following Uncle Charles's talk; in the moonlit night outside the house, as Charles attempts to confront Charlie and then again at the top of the outside stairway as she glares into his face in silhouette. The illumination is relentlessly sharp and hungry, picking out relevant details of expression or posture, of architecture or natural setting, as

---

[31] "Hitchcock was so touched by [Thornton] Wilder's abilities, in fact, that he gave him special credit in the titles," writes Auiler (*Notebooks* 103).

though each moment of the film constitutes a kind of symptom of rural embedding and intelligence caught in the margins of war.[32]

Secondly, and very powerfully, in a chain of telling close-ups Hitchcock reveals the American face as a kind of moral space itself, indeed a space troubled by deep fractures (like the State of California) and vulnerable humanity. When she learns that her brother must leave Santa Rosa, Emma Newton loses control at her little party. The camera gives a pregnant close-up, showing her as a little girl again, hope and dreams twinkling in her teary eyes, and also as someone who has never gained a sense of self independent of her family. At the dinner table, as Charles expounds bitterly on the moral corruption of American life, the camera swoops into a macro close-up that reveals his brittle (perhaps crumbling) façade, his inner vacuum, the soft and etiolated flesh that grew out of boyhood without guidance and purpose. For William Rothman, "The poetry in his voice disappears as his speech turns to an indrawn, private vision" (216). When one night Charlie slips on the outside staircase (because it has been sabotaged), we get a close shot of her face as she bends to examine the dislocated step: something is strange, something is not beautiful and natural and ordinary here; a dark spot has come into her world.

Hitchcock had been preparing personally to handle dark spots like this. Six months before *Shadow* opened, he obtained "Special Deputy Sheriff of Sonoma County State of California" identification card No. 0551, giving him "the right to make arrests as provided by law" but not "the right to violate the law himself."

---

[32] In some of the street scenes, writes Bill Krohn, conscripts appear as "mute witnesses" (Alfred 42–3) but "dialogue references to the war were avoided because they 'might date the film'" (*Work* 71). Krohn notes that some of the script was written by Patricia Collinge (*Work* 63).

Patricia Collinge as Emma Newton in Shadow of a Doubt *(Universal, 1943) at the moment she is faced with her brother's plan to leave Santa Rosa. Digital frame enlargement.*

City Movements

For the Romantic imagination the city was a quintessential "dark spot," a festering vortex of disease, deprivation, abject poverty, and pollution (the gas lamps of the late nineteenth century were alone responsible for grime, explosions, and malady), but it was as a city boy that Hitchcock had grown up. In his great explorations of New York and San Francisco, *North by Northwest*, *The Wrong Man*, and *Vertigo*, he brings to the screen a precise and fond acknowledgment of urban detail. If in *Vertigo* San Francisco does not achieve the status of a redeeming sanctum – Scottie Ferguson must flee it for an old Spanish mission in order to come properly to the end of his story – it remains an alluring, mystifying, and gleaming jewel on the Pacific; and, of course, as I have listed above, it is shown to us by way of very precise and carefully viewed locales. As for New York, we see in *North by Northwest* a city of energizing traffic and purposiveness, a riotous cacophony that twists and entangles events, personalities, and intentions in furious, sometimes desperate, motion. In *The Wrong Man*, focused largely in the borough of Queens, there is a somber, stoic, and stony sense of institutional process, enduring and monolithic structure, gloomy doubt. But New York is always for Hitchcock a place out of which action springs with a kind of natural inevitability, and there is always a confounding multiplicity of action and event there, with Roger Thornhill racing across town between the Plaza Hotel and the United Nations and Grand Central Station to avoid kidnappers and murderers, all the while surrounded by the immense throng that is the modern crowd, an undifferentiated and shuddering organism going everywhere at once, always fascinating to watch; or with Manny Balestrero enduring the humiliating procedures of arrest, arraignment, and incarceration before trial while another man[33] – invisible at first but gradually and mortally changing into a tactile presence before our eyes – is also at work, also in movement, creeping along his own dark course in the twilight streets.

 The New York City area was by the middle of the twentieth century, and remains today, one of the prime examples of not only metropolitan but also suburban development, especially with the construction of the Long Island Express-

---

[33] The role was played by Richard Robbins, who had appeared on Broadway with Judy Holliday in *Born Yesterday* and who read in Walter Winchell's column "that producer-director Alfred Hitchcock was seeking an actor who resembled [Henry] Fonda. He sent him his photograph and 24 hours later was playing the holdup man for whom Fonda is mistaken in the story" (*Wrong Man* Publicity).

way and the Parkway system and with the growth of such exurban communities as Levittown, Great Neck, Hempstead, Garden City/Roslyn, and, further out, Amityville, Babylon, Patchogue, and the Hamptons (see Caro). By including in his diegesis for *North by Northwest* a scene of Vandamm's henchmen driving the kidnapped Roger out to Old Westbury, particularly a handsome mansion reposing inside a vastly expansive green sward and forest, Hitchcock shows a kind of "second America," an America bordered off from and elevated above the workaday world of cramped skyscrapers and scurrying throngs in the city and commanding the economy from a quasi-baronial distance. It can never be overstressed how much Hitchcock was sensitive to, and aware of, social class and the systematic arrangements that followed its division. Roger needed to meet "Lester Townsend" not anywhere but precisely in his capacious Long Island retreat; then later inside the United Nations,[34] symbol not only of postwar Unity but also, perhaps more pointedly, of America's open-arms attitude toward the rest of the world. As to classes, the contrast between them and between urban sophistication and rural simplicity would never in Hitchcock's work be more sharply illustrated than in the paired sequences of Roger's gallivanting around the Plaza Hotel – the staid Oak Bar, the marbled lobby, the

---

[34] Built on set for the project, after the U.N. refused permission for shooting on site. "When authorities at the United Nations read the final screenplay of *North by Northwest*, they turned thumbs down. They would not allow us to film anything on or inside U.N. property. ... We couldn't put an open camera on the curved driveway, so I used a station wagon filled with luggage and clothes hanging from hooks all along the windows. Hidden under the luggage were the cameraman and his assistant. The driver of the station wagon and his passenger were dressed like California tourists. The passenger got out and began shooting pictures in every direction. Meanwhile, the cameramen [*sic*] slipped a suitcase aside and began filming the scene" (Coleman, *Hollywood* 282; 283).

gilded elevator – and his later adventure in the Indiana cornfield, where his only social encounter is with a gentleman born to the land, alien to urban sophistication, plainspeaking in the extreme,

> ROGER: Hi.
> FARMER: (Silence)
> ROGER: Hot day.
> FARMER: Seen worse.
> ROGER: Are you supposed to be meeting someone here?
> FARMER: Waitin' for the bus. Due any minute.
> ROGER: Oh.
> FARMER: Some of them crop-duster pilots get rich. If they live long enough.
> ROGER: Yeah. Then, uh . . . Then your name isn't Kaplan?
> FARMER: Can't say it is, 'cause it ain't.

all this straight out of Carl Sandburg.

Nor was Hitchcock oblivious to urban workers, as we see in the Grand Central Station sequence in which a ticket vendor displays a canniness and make-do acumen typical of New Yorkers who must struggle for their daily bread along with millions of competitors; and in the sequence at the La Salle St. Station in Chicago, where hundreds of red caps mill around with baggage in an echoing vault (Roger, in disguise, among them). Not only is there a lot of traffic in the main rail terminals of America, but the servile class is overpopulated there; one receives – even in the brief few seconds of this shot – the distinct impression of workers struggling against one another to make pickups and a little cash. The argument that any director shooting in a major railway terminal would undoubtedly get something of the same picture needs only the rejoinder that Vincente Minnelli (an American by birth) shooting in Pennsylvania Station for *The Clock*

(1945) didn't give a comparative picture of laborers in action at all, nor did Rudolph Maté making his *Union Station* (1950) at the Union Station in Los Angeles.

Location sequences in *The Wrong Man* show a tenderer New York. We begin at Sherman Billingsley's Stork Club (formerly on East Fifty-Third Street, near Fifth Avenue, now the site of Paley Park), but hardly in the swing of mid-evening hilarity and joie de vivre. It is well after midnight.[35] The party is over. The air is palpable, looks stale, and the dancers are wearing out and departing, with the band doing its last number and wrapping just at the point the credits conclude. Manny Balestrero (Henry Fonda)[36] soundlessly treads away with his double bass, then descends into the subway to catch an "E" train for the long ride out to Queens. We have enchanting but also eerie shots of the glaring lights as he descends the long escalator down to the track at Fifth Avenue, then harshly illuminated shots on the train itself as Manny sits to work on his racing form – his nightly habit. At the Roosevelt Avenue/Jackson Heights station he visits the Victor Moore Arcade,[37] settles into Bickford's, a tiny all-night coffee spot (photographed April 16, 1956), and, calling up an image of Edward Hopper's transcendentally silent and enveloping *Nighthawks* (1942), takes his toast and coffee in

---

[35] A typical Hitchcock question to his researchers: "What would the waiters be doing at 3:30 A.M. and how many of them would there be?" Or this, which bears directly on the opening credits sequence: "When the band stops played [*sic*] does it sign off or does that only happen when there are a lot of people dancing? If there are a few people dancing and it is 4:00 A.M., should we say, do they stop or do they have to continue until there is only one couple or so on the floor?" (Questions on Script).

[36] Fonda is portraying the real Christopher Emmanuel Balestrero, whose wrongful arrest in 1953 was the story of the film.

[37] Named for the actor Victor Moore (1876–1962), a local resident, who starred in *Swing Time* (1936), *Make Way for Tomorrow* (1937), *The Seven Year Itch* (1955), and numerous other films.

delicious solitude before making his way home. He will return to this Arcade, ironically enough, to visit an insurance company[38] in hopes of getting some money on his wife's policy so that she can have dental work done; and then later with police accompaniment, charged with robbery and faced with the secretaries who, Harpies both, will scornfully identify him.

Much later, seeking a witness who could place him out of town at the time of the robbery in question, he is standing on the sidewalk on West 178th Street, just beside the Manhattan entrance to the George Washington Bridge, while in a sumptuously provocative foggy twilight its beacon lights radiate in the background. This isn't merely a case of Hitchcock's assistant director or location manager finding an interesting spot; it's a case of finding the perfectly evocative spot, with Manny's identity vulnerable to sudden and perhaps enduring redefinition as he panics at the thought of not finding the witness here and the bridge calling up the endless movements and transformations, the endless chain of hopes, inherent to life in New York. The

---

[38] Hitchcock's penchant for meticulous research is evident here. For example, since the Prudential Insurance Company was mentioned in an early script and Carl Milliken Jr. of the Warner Bros. Research Dept. had warned associate producer Herbert Coleman about likely rights problems, a considerable list of "Substitute titles" was offered the next day, including Peoples' Life Assurance Company, Long Island Life Insurance, Home Owners' Casualty, New York State Insurance Corp, Life & Casualty Insurance Co. of Queens, East Coast Life Insurance, Hudson Home and Life Insurance Co., and Insurance Services, Inc., but not Associated Life of New York, which was finally used. All these possible names would have rung with Hitchcock and his associates bells of fidelity to the actual sorts of companies active in New York City at the time, a requirement for Hitchcock's persistent need to create a "real" screen world. Numerous other potential problems are cited in the Milliken memo, including the need to obtain full permission from the Balestrero family for use of their names.

lighting makes the scene half unreal – as it must seem to our protagonist – and at the same time embeds it in a climatic actuality, a freak manifestation of the weather that makes for the lushly radiant fog, the bleary, almost weary streetlamps, and an atmosphere of wonder mixed with doubt that precisely captures Manny's dislocation and anxiety now that he has fallen afoul of the law. Hitchcock had been expressly directive to his cinematographer, Robert Burks, about the manner of shooting these settings: "I want it to look like it had been photographed in New York in a style unmistakably documentary.... Perhaps you may not want to do this picture, Bob. I wouldn't want the stark, colorless documentary treatment I expect to reflect on your reputation as a photographer" (qtd. in Foster 85). Frederick Foster indicates that "Hitchcock not only visited, measured and inspected every real-life locale of the story, but also had his staff record with stop-watch accuracy the way the

West 178th Street, the Bronx: an establishing shot for The Wrong Man *(Warner Bros., 1956). "Like it had been photographed . . . in a style unmistakably documentary." Digital frame enlargement.*

subway ran at the time of the events depicted in 'The Wrong Man,' the block-by-block itinerary of the hero and the experiences of all the principal characters in the drama" (112).[39]

In *Vertigo*, Hitchcock's use of San Francisco shows precisely the kind of highly intentional playfulness and deep-rooted familiarity with place that could have characterized a recent newcomer to the neighborhood impassioned about his surround. Charles Barr notes an "unusually rich texture of topographical allusion" and "the film's intense and rather magical quality of rootedness: in the city and its environs, in its historical past and in the uncanny dimensions waiting to be explored within and around it" (34). For the filmmaker this was well-known territory: he had purchased a second home near Santa Cruz (just south of San Francisco) in August 1942 (Spoto 272) and would have been more than familiar with that part of the country. His achievement in adapting the Boileau/Narcejac novel *D'Entre les morts* was to add a dimension, that of verticality. The difference between the powered controlling class and the middle and working classes became essential to the story, as it pivoted around the tale of a woman "owned" by a city man in the nineteenth century, abused and wasted by him, then discarded like abject trash. Hitchcock had to connote this social ladder. But he was also interested in the difference between the present and the past, and in the idea of "falling back into" history, a theme evoked repeatedly in the film but most poignantly after Madeleine Elster's death when Scottie, still obsessively in love and unable to get her out of his mind, sees simulacral doubles all

---

[39] Foster quotes Burks as crediting Kodak Tri-X stock and the newly developed Garnelite lamp, with its compact size, intense power, and portability, for much of the success with the cinematography of this film. "We actually lit streets a block and a half long with this equipment" (114).

over town and is hurled into the pit of reminiscence. The very acrophobia which is registered in the film's title involves a powerful vertical experience, as does the idea – central to Scottie's knowledge of both Madeleine and Judy (a shop girl who somehow recalls her to him) – of a mask or face riding on top of, and thus surmounting, a lingering underworld of personality and biography.

Writes Lary May with an eye on cinema, race, and urban tensions, "Just as the dark cinematic style and current cultural wars dramatized the fear that to give into one's dark desires was to become no better than nonwhites, so reason and experts armed with science and the law brought light and happiness. No doubt the master of this duality was Alfred Hitchcock.... Hitchcock showed that just beneath the surface of wartime patriotism lay danger, spies, and hidden enemies" (222). Of course, wartime patriotism outlasted the war. While the novel was set primarily in Paris and Marseilles, neither of them especially vertical locales, the vertical dimension would become a figurative key to Hitchcock's constructions, San Francisco constituting a perfectly apt setting for making believable these narratological "drops": Scottie's car in descent from the Top of the Mark down toward Union Square or climbing up to the Palace of the Legion of Honor; the retracing of steps back into deep historical time in the redwood forest. A vital (and vertical) interaction that takes place underneath the Golden Gate Bridge[40] is not only about bridging a past to a future and a woman to a man's heart, but about the power of the towering

---

[40] The bridge stands 746 feet high and opened May 27, 1937. The spans were forged and prepared in Vancouver, then ferried to the site for erection. Later, the construction facility was converted to Vancouver's Bridge Studios, a motion picture studio where in 1985 Ridley Scott had Assheton Gorton build him a magical forest for *Legend*.

superscape and the peril of a channel that runs far beneath. If all of this were not enough, the vertical arrangement by which we fall through a story as we engage with it – Paul Goodman's idea of stories proceeding along a line of steadily increasing probability – is mirrored in Scottie's whole experience with Madeleine, nothing if not the princess elevated at the heart of the fairytale, and also invoked powerfully with the tower sequences at San Juan Bautista, where the idea of falling (but not falling itself) is conveyed through the celebrated zoom/dolly combination shot that makes the ground appear to swoop into our face as though we are cascading toward it.[41]

American Paradise

In *The Trouble with Harry*, a gaggle of characters inhabiting a charming Vermont town confront, one by one, the pathetic reality of a corpse found lying on its back without its shoes up in the low hills where little Arnie Rogers (Jerry Mathers), "an energetic, forthright little male explorer in life," pretends to hunt for rabbit (July 27, 1954, script). What interests me here is less the pretext and plot of this film – virtually

---

[41] "The viewpoint must be fixed, you see, while the perspective is changed as it stretches lengthwise," Hitchcock told Truffaut. "I thought about the problem for fifteen years. By the time we got to *Vertigo*, we solved it by using the dolly and zoom simultaneously. I asked how much it would cost, and they told me it would cost fifty thousand dollars. When I asked why, they said, 'Because to put the camera at the top of the stairs we have to have a big apparatus to lift it, counterweight it, and hold it up in space.' I said, 'There are no characters in this scene; it's simply a viewpoint. Why can't we make a miniature of the stairway and lay it on its side, then take our shot by pulling away from it? We can use a tracking shot and a zoom flat on the ground.' So that's the way we did it, and it only cost us nineteen thousand dollars" (246).

every inhabitant of the town assumes a guilt-ridden responsibility for this mysterious death – than two particular aspects of it, desired by the filmmaker with sufficient urgency that in the early fall of 1954, having just completed his last takes for *To Catch a Thief* in Nice, he flew immediately to the American northeast to commence principal photography without delay.[42] First, we have in this film the absolute commingling of two great American characters, the agrarian prophet and the urban sophisticate, sometimes in the persona of a being who began life in the city and now, having lived away from it for several years, has begun to abandon an urban attitude in favor of a rural one (as Lydia Brenner did in *The Birds*). Principal among these is Sam Marlowe (John Forsythe), a charming gadabout painter – and "a young man, carved it seems, from solid gold" (script) – who has befriended everyone (with the garrulousness only the urban type could show) and fallen for Arnie's mother, Jennifer (Shirley MacLaine, in her first screen role). What is rural about Sam is his chatty familiarity with the whole community, his skepticism and dogged way of clinging to Jennifer and Arnie. What is distinctly urban is his manner of painting, heavily influenced by abstract expressionism (a style born in New York and Long Island [see Rosenberg 213–28]) and the sharp wit evidenced in his conversation and his canvases. Harry himself, dead though he may be, was nothing but an urban type, now planted and dug up a dozen times under the bucolic loam of the Vermont hills. Jennifer herself seems to

---

[42] Spoto attributes to Mildred Dunnock the account that "Hitchcock was anxious to photograph the autumn landscape colors in full glory; the fall foliage was, he told her, the real reason for insisting on the actual locations for a film that could otherwise have easily been shot in the Paramount studios" (380). Krohn states that much of the material intended for location shooting was indeed shot in Hollywood, using foliage borrowed from Vermont, as the local weather was inclement (150).

have emerged from an urban locale, while the keeper of the general store, Mrs. Wiggs (Mildred Dunnock), her lanky and suspicious sheriff son Calvin (Royal Dano), and the town spinster Miss Ivy Gravely (Mildred Natwick) all give airs of having lived their lives in the country. The ancient suitor of Miss Gravely, Capt. Wiles (Edmund Gwenn), clearly hails from across the sea (but not from a city there, his delicacies reveal). As these folk interact in pairs and groups throughout the turning of the (comedic) plot (which is essentially the game of hiding Harry's body from the

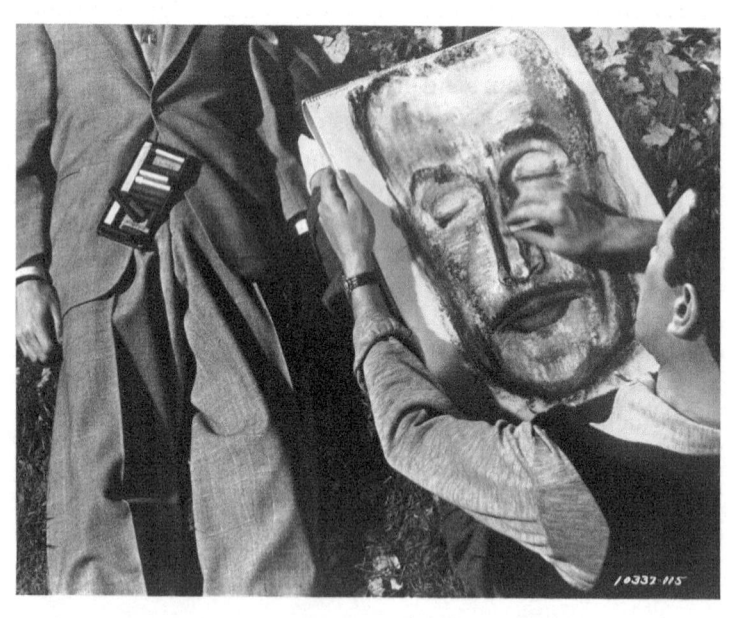

Sam Marlowe (John Forsythe, r.) using pastel crayons for a quick sketch of the dead Harry in The Trouble with Harry (Paramount, 1955). "Everyone," wrote Walter Benjamin, "praises the swift crayon of the graphic artist" ("Paris" 41). Late in this film, Sam's "swiftness" with that crayon will prove lifesaving. Courtesy Academy of Motion Picture Arts and Sciences.

authorities while at the same time trying to figure out who he is – or was!), there are continual rises and falls in the melodies of speech, the language, and the attitudes, as city and country voices contend against one another, then harmonize, and finally become indistinct. But this admixture of cultural types, and thus scenic forms, is not the most amazing thing about this film.

Hitchcock needed to rush to Vermont because he wanted to photograph at least establishing shots for *The Trouble with Harry* at the precise time of autumn when the foliage, at its apogee, would explode with scarlets, vermilions, tangerines, golds, sienna browns, and lush acid greens.[43] The net effect is that we watch this tale of death and resurrection, guilt and intuitive innocence, spread across a backdrop of vast and apparently limitless death and decay, the decay of vegetation in its annual cycle and the spectacular, even mythical glory produced through this process. In *Libération*, Simone Dubreuilh reacted with almost instinctual sensitivity: "The action is simple, almost Virgilian. Autumn, the dead leaves." There is no more picturesque or colorful Hitchcock production. Further, the film was shot in VistaVision, processed in three-strip Technicolor (at a time when Technicolor matrix manufacture

---

[43] Associate producer Herbert Coleman had assured unit production manager "Doc" Erickson that he was airmailing a 1953 foliage chart for New England, and estimated a period from early September to mid-October when leaves would be changing (production notes from telephone call, August 9, 1954). The script had originally called for an elaborate special effects transformation shot behind the main titles beginning with a slim branch of a maple tree ending in a pale green bud, then moving through the seasons until we have darkening, stiffening veins holding up the leaf "with Autumn's regal pride before the death of winter" (July 27, 1954). But according to Erickson, the filmmaker decided the backgrounds would "not be as appear in script – just trees and scenes. Hitch wants it all scenic" (Erickson note, October 14, 1954).

from Eastman Color negatives was in its glory), and then in limited theaters projected in large format. The effect of seeing this was deeply involving: the film was the best kind of view of a bucolic America slowly disappearing (just as the greenery was doing onscreen). A paradise of tranquility and stability was being replaced by something more urgent even than mortality, something impending and energizing and disconnected, the anxious future.

2

HITCHCOCK'S AMERICAN PERSONALITIES

"I often tell people, there are no Americans," Alfred Hitchcock admitted to Ian Cameron and Victor Perkins. "You become very audience-conscious because there are so many different types of people" (53). While he was growing up in England there were many different regional styles, vocalizations, and patterns of mannerism, not to say many local cultures even in London itself, but the fairly rigid social organization according to a strict class hierarchy meant that there really were not so many types of people. Whether in Hartford, Hereford, or Hampshire, the landed aristocrat was uniformly distanced from, and by at least his own estimation superior to, the tenant farmers and village laborers who surrounded him. When his stellar career as a filmmaker took Hitchcock from the High Street, Leytonstone, to a middle-class sub-baronial garden estate in Surrey, therefore, he had as though ridden in an express elevator unavailable to most Cockney lads.[1]

America offered another sort of palette altogether, with coastal, plains, mountain, urban, and agrarian types varying widely according to geography, ethnic background, and class. As Tocqueville had it, pointing to the many variant pathways they took in progressing toward success, "It is strange to see with what feverish ardour the Americans pursue their own welfare; and to watch the vague dread that constantly torments them lest they should not have chosen the shortest path which may lead to it" (2:161). Yet, as we can detect by examining a number of types seen through Hitchcock's eyes and framed as central characters in his dramas, there is something optimistic, unadorned, even urgently aspiring about the Americans he had come to know. It was as though in the American personality distilled and purified under the pressure of exigent necessity and ardent dreams one could meet, again and always, a fresh and modern spirit.

Melanie

"It is the same old thing as in all Americans," writes D. H. Lawrence about Herman Melville's masterpiece *Moby Dick*. "They keep their old-fashioned ideal frock-coat on and an old-fashioned silk hat, while they do the most impossible things" (154–5), a comment, perhaps, about latent conventionality underlying a skin of boisterous adventurousness. Or about their willingness, those Americans, to go anywhere and

---

[1] One of the very astutest and most sharply written evocations of class division in the England where Hitchcock came of age and did his earliest work is Orwell's *The Road to Wigan Pier*.

do anything in the same old clothes, the same everyday garments never gussied up for presentation. Or even about just their unbounded capabilities – unbounded because like Shakespeare's monster each of them might impetuously sing, "'Ban, 'Ban, Ca–Caliban / Has a new master. Get a new man! / Freedom, high day! High day, freedom! Freedom, / High day, freedom!" (*Tempest* II.ii.192–5). That, looking rather ordinary and proceeding almost always without ceremony, they manage to put up with the greatest torments, to climb to the highest peaks of achievement, to accomplish what ostensibly cannot be accomplished with a technique that is the key to opening history and possibility in every waking moment. Call it the practical spirit. While Europeans were convicted in ceremonial and signification, Americans took off and got things done.

Consider in this light the case of a persistent young woman ('Tippi' Hedren) who lives in San Francisco (probably on Nob Hill). Sired by a newspaper magnate, abandoned by her mother, she flew off to Europe, a quintessential American girl, a Daisy Miller, and exploited Western cultural history and her own frangible emotions by dunking herself naked in public fountains.[2] Grown older now, she has become smartly serious, a wearer of expensive lipstick and sleek mink. She takes herself window-shopping in the bird room of Davidson's Union Square pet shop (also frequented by Alfred Hitchcock and his twin Sealyham terriers), there making the acquaintance of a debonair and articulate young lawyer, Mitch Brenner (Rod Taylor), who, having read the newspapers, knows all about "Miss Melanie Daniels" and her "gilded

---

[2] Federico Fellini's *La Dolce Vita* had been in American circulation since April 1961. The scene in which Anita Ekberg steps into the Trevi Fountain – fully clothed – could have inspired the scriptwriting of Evan Hunter.

cage."³ After teasing her a little, raising Melanie's pique, Mitch zooms away in his car but not before she can abscond with his license plate number and use her contacts to find his local address. There is an idea brewing under her golden curls: having purchased a pair of lovebirds, adorable and green, she will leave them for him – perhaps as a mollifying token or come-on, perhaps merely to be kind, perhaps as a way of seeing what might eventuate from so casual an encounter. But Mitch has gone up to Bodega Bay for the weekend. So it is that Melanie hops into her little green sports car and weaves back and forth up the hilly country road away from the city, the little green lovebirds in their little cage down by the gearshift and swaying happily back and forth as the car takes its curves.

Receiving directions in the little fishing town, Melanie rents a rowboat and makes her way to the Brenner place across the bay, silently docking there, creeping into the empty house, leaving the birds with a note on the coffee table (aimed at Mitch's little sister), and retreating. But as she makes her way back to town a solitary seagull swoops down and grazes her temple with its beak. Mitch sees this, watching through binoculars back at the house, and drives around the edge of the bay to meet her at the wharf. He brings her into The Tides restaurant so that her bleeding head can be bandaged. She is persuaded to stay in the town, join his family for dinner, and then remain overnight. Over the weekend – what turns out for the residents of Bodega Bay to be a weekend from hell – there are several severe bird attacks, commencing with a flight of linnets down the

---

³ We may find ourselves pleasurably wondering whether the newspapers Mitch has read include the one(s) in her father's control, thus, whether the father is publishing ticklish stories about his own daughter.

Brenner chimney after dinner, proceeding the next day at the birthday party of Mitch's sister Cathy (Veronica Cartwright) with a gull attack upon the children, building through an attack of ravens outside the local schoolhouse, and culminating in an all-out gull attack upon the center of town. By film's end, the local schoolteacher (and Mitch's old girlfriend) Annie Hayworth (Suzanne Pleshette) lies dead in the road, the town is littered with avian corpses,[4] the children are terrorized, and the Brenner family, with its new "child" Melanie, is besieged in the old farmhouse. Mitch has boarded over all the doors and windows. But upstairs somewhere there is a noise. While everyone dozes, Melanie slowly ascends the stairs – has she been beckoned? A door at the top masks the source of the sounds. She opens it – is she lured? There is a tremendous rush of bird violence – the gulls have torn off the roof and are poised in the rafters. They fly at her face, her arms, her thighs. She is down and being pecked to death when Mitch pries the door open and rescues her. He guides the dazed Melanie downstairs and settles her on the couch where, awaking to reality, she recoils. Hitchcock explained to François Truffaut, "The inspiration that gave it to me was being in an air raid. I was in London during the War and I used to be alone in the Claridges Hotel" (Krohn, *Work* 238). In the finale, as myriad birds of many species wait in silence all the way to the

---

[4] The production had trouble with animal rights activists, even though there were very few bird fatalities and tremendous care was taken to protect all the creatures used. "We were setting up and we had all the bleeding birds and all the blood hanging out from the windows," said Robert Boyle, referring to fake birds and special effects, "we had dead chickens all over the road ... And then that woman who came from the animal society" (Krohn, *"Birds"* 2).

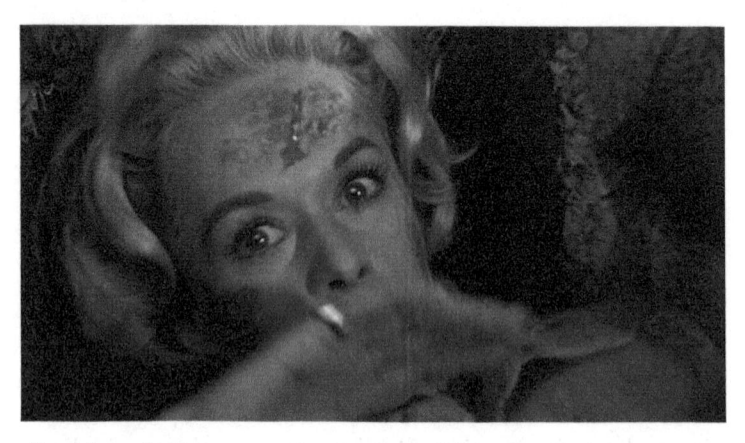

Settled on the Brenner couch after the gulls have ravaged her upstairs, Melanie comes to and recoils in The Birds *(Universal, 1963). Hitchcock was thinking of being alone during the air raids in World War II. Digital frame enlargement.*

sun-streaked horizon, our little family manages quietly, as it were with breath suspended, to drive off.[5]

As Melanie, Hedren seems to have followed Lawrence's guideline to a T, dressed as she is through practically the entire film in a single (and elegantly simple) pear green

---

[5] The bird attack shots all involved special effects, including, as Hitchcock's assistant Peggy Robertson recalled, "Bluescreen, sodium vapor, and front-process and back-process" (Hall 253). For a good discussion of "back-process" or normal rear projection; and the newer front projection, see Rickitt 82–4 and 84–6, respectively. Blue screen mattes are discussed on 64ff. The sodium vapor process for making mattes used a vivid yellow, not a blue, muslin ground and a special prismatic lens, and was proprietary to the Walt Disney studio. A special duplicate of the lens had to be made (253), and a contract struck with Disney on March 21, 1962, whereby Disney would supply the sodium vapor lamps and the necessary technical personnel and Hitchcock's production company at Universal would arrange for, among other things, the Technicolor sodium process D-7 camera (contract). Speaking about the film ten years afterward, Robert Boyle recalled the case differently. In his view, funding was not available for making a second prism, and so they had relied on the Disney equipment (Krohn, "*Birds*" 7–8).

Chanel-style suit designed for her by Edith Head (and that Hitchcock thought "hinted at a personal reticence" [McGilligan, *Darkness* 621]).[6] "She is in spring colours of light brown and pastel green, as if she were signaling œstrus, the promise of fertility," writes Camille Paglia somewhat archly. "Further, her green suit is color-coordinated with the parrot-like green lovebirds, who are capped with a splash of vermilion. She too will be christened with blood-red in the boat in Bodega Bay" (28). We never see her take that suit off (although in the general store she has purchased a horrific flannel nightgown that she models for Annie), quite as though, far from being a product of human endeavor, it constitutes a natural covering, like feathers upon birds. Melanie seems one of the flock, to be sure, close to nature in her willfulness. Creatures of the wild – Melanie has been and remains one of these – don't "dress," as though preternaturally in agreement with Thoreau's dictum, "Beware of all enterprises that require new clothes" (66). Sitting at the Brenners' piano to play Debussy's Arabesque No. 1 (from 1888; and that Hedren practiced on a dummy piano before shooting), or running down the street from the local school with children under her arms as the birds attack, or descended upon by an army of birds as she cowers in a telephone booth with the town afire around her, or victimized without mercy in that Brenner attic, she remains always in her pallid green sheath, always clothed for action, always showing – as many early observers of the film felt – "tremendous poise" (McGilligan, *Darkness* 634).

It would be a mistake to claim that Melanie shows off any particular technical skills as she contrives to survive the bird

---

[6] Head claimed that Hitchcock "virtually restricted" her to two colors, blue and green, and that "he uses color like an artist, using soft greens and cool colors for certain moods" (McBride 167). Twenty years after *The Birds*, she could "barely remember what [Hedren] had on" (Head and Calistro 139).

attacks, or indeed to claim that her social position is of much worth to her here, mixed in as she is among working- and middle-class individuals who are as enmeshed with, and threatened by, the inexplicably massing birds as she is. What she exhibits is a kind of naturalism, call it the "naturalness" of the American type: social organization does not benefit her much, nor do her wealthy background, her rings of friendship (all outside the orbit of the film), her social capital at large. Hitchcock noted to Hedren in preparation for filming that, coming up to Bodega Bay from "various groups she's been among in San Francisco whether socially or what have you, . . . there's a kind of toning down" (tape recording, February 24, 1962, qtd. in Auiler 390). In the moments that call for the greatest strengths, she is only – yet fully – herself, the girl who will not be daunted or put off, the one who looks you straight in the eye when she talks, the one whose voice is crisp and tidy, whose dialogue is succinct, direct, well articulated, and identifiable by its tone. "American girls are the best girls," as Winterbourne says of Daisy Miller.

We could hardly call Melanie a bird, yet she is closer to the birds than to the other people in this film. Early on, for example, she is curiously discomfited when a bird gets loose in the pet store, as though sensing its anxiety just as she mirrors it (see Pomerance, "Thirteen" 271). When finally the birds come for her, it is as though they act out of some strange recognition.

Melanie is not – cannot afford to be – put off by decoration, ostentation, or ceremony, though she has been brought up with all of them. She sees with eyes wide open, the way Mitch's mother Lydia (Jessica Tandy) sees, by looking directly at the world, confronting it for what it is: "I don't think I could bear being left alone." Many have thought of this attitude as the pioneer spirit, the ability to take things as they are and not as one would imagine or wish them to be coupled

The climactic bird attack on Bodega Bay included a "God's point-of-view" shot made through a rotoscope-traveling matte composite. (a) The matte painting of the town seen from on high was accomplished by Albert Whitlock on a canvas roughly thirty-six inches wide, with the central area blacked out. Live action shot on a Universal parking lot would be incorporated there, including the fiery stream of gasoline. (b) Seagulls were photographed off the cliffs of Santa Cruz Island, then rotoscoped: copied onto cels and laboriously hand-painted frame by frame – over a period of three months – for incorporation in (c) the final composite shot (see Krohn, Work 252–5). Courtesy Academy of Motion Picture Arts and Sciences.

with a deep sensibility toward the chilling vacuum of the untamed and unknown. It is finally a practical spirit, perhaps even to the extent of surpassing (while suppressing) emotion. Melanie often suffers in this film but never reacts to or demonstrates her own suffering to gain attention or blessing from others. And confronted with the suffering of others, she is sensitive, active, responsive. Lydia, for instance, gets a visit from Melanie as she lays abed debilitated from one of the attacks. Melanie has had no reason to believe the old lady trusts or likes her. But their eyes meet in a room lit only by filtered daylight, and in two straight gazes they recognize and know one another as conspecific. "There I think she regains her compassion for the woman," suggested Hitchcock (in Auiler 410). Melanie's serving Lydia a soothing cup of tea is purposive, not expressive, the action of an engineer devoted to erecting a structure of amity and accord.

By film's end, in a scene that is decidedly tranquil, almost utopian, those innocent lovebirds are riding in a car again, this time sandwiched *en famille* with Lydia and Melanie and Cathy as Mitch slowly drives off. "They haven't hurt anybody," pleads Cathy. Neither, in truth, has Melanie, the one who found them, bought them, brought them to Bodega Bay. Perhaps with some arcane magnetism that is never apparent but always implicit in the film, Melanie has brought the other birds, too, the whole *genre*, just as the anxiety-ridden and immoderately strident local citizens at The Tides suspected. Remembering the traces of the little fishing town as we follow Mitch's car off to the twilit horizon – in an improvised ending, since Hitchcock had planned a summative bird attack on the car but "threw the whole lot away" (Krohn, *Work* 240) – we know we have seen death, experienced *agon*, yet even if the birds did come in response to her "call" Melanie herself hasn't hurt anybody. A conversation between Mitch and his little sister:

CATHY: Why are they trying to kill people?
MITCH: I wish I could say. But if I could tell you that, I could also tell you why people are trying to kill people.

Dr. Ben

The American social philosopher Max Lerner wrote of the mid-1950s family as "a caricature of itself, since it always seems to be parading its excesses" (550). It was nuclear in form, he notes, because it "shed in-laws, grandparents, cousins, aunts, and retainers; it handed over production to the factory and office, religion to the churches, the administration of justice to the courts, formal education to the schools, medical attention to the hospitals. . . . It has been stripped down to the spare frame of being marriage-centered and child-fulfilled" (552). As to the American patriarch of the epoch, he "has accepted his diminished authority partly because his work takes so much of his time and energy, partly because his role fits into the spirit of his society as a whole" (555). Many parents in middle-class families of the 1950s, Lerner informs us, "had come from farms and small towns, many others were of immigrant stock. . . . Having achieved income and position, and seeing limitless vistas ahead, they hoped their children would keep moving upward and fulfill the dreams they had themselves fallen short of" (566). By the mid-1950s, "the child panic, as one might call it, was relaxing" and "the cult of the child was giving way to a new perspective" (569). Parents had again become interesting in themselves, as much worthy of attention as their children. Adulthood was being critically examined for its failures and potentialities.[7] And by the early 1960s, it had become possible for a critical historian to complain openly of American schooling that "ours is the only educational system in the world vital segments of which have fallen into the hands of people who joyfully and militantly proclaim their hostility to intellect and their eagerness to identify with children who show the least intellectual promise" (Hofstadter 51).

The year 1955, however – when Nicholas Ray's classic tale of adolescent angst, *Rebel Without a Cause*, came out – was still a time when the child was upheld as principal family value, principal focus of interest, principal locus of concern. Hitchcock was hard at work preparing and filming *The Man Who Knew Too Much* (1956). This film can be studied as an essay on the American family dynamic, seen from the point of view of two loving but slightly incompatible adults raising a precocious little boy but centered essentially on the

[7] For example, by Paul Goodman in his *Growing Up Absurd*.

At the taxidermist Ambrose Chappell's establishment in Camden Town, Ben has lost control of his temper and is manhandling the proprietor's proprietary son, Ambrose Jr. (Richard Wordsworth). This is the beginning of a signal degradation of character in the American ex-soldier, whose holiday abroad is in ruins. Courtesy Academy of Motion Picture Arts and Sciences.

anxiety-ridden father, a man panicked about the way he looks to his wife and to the eyes of the world. When his child is kidnapped during a family vacation in Morocco, Dr. Ben McKenna (James Stewart) becomes a textbook example of a figure whose authority has waned, whose ability to marshal his personal forces toward controlling and shaping events, has reached its utter limit.[8] From a casually domineering and

---

[8] Stewart had been involved with the picture from the start, having formed the production company that would make it, Filwite, with his friends Hitchcock and Lew Wasserman (agent to them both, and president of the Music Corporation of America since 1946).

apparently good-natured tourist, clumsy out of his element but persistently charming, we see him degenerate into a temperamental and desperate man out of touch with the forces that shape his destiny and that of his family.

Without his son under his protection (and available for display), Ben is entirely at loose ends. Having sedated his wife Jo to keep her from exploding into uncontrollable grief, he decides while she is in a stupor that they must leave Marrakech and head for England, a terrifying prospect since in truth he has no inkling on what continent the child might be found and knows only that he has been warned of an impending assassination in London, about which he is to keep Scotland Yard in the dark. The murder of a visiting prime minister from an unidentified foreign country is indeed attempted, during a concert at the Royal Albert Hall[9] (and in a sequence that has become legendary of Hitchcock's masterful ability to set dramatic tensions in fabulously entertaining or bizarre social contexts), but it fails thanks to Jo's rather spectacular screaming just before the downbeat on which the assassin has been primed to shoot. The McKennas then find themselves invited by the grateful prime minister to visit him at his embassy. But it is precisely there that the villains have secreted Hank, and in an emotionally wrenching conclusion that involves Jo reprising her pet melody for her son, "Que Sera, Sera (What Will Be, Will Be),"[10] the

---

[9] A performance of Arthur Benjamin's *Storm Clouds* cantata, with Barbara Howitt, mezzo-soprano, and the London Symphony Orchestra and Covent Garden Choir conducted by Bernard Herrmann.

[10] Inspired by a telling moment in Joseph L. Mankiewicz's *The Barefoot Contessa* (1954), which they were watching together in a theater, the song's composer Ray Evans and Jay Livingstone dashed home and scribbled it in half an hour. Hitchcock was instantly pleased when he heard it, but Day balked a little. After recording the melody for Columbia with Frank DeVol, she muttered, "That's the last time you're gonna hear *that* song!" – one of the great miscalculations in Hollywood history.

Jay Livingston (c.) and Ray Evans (at piano) rehearsing their song "Que Sera, Sera (What Will Be, Will Be)" with Christopher Olsen. Olsen, born in 1946, made films with Nicholas Ray and Vincente Minnelli, among other directors, but stopped film work in 1960 for another career. Courtesy Academy of Motion Picture Arts and Sciences.

boy is reunited with his parents in a wholly satisfying harmonic tableau.

Not only is Ben anxious about the missing child, he is displaced from a clear perspective on his wife. All through the film we witness his questionable consideration for and fragile position vis-à-vis Jo and her concerns. Riding to their Marrakech hotel in a horse-drawn carriage, for example, Jo and Ben banter about Louis Bernard (Daniel Gélin), a mysterious Frenchman they've met on the bus. Jo, we can see clearly enough but Ben cannot, is far more perspicacious and observant than he, since she notices how much he told the stranger about himself without learning anything in return. Later, at a local restaurant "where the food is different and the manner of eating exotic," they find themselves chatting with two British tourists, the Draytons (Bernard Miles and Brenda De Banzie). Like sheepish fans the world over, these two have recognized the "famous Jo Conway." Jo makes clear to them one of the central dissatisfactions of her married life, that although she would like to reignite her stalled stage career it is "difficult" to do this from Indianapolis, Indiana. "What Hitchcock did with the career idea," writes Krohn, "was to let it haunt around the edges of the couple's banter, which he encouraged [writer John Michael] Hayes to develop in the restaurant scene in his best comic style. Everything in that scene – extended by Hitchcock via improvisation on the set – is played for laughs" (*Work* 162). The next morning, strolling through the *souk* with Ben while the Draytons occupy Hank, Jo makes it plain that even though he keeps refusing she would like to have another child. Ben is, in short, the perfect model of a dutiful and gracious husband while being at the same time something of a folksy Bluebeard who has stolen her artistic career, trapped her in a hopelessly boring cell in the Midwest, and refused to assist her even in furthering her motherhood.

Nor can Ben muster the aplomb, dexterity, or grace to show himself as an athletic hero, full of energy and dash. Seeking out a mysterious taxidermist, Ambrose Chappell, in the Camden Town section of London because he suspects Hank is being kept there, he creeps trepidaciously along a street rather than marching forward with purpose. When he finds the place he is befuddled by the bevy of stuffed animals and fish, the simple diligence of the workmen, and the apparently innocent mien with which both the proprietor and his son indicate they know nothing of a kidnapped child. Soon he is wrestling his way out of the place, and ends up with his arm stuck inside a lion's maw.

The American abroad cannot trust even to his language. Being interviewed at London Airport[11] by Scotland Yard Inspector Buchanan (Ralph Truman); then later encountering a jabbering quartet of Jo's old friends at the Savoy; still later arguing with the taxidermist Ambrose Chappell about the whereabouts of his son in a "comic misunderstanding" (Krohn, *Work* 158); and after this, when Jo has realized the meaning of Louis Bernard's whispered dying words, that "it's not a man, it's a place!" making way to Ambrose Chapel in Bayswater – "The Ambrose Chapel solution was too elegant (and too anti-Protestant) to abandon" (159) – and bellowing viciously at Drayton within its shabby precincts Ben repeatedly exhibits a kind of stuttering drawl, going far beyond Stewart's trademark performance style, in which he repeats phrases, holds back from speaking, cannot quite get words smoothly out of his mouth, and generally gives an acoustic display of well-meaning but bumbling incompetence. Even in the conclusion, as Ben saves Hank from Drayton's clutches on an elegant staircase at the embassy, it is more the force of gravity than any deft action on Ben's part that makes for a happy ending, and he has nothing significant to say. In short, as he is portrayed in this film Ben McKenna only begins as a version of the Jefferson Smith character Stewart had incarnated for Frank Capra in 1939, an "earnest and quiet man" (Hitchcock qtd. in Truffaut 228), entirely well meaning in some slightly patriarchal way, hailing from small-town America but caught up in big-city politics, humble, attractive, and slightly unsure of himself; yet positioned in depths far beyond his ken and power.

---

[11] London Airport was opened on May 31, 1946, and came later in the 1950s to be known as "London Heathrow."

Under extraordinary anxiety he develops as a nervous, frightened man too quick to snap and helpless in the impotence of his substantial learning. We may reach out to sympathize and identify with him, and feel a certain comfortable reliance at his tough-minded determination and no nonsense stridency, yet for all this he is the American personality on show principally for its weaknesses and vulnerabilities, an entirely amicable sport trapped in unfamiliar territory and confronted by a sophisticated strategy he can confront only through a kind of flailing persistence. Back at home he was adept enough with Herbie Taylor's ulcers, Alida Markle's asthma, and Mrs. Yarrow's triplets, but here on the other side of the pond, with only his family to support his identity (one of them missing perhaps forever and the other a sometime unwilling ally), Ben McKenna is the Lost American, one of those who "have no conception at all of what is meant by moral, since we recognize no ground our own" (Williams, "Père Sebastian" 109).

In the mid-1950s, Americans were shuttling in droves to visit Europe and other World War II sites in which soldiers had discovered the exotic allure of an older world.[12] The confrontation was almost inevitably with one's deep cultural past, a language, an aesthetic, and a politique that seemed hereditary, even parental, to these citizens of a relatively young nation that had been established with an eye upon the future, not the past. As William Carlos Williams wrote it,

---

[12] Nellie Perret has suggested to me a reading of Ben as typical in many ways of a generation of American men who had fought in the Second World War and, back home in the U.S.A., were somewhat displaced from cosmopolitan memories. The war for them would have been brutal and shocking, certainly, but the cultural locale they had to have grown to know would have been a revelation to those who had not visited Europe, Africa, or Asia before and were now unable to enact back home the desires foreign interactions had raised in them. Ben's experience had been in French-controlled Morocco.

"Two cultural elements were left battling for supremacy, one looking toward Europe, necessitous but retrograde in its tendency ... and the other forward-looking but under a shadow from the first" ("Background" 135). In buying, and having, the European experience, the American returns, as Leslie Fiedler puts it, "to the Old World (only then does he know for sure that he *is* an American), his Old Home, the place of origin of his old self, that original Adam, whom the New World presumably made a New Man" (*Return* 19). In making this kind of voyage, and then in having to negotiate a search for a missing child in territory so *unheimlich*, Ben will require, above all things, the powers of the tongue. And here we must recall that in his interactions with Bernard on the bus, and later with the Marrakech police commissioner (Yves Brainville) regarding the man's sudden death, Ben McKenna is in dialogue not with Africans but with the French, epitomes of the classical European personality, who have colonized Morocco (Hitchcock and his crew were tasting the hospitality of the French-installed Glaoui of Morocco as they filmed sequences on location there).[13] He has also been given occasion to chat sociably with the voluble,

---

[13] Permission for the Marrakech shooting was obtained from the Glaoui, who was sympathetic to the French, by Édouard de Segonzac, managing director of Paramount's Paris office, and Hitchcock's team was informed on April 25, 1955 (Caffey wire). Months earlier, Segonzac had identified the Glaoui as a longtime friend of his uncle's. Filming local citizens would not be a problem, and extras could be paid three to five hundred francs per day (Segonzac to Holman). A primary requirement was that all shooting had to be completed prior to the commencement of Ramadan, a condition that put a crimp in the preparations since it meant that the script for the Morocco scenes would have to be completed very quickly. As finally, "armed soldiers were on the rooftops overlooking the [Souk] area. By noon the crowds were becoming hostile," the filmmakers were recommended to suspend filming immediately and get their cameras out of sight. (See Coleman 213ff., 220.) The Marrakech production occurred between May 13 and May 23, 1955.

chirpy Draytons, an experience of pure linguistic torture for anyone like Ben whose mother tongue has been borrowed from theirs at a distance. For mid-Americans, speaking to the British is an exercise in self-consciousness at best. Once he and Jo move to London, Ben must show his untutored simplicities (adorable for American audiences, especially in these revelations) first to Inspector Buchanan, a clipped and well-spoken Londoner if ever there was one; then – and completely without warning – to the effete and garrulous Val Parnell (Alan Mowbray), Jo's old patron, a man who means nothing but to be polite and welcoming but whose polish would be appropriate for Windsor Castle; then to the older and younger workmen, stolidly middle-class Ambrose Chappell and his painfully taciturn son; then yet again to the articulate Drayton, this time "a wolf in sheep's clothing" since he has donned the collar of the clergy. The visiting foreign prime minister and his British ambassador (Alexei Bobrinskoy and Mogens Wieth) also speak a more fluid, more grammatical, more elegant English than Ben does, and, indeed, one could make the case that even Jo, with her elocutionary training and singing voice (a voice that involves diaphragm control) has a more relaxed and articulate expression than does our hero. In short, this innocent abroad signals through his bumbling and stuttering, his hesitation and his genuinely felt tone, a type home audiences yearned to approve of but could not really see as more than a rude child on a world stage.

Beyond Baedeker

In *Foreign Correspondent* (1940), Hitchcock's paradigmatic American is also an American abroad, Huntley Haverstock (Joel McCrea), freelancer for a major New York newspaper whose prescient publisher (Harry Davenport) anticipates war in Europe and sends him to find out when the Allied forces will join in. (For the lead role Hitchcock wanted Gary Cooper, who had just shot two films for DeMille, but Cooper said no [Krohn, *Hitchcock* 36].) Huntley's specific mandate is to seek out a celebrated Dutch philosopher, Prof. Van Meer (Albert Bassermann), privy to a secret treaty clause with the Germans and working in Holland along with a British peace organization headed by an obscure aristocrat, Stephen Fisher (Herbert Marshall) and his impressionable daughter, Carol (Laraine Day). The hunt for the "treaty clause" is an old Hitchcockian device, by which a film is arranged as a complicated chase after something that appears to be of immense narratological value but that in the end turns out to be, at best, a trifle.

This "MacGuffin," as Hitchcock named it, after the subject of an old joke about a device for capturing lions in the Scottish Highlands (see Truffaut 138), shows up again and again in Hitchcock's work – the uranium in the wine bottles in *Notorious* (1946); the secret meaning of "the 39 steps" in the film of the same name (1935); the mysterious George Kaplan in *North by Northwest* (1959) – so its mere presence in *Foreign Correspondent* in the form of the clause is not especially revealing of the filmmaker's intent. More informative is the link between the MacGuffin and the personality of Huntley Haverstock, since the challenge of eliciting information from Van Meer – possessing the MacGuffin and transmitting it from Europe to America – is made onerous not only because the philosopher has been kidnapped but, much more interestingly for students of Hitchcock's American vision, because Huntley lacks the etiquette and cultural understanding to discern the difference between sincerity and posture when he is being faced with British manipulators. He is, as Ina Rae Hark suggests, "an 'innocent' compared to the European [characters]" (292). As an adventurer, he is generally canny about duplicity, and about the way an enemy espionage network might work to present itself through a front; but as an American he is easily caught by his own high regard for – even fandom of – the British culture that America only pretended to itself it had left behind. If through his condescending veil of aristocracy Fisher has found the ideal cover for hiding his German connections from his own countrymen, he has also adopted the masquerade most likely to impress this foreign journalist, whose manner is jaunty and casual, whose attitude toward strangers is all plain-speaking openness, and whose conviction it is that Englishmen – just because they are English – are stalwart and honest.

Huntley's unsure footing on foreign soil is emphasized when in London, and on the nefarious Fisher's recommendation, he meets a pudgy "bodyguard" named Rowley (Edmund Gwenn). Rowley has worked with Fisher before on cases plenty dirty. Here the well-mannered thug is tasked with the challenge of quickly and unobtrusively murdering our reporter hero, since the American has become an irritation by probing around for the vanished Van Meer (although the professor was publicly "assassinated," Huntley remains certain that a double was used, and his discovery of a conspiratorial meeting in an abandoned windmill convinces him even more). Rowley tries unobtrusively shoving Huntley in front of a moving omnibus but that doesn't work. Then he chummily leads him to the top of a tower at Westminster, planning – as soon as a group of schoolboys finishes up a little tour there – to hurl him to his death. That at the crucial moment, as grimacing Rowley makes toward Huntley's unprotected back with his hands outstretched, Huntley has an unaccountable premonition, turns around, and quickly steps aside – so that it is the henchman who goes flying to his end – is hardly as significant as the deeper and broader truth that the American was altogether an innocent abroad, entirely clueless as to the true intentions of the "chummy," "affable" Englishman. He has been saved from a trap revealed by Debra Fried: "The mistake ... is to doubt the power of ordinariness, in its power both to harm and to sustain" (26), yet he seems hardly aware.

Meanwhile, the English language Huntley hears spoken in London, with its singsong rhythms and amicable slangs, is not only a means of expression but another way of masking plans, since for this American not free from its enchantments the British lilt is first, and always, irresistible, undeniable, and authentic. To put himself in killing position Rowley needed no camouflage at all. Just be the good-natured English bloke American blokes are so eager and happy to like and listen to.

A third signal European presence comes in contact with Haverstock. This is the rather quiet and unassuming Ffolliott (George Sanders), an associate of the Fishers who befriends our hero without seeming to offer any motive at all. Ffolliott does not particularly interest Huntley, as either a person or a type, possibly because he mumbles a good deal, looks askance, has very little wit or charm, and is always dutifully helpful without asking any questions. He seems, in short, the perfect majordomo. It is only toward the end of the film, and at a point when it is almost too late to do him any good – almost, but not quite too late – that Huntley discovers Ffolliott for the truly heroic man he is, an agent who has for some time been out to trap Stephen Fisher and now thinks that with Huntley's help he finally can. Ffolliott is the steadfast but quiet Englishman America really did need, finally, to rely upon; and who in his turn really did need to rely upon America. But he doesn't appear to stand out, isn't, in fact, recognizable to Huntley even though our every encounter with the man reveals his directness, his skill, his precision of diction, his calmness of manner, his sweetness of affect, and his loyalty. The film, claimed Joseph Goebbels – something of a specialist in propaganda – on January 22, 1942, "is a first-class work, in the style of a police thriller that will certainly have an effect on the public at large in enemy countries" (Lesch 25).

In thoroughly misperceiving and misestimating Fisher, and in failing to see both Rowley and Ffolliott for what they are, Huntley blunders into one catastrophic situation after another, the diegesis being a series of his sometimes artful and sometimes just lucky escapes from various social and physical confinements. The American here means only to do well and honorably, and finally casts himself even into the sea to save the day with characteristic panache.[14] In the film's concluding moments, we find him standing at a microphone in a London studio during the blitz, as his co-workers rush to evacuate to the shelters. "Keep your lights burning, America," he calls into the microphone with unwavering conviction. "They may be the only ones we have." But Huntley's conviction and articulateness are not tempered by any nuance of embarrassment or relief in the face of his own brittle ignorance. He seems completely unaware, even now with his voice calling across the Atlantic heroically to awaken America to interventionism – and while on the sound track "The Star-Spangled Banner" sounds (a decision of producer Walter Wanger and writer Ben Hecht

---

[14] Hitchcock was extreme in his pride about the accomplishment of the thrilling airplane crash sequence, which involved rear projection onto a rice paper screen behind which 2,700 gallons of water waited to be dumped upon a stage set cockpit on Hitchcock's signal (see Truffaut 135–7; Knight 173–4; and Warhol 201–2).

The bombers are overhead but Huntley Haverstock (Joel McCrea) will not abandon the microphone that is carrying his voice back to America, in Foreign Correspondent *(Walter Wanger, 1940). Improbably for a radio broadcast, he has his trusty girl at his side (Laraine Day). Huntley is modeled on Edward R. Murrow (1908–1965), whose broadcasts from Europe during World War II roused American consciousness of the battle against Nazism. Courtesy Academy of Motion Picture Arts and Sciences.*

[Samuels 148]) – that England and Europe are territories he doesn't fully comprehend and never will, having relegated both, as all true Americans continually did, to the crumbling past.

As with Huntley Haverstock, Mark Twain's American tourists in *The Innocents Abroad* enter the world outside their perimeter with an impressionability and foreknowledge that work to blot out the careful apperception of the present that can lead, if not to full knowledge then at least to unveiled experience. In Paris, the narrator's friend Jack is having a particular problem with his journal, not very unlike Huntley's trouble as he strives to grasp and record events in London and Holland. Jack, however, recognizes the condition he's in whereas Huntley does not: "I reckon I'm ... behind ... I haven't got any France in it at all. First I thought I'd leave France out and start fresh. But that wouldn't do, *would* it?" (41). Searching Europe for the key to war, Huntley is like this young journalist struggling to put France into his logs. If only there were an easy way to copy it all! Huntley, of course, is looking for a Europe that he can recognize, a European he has read and dreamed about that now he can meet and converse with about the great subjects of peace and war. Beyond protecting sweet and right-thinking Carol Fisher, with whom, of course, he has fallen in love, his sole desire is to find and redeem the old Dutch professor hidden away somewhere in London. He will help Huntley save the world, if only, tortured and drugged instead of murdered, he doesn't actually die first!

But how energizing it is, through all of this, and how enlightening – for Huntley and for us as we observe him – to be American! "None of us," writes Twain, "had ever been anywhere before":

> *Travel was a wild novelty to us, and we conducted ourselves in accordance with the natural instincts that were in us, and trammeled ourselves with no ceremonies, no conventionalities. We always took care to make it understood that we were Americans – Americans! When we found that a good many foreigners had hardly ever heard of America, and that a good many more knew it only as a barbarous province away off somewhere, that had lately been at war with somebody, we pitied the ignorance of the Old World. (645)*

Step Jumpers

An interesting reprise of *Foreign Correspondent*, especially in terms of its American hero wandering the pathways of Europe in search of a buried and vital secret, is the Cold War drama – or choreography, as I have called it (*Eye* 97–107) – *Torn Curtain* (1966). Here we find a young and brilliant American theoretical physicist, Michael Armstrong (Paul Newman), accompanied by his erstwhile postgraduate assistant (and fiancée) Sarah Sherman (Julie Andrews), voyaging to Copenhagen for an academic conference. This trip is merely his cover, however, since beyond even Sarah's ken Michael plans to defect across the Iron Curtain in order to work in Leipzig with his East German counterpart, Dr. Gustav Lindt (Ludwig Donath).[15] The Americans, he complains, have not believed enough in him, not provided sufficient funding for his intellectual escapades. But we discover along with Sarah, who has followed him to the East, that the defection story was only another cover. Michael is a secret operative of American Intelligence intending to extract from Lindt the zealously guarded formula for Gamma-5. Like Huntley Haverstock, then, but equipped with a considerably more articulate armature of language, theory, and scientific understanding, Armstrong must encounter, unobtrusively debrief, and thus in effect eviscerate his European forbearer, a man old enough to be the senior scholar a bright young academic like Armstrong would slather to work with under any other circumstances.

[15] Hitchcock's assistant Peggy Robertson wrote to Hansjörg Felmy of Donath, "Professor Lindt is being played by a very fine actor named Ludwig Donath. I am sure that you have heard of him. He came from Germany to New York where he has lived for a number of years. He is a most charming man and I know will be a perfect Professor Lindt" (Robertson to Felmy).

If in *Foreign Correspondent* the most salient characteristic of the American hero, beyond his perduring innocence, is his well-meaning amity and openness to human relationship, in *Torn Curtain*, filmed in response to the Cuban Missile Crisis and the intensification of hostility between American and Soviet power bases concentrated around the Berlin Wall, we have a figure without particular social charm and more innocent of the dangers he is positioning himself to encounter as a spy than of the complexity and untrustworthiness of human interaction in general. He knows how to watch out for the East Germans and their polite machinations, for example. Hitchcock goes to lengths to cast, script, and photograph the official types Michael will have to encounter – Gerhard, the Director of Security (Hansjörg Felmy),[16] Armstrong's bodyguard Gromek (Wolfgang Kieling), and even the obsequious Prof. Manfred (Gunther Strack) – as attractive, more or less erudite, socially charming, and unfailingly polite people,[17] by contrast with whom Michael seems as boorishly out of place as did the prototypical 1960s middle-class American tourist (lampooned by the sculptures of Duane Hanson) in Europe: the boob who comes to photograph instead of looking, chats always about himself, and compares everything to the superior reality he finds back home.[18]

Armstrong is the soft imperialist who wants American bureaucracies to possess, dominate, and control Europe in

---

[16] Although the actor's name is spelled Hansjoerg in the credits and most publications about this film, I here use his own spelling.
[17] Interestingly, relatively early script material had stultified and calcified these European types, but a consultant sent clear advice for correction, noting that taking snuff, wearing robes in academic life, drinking Moselle wine, calling people "Herr Doktor Professor," and bowing were distinctly out (Stoiber to Ludmer).
[18] As Ben McKenna does in *The Man Who Knew Too Much* by acknowledging to his son and wife that Morocco really does resemble California.

his name, until a climactic moment late in the film when, completely by chance, he and Sarah meet a notably pathetic figure, the Countess Kuchinska (Lila Kedrova), desperate to find sponsors who will help her leave Germany and move to the United States of America. It is through Michael's at first condescending but soon enough genuine offer to help the Countess, his willingness to reach out with kindheartedness to a stranger and offer the treasure of his country's freedom, that his American identity is elevated, ennobled, and enriched. Fleeing for their own lives from

Lila Kedrova (1918–2000) was one of the older and more experienced actors Hitchcock could work with on Torn Curtain *(Universal, 1966), so he favored his moments with her. Here he takes time for meticulous directorial comment about a tiny scene, which is one of the few Countess Kuchinska would have in the film. Courtesy Academy of Motion Picture Arts and Sciences.*

the security police who are on their tail, frantic to get back across to the West, Michael and Sarah pause for a moment of distinct generosity, compassion, and trust, a gesture that clarifies and purifies the American spirit even as it moves the story forward. The poor countess soon falls behind, however, and we never learn whether she manages to climb out of the political darkness of East Berlin or not. (Generally unimpressed with *Torn Curtain*, Hitchcock's biographer Donald Spoto cavils that with Kedrova, the film "substitutes an eccentric, bravura performance for a potentially powerful situation" [517]).

Michael Armstrong is described in an undated writer's memorandum as "the sort of man who believes that if one wants something done well, one has to do it oneself. . . . He is uncommonly dedicated and serious, brave to the point of recklessness, and capable of showing his temper. . . . He is a man with a vision and he will stop at nothing to realize his vision. His own career, his private life, even his skin, are secondary to his realization of his goal" (Memorandum). In some ways he is not unlike Hitchcock himself, as the scriptwriter Brian Moore saw him: a man committed to his project in the face of everything, and who might well be willing to bustle forward with "characters and much of the narrative unbelievable" (Sampson 175). In other ways Michael certainly reflects the American hero so many filmgoers living in the shadow of the "heroic" Kennedy presidency could have imagined themselves to be.

The film contains a beautiful moment of revelation, in which Hitchcock's own affiliation with the American hero is manifested. We need remember that Gamma-5 is some sort of rocket fuel or process that the Americans and East Germans have both been racing to perfect. As Armstrong finally gains Lindt's confidence it becomes clear that the batty old physicist has in fact derived a workable formula, and that he is now

Ludwig Donath (l.) with Paul Newman in Room 29, working through the arcane problem of Torn Curtain. *Courtesy Academy of Motion Picture Arts and Sciences.*

about to show this defector – as he thinks Armstrong to be – the details of it. We enter Room 29, Lindt's classroom/sanctuary in the basement of a building at the University of Leipzig. In a manner that will be recognized by anyone who has studied the higher sciences, Lindt swiftly fills all the blackboards with the arcane mathematical theory that he knows how to write, Armstrong knows how to read, but that can only baffle us.[19] Suddenly something on the board seizes Armstrong vitally, and to show the character's amazement Hitchcock's camera swoops into his widely opened sky-blue eyes.

---

[19] There is a page filled with such formulae—the terms Michael inscribes on Lindt's board and which Lindt augments—in *Torn Curtain* file 926, Alfred Hitchcock Collection, Margaret Herrick Library.

"My God! That's brilliant! You jumped a step, didn't you?" he cries.

"Of course it's brilliant! It's genius!" barks Lindt. "The Russians thought I was crazy. They didn't know I'm Lindt."

In working out his formula, then, the German has forsaken his traditional obligations to proper form, has in fact utterly relinquished all of the strict and stiff proprieties of classical convention and thrown himself forward with a purely creative spirit – the spirit that is properly Hitchcock's. He is both wondered at and admired by the American for having done this. *"You jumped a step!"* – expostulated with the amazement and restrained excitement that Newman brings to his line reading – points out not only the brilliant theorizing the diegesis indicates but also the brilliant editing and unfolding of this story, for which credit goes to Hitchcock. A step has been skipped in the narrational flow, too, since the vital sharing of thought occurs through – and only through – an abstract mathematical language to which the audience has no access.

But at a central moment a little earlier, when Michael confided to Sarah his true purpose in coming across the Iron Curtain and she turned to regard him with stars in her eyes, the filmmaker also "jumped a step." Michael was being interrogated by academics in a lecture theater. As the session recesses because of an interruption from German security, he goes out into the garden with Sarah and retreats with her up a tiny hillock and past a planting of flowers. Hitchcock avoids sweeping in for a telltale close-up of this conversation but instead keeps his camera down at the bottom of the hillock so that we see Michael and Sarah only in profile and interpret their conversation only through their pantomime (as in silent film). The kiss that concludes it is all we need in order to know that Sarah has now been brought into Michael's innermost reality.[20]

Michael's susceptibility to Lindt's magic in *Torn Curtain* is based in the same ferocious spirit of innovation, ingenuity, and spontaneity that made David O. Selznick and Walter Wanger, Hitchcock's first producers in America, fall into admiration for his: not only could Lindt bravely "jump a step" but Armstrong could bravely ascertain that he did, and admire him for it. America is all about "jumping steps." The wizened European professor had Americanized himself. He had learned to throw convention away and work through the commitment of the jump in such a flamboyant way that the quintessentially American Michael Armstrong, himself an advertisement for flamboyance, could read him, approve of him, and make him his own. Lindt is as much an American in spirit and style as Michael is, but secretly so.

The Working Type

Scattered through Hitchcock's films are examples of Americans as solidly working-class types. These folk lead humdrum, repetitive, routinized lives, and can be predicted to labor methodically and ploddingly so that notable others can dramatically ascend and descend the scales of suspense and intrigue. To give only a few examples: in *Saboteur* (1942), the truck driver (Murray Alper) who helps Barry Kane escape from Los Angeles or the freak circus performers in the caravan, with whom he and Patricia Martin hide;

---

[20] The structure of the scene recalls the mountaintop murder, seen in silence and at a great distance, in *Secret Agent* (1936). Hitchcock is, here and always, a master of self-reference.

in *Spellbound* (1945), the boorish Dr. Fleurot (John Emery), forever trying to seduce Constance Petersen (Ingrid Bergman) at Green Manors; in *Rope* (1948), the housemaid Mrs. Wilson (Edith Evanson) dutifully trucking food into and out of the protagonists' dining room. There is also Guy Haines's tedious wife Miriam (Laura Elliott), stuffed with malevolence, in *Strangers on a Train* (1951); that hapless composer (Ross Bagdasarian), persistently hacking away at that sweeping tune in *Rear Window* (1954); the saleslady at Ransohoff's (Margaret Brayton) who in *Vertigo* (1958) doggedly works to outfit Judy Barton in exactly the right gray suit – "The gentleman certainly knows what he wants!" – or the hapless cop (Fred Graham) who falls to his death at the film's outset; the powerful but also completely colorless Professor (Leo G. Carroll) in *North by Northwest*, orchestrating Roger Thornhill with all the panache of a plastic mannequin; in *Psycho* (1960) the used car salesman (John Anderson), not so perplexed by Marion Crane that he cannot transact a vehicle transfer without ceremony; in *The Birds* the proprietor of The Tides restaurant (Lonny Chapman), a plain and ordinary working fellow confronted by happenings beyond his imagination; Cousin Bob (Bob Sweeney) in *Marnie* (1964), a man whose thoughts have never strayed outside a ledger book; the CIA contact (Mort Mills) in *Torn Curtain*, disguised as a farmer and chatting to Armstrong while they take a portentous ride on a tractor. In all of these, as in other characterizations, Hitchcock portrays workers without allure, common-man types, who at once move the country, its infrastructure, and the plot of the film. Each is a mere cog in the massive social or dramatic machine, while being, in his or her own version of the universe, a star.

The England that bred Hitchcock and the America that nourished him were two different cultural environments,

England crammed into a tiny island and reflecting through all its institutions and patterns a high valuation of the etiquette that keeps people from irritating one another at close proximity, and America by contrast a vast and open field of possibilities, where social encounters and collisions seem rare in an ethos of spaciousness, strangeness, and mobility. What the English workman exemplified on a consistent basis was not personality, a substance and structure that could threaten or alienate if projected at too close a distance, but the rationalizing and containing cast of position, class, and profession. Each law-abiding man behaved more or less as was appropriate for his status in a social class and a trade. Thus, for example, the pathetic character we know by his stage name as Mr. Memory (Wylie Watson) in *The 39 Steps* (1935) shows only the barest modicum of personal feeling, and more generally restrains himself to demonstrating the talent he claims for himself in his act, that he can recall information dutifully, meticulously, truly, and with speed. Earlier in the same film we meet a milkman (Frederick Piper), who is willing to exchange clothing with our hero Hannay (Robert Donat) and to briefly share with him a male joke about sexual infidelity: but rather than learning about this man's personal nature we are given to noticing and apprehending his fluid routines as a deliveryman.[21]

---

[21] In *North by Northwest*, Roger Thornhill exchanges his clothing with a Pullman porter on the Twentieth Century Limited, but the porter is paid in cash. This brief scene shows many things at once: that the porter knows Roger isn't a class mate, and so feels no need to reach out in his aid with nothing but charity – the porter does make a point of stalling before informing the detectives who are on Roger's tail that the tradeoff was made, and keeps the money secreted for himself; that in America, money will buy anything, including class demotion if one wants to acquire it. As to Roger paying off: this is one of the very few times in the film when money appears to have touched his hand.

In America, however, workers' identities are American before they are occupational. With so many of Hitchcock's working characters we come to an appreciation of their stoic patriotism, their self-consciousness, their vociferous opinions about the world. Each of these – the trucker in *Saboteur*, the aging ornithologist in *The Birds* (Ethel Griffies), even the plodding detective in *Rear Window* (Wendell Corey) – says in effect, "I am as much a center of attention as the hero you insist on watching. This place, this culture, this particular story is also mine." Note for instance how the conductor who is guarding the gate at Grand Central Station in the conclusion of *Spellbound* (Irving Bacon) winks with avuncular approval and pleasure at the couple formed by Ballantine and Constance, or how in *Vertigo* the shopkeeper Pop Leibel (Konstantin Shayne) becomes not only a source of information but a self-aware raconteur; how in *Lifeboat* (1944) the wounded sailor Gus Smith (William Bendix) speaks in such a way as to announce with every breath not what he does well, not how he came to learn it, not what position his parents held in society and he after them, but the fact that he is from Brooklyn and that Brooklyn has infused his character with its "spirit."

The American is perennially present announcing the self – and social class be damned. A person's cognizance of his own class status, indeed, is often taken as a sign of etiolation, regressiveness, European archaism (as with the wealthy Nazi Tobin in *Saboteur*). While the argument may of course be raised that Hitchcock's American characters owe their rich display of personality to the personnel available in the studios for character casting, and the same in the United Kingdom, this hardly diminishes the point that Hitchcock knew what sort of national themes had to be reflected through his characters in order that his films might take on the cast of reality; and knew what actors to use in order to reflect those themes.

Edith Evanson (1896–1980) did more than a hundred character parts, including Mrs. Wilson the maid, seen here with James Stewart's Rupert Cadell in Rope *(Transatlantic Pictures/Warner Bros., 1948), and Rita the floor cleaner in* Marnie *(Universal, 1964). Digital frame enlargement.*

She

If Henry James's Daisy Miller, voluble, opinionated, passionate, flirtatious, unselfconscious, and fully "natural," models a certain sort of American woman, this type is rarely to be found in Hitchcock's oeuvre. Excepting little Ann Newton in *Shadow of a Doubt* (1943) (Edna May Wonacott),[22] who not only reads a great deal but shares her every observation with anyone around, and the vapid partygoer

---

[22] Miss Wonacott's casting photograph of July 25, 1942, identifies her as residing at 1132 Neal Drive, Santa Rosa, telephone 3058. She was at the time ten years old, four feet tall, and in the lower sixth grade.

Mrs. Cunningham in *Strangers on a Train* (Norma Varden), giggling like a schoolgirl as she becomes the subject for a demonstration of strangling, we are left with relatively taciturn (or manipulative) types. There is impetuous, controlling Patricia Martin (Priscilla Lane) in *Saboteur*, the sentimentally nostalgic Emma Newton (Patricia Collinge) or her reflective, silently observing daughter Charlie (Teresa Wright) in *Shadow of a Doubt*, silently perspicacious and modestly eloquent Constance Petersen in *Spellbound*, patriotic, but also romantic Alicia Huberman in *Notorious* (her expressions are all tied to her uncontrolled feelings, not her thoughts), loyal and retiring Ann Morton in *Strangers on a Train* (Ruth Roman), or her eager younger sister Barbara (Patricia Hitchcock).

The Hitchcock heroines, especially the frequently celebrated "Hitchcockian" blondes, are poised more than expressive – Grace Kelly in *Rear Window* is the exception that proves the rule. In *Psycho* Marion Crane (Janet Leigh) is modest and guilty; she says little. In *Marnie* the central character is reclusive and guilty; she speaks mostly in self-defense. In *Vertigo* our beautiful focus of attention (Kim Novak) is at one point aristocratic (that is, withdrawn) and oneiric, at another point clumsy and desperate, yet never very talkative. In *North by Northwest* Eve Kendall (Eva Marie Saint) is almost always secretive, until she finds herself clinging to Roger Thornhill from the face of Mount Rushmore, when she becomes hushed by dread. In *The Birds*, Melanie Daniels seems to be a point of focus for all the sounds around her – especially bird sounds.[23] Shots could be made,

---

[23] An early memorandum (occasionally self-avowedly morbid) from the man who would gather and train the birds for Hitchcock proposed, "The introduction of birds *pecking* and *tapping* on a window can be dramatized photographically. Such a bird, already trained, is available for demonstration. In the way the story suggests, birds can be made to *peck* and *claw* at a door or roof top, or to dislodge shingles and loose boards" (Berwick).

Hitchcock's bird trainer proposed, of "a single large bird attacking the face of a prone human. In this instance (with the use of parts of animal anatomy from the market) it can conceivably be tearing out an eye or dissecting an ear" (Berwick). In this way, Hitchcock could dramatize the transition from Melanie's initial aloofness to vulnerability and finally helpless victimization, but even in victimization she does not scream.

Beyond evincing a kind of "uncanny otherness" that permeates their presence in relation to men (Modleski 92), Hitchcock's American women are gifted with prescience and sensitivity in their reserve or hesitation, an attachment to the nuance of the moment and to the currents of life that marks them as forces of heroic love.[24] Consider a moment involving Emma Newton, a paragon of domesticity (Bill Krohn calls her an "Invisible Woman" [*Work* 68]) who cannot serve a platter of deviled eggs without apologizing, "It's the paprika makes it pink." She is a slave to the kitchen: when her brother Charles comes visiting from the east, she wakes him on his first morning with a splendid breakfast

---

[24] One might go beyond reserve and hesitation and add modesty, a quality shared by characters and actors alike. Discussing her wardrobe for *North by Northwest*, Eva Marie Saint told Walter Raubicheck, "Because Mr. Hitchcock did not like the wardrobe that was made for me . . . he took me by the hand and took me to Bergdorf Goodman and picked out the wardrobe, and it was the first and last time that I ever had a sugar daddy. At one point he said, 'Do you like the black dress with the red roses embossed?' and I said, 'I love that dress.' And he said, 'Well, just wrap it up for Miss Saint,' and there it was – my dress. One day on the set – it was during the auction scene and there were many, many extras around – I started to get my own coffee in a Styrofoam cup. That's what actresses do, and he said, 'Eva Marie, I don't want you to get your coffee in a Styrofoam cup in the $3000 dress. Someone should bring it to you in a china cup and saucer.' And I thought, 'Well, that's really nice.' No one has ever said that to me on a set before or after" (32–3). Herbert Coleman claims it was he who took Saint shopping at Bergdorf's (281).

tray, spoiling him and yet also openly manifesting her commitment to hospitable servitude and grace. Late in the film, confronted now by a niece who has discovered evidence that he might be the serial killer police are searching for, Charles announces that he is going to leave Santa Rosa, abruptly, tomorrow. The camera swoops into Emma's face, as tears slowly well and then flood out of her eyes. She recalls how happy they were in childhood in a voice that is palpably given over to grief, one that announces between the lines, "I know we will never meet again." And as the scene slowly fades to black, it is Emma's voice (in a speech written by Collinge herself [69]) we hear trailing away in reflection: "Then you know how it is. You sort of forget you're you. You're someone's wife . . ." This is undoubtedly one of the most powerful statements about women's position in American culture ever put to film. Earlier, Emma had held in her hands, and meditated about, the one photograph of Charles that exists, him as a little boy, sweet and happy, before he had that accident falling from his bicycle and hitting his head (and was never, we can presume, the same person again). The elegiac quality of Emma throughout the film, and especially in this moment, may well reflect the fact that, as Krohn reveals, the character was "named after Hitchcock's mother, who was very ill in England while *Shadow of a Doubt* was being made" (*Work* 63).

It is Hitchcock's mise-en-scène in *Shadow of a Doubt* that gives weight and moment to his characters, since very like Emma (and with the sole exception of the pedantic Charles, a man who sermonizes his pathetic misanthropy) they speak briefly and with deep feeling, conveying most of their attitude toward one another and their situations through gesture, silence, and posture. The powerful statement of Emma's vulnerability and sweetness that is her reflection on marriage – for Paula Marantz Cohen, what the film seeks is "the delineation of a family idea" ("Conceptual" 129) – is not even delivered while we look at her, but comes at a moment when the film has turned away, moved on to "more important things."

Equally poignant, but imbued with a wholly different emotional quality even while it reflects Emma Newton's profound gentility and love, is the confession of Marnie's mother (Louise Latham) to a daughter utterly broken by memory, need, and loss. Marnie has been stealing, and has fallen into the gentlemanly clutches of Mark Rutland (Sean Connery), the scion of a wealthy publishing magnate who has decided to "tame" – that is, in a way, possess – her. "There is a powerful need for Hitchcock's camera to possess Marnie," writes Joe McElhaney, "to offer her up as something which cannot only be viewed but physically touched as well" (97). Under Mark's protection, and pressured by his desire that she overcome an enormous emotional block, she comes to visit the house of her dreaded and resented mother, the icy and forbidding figure who would never give Marnie a mother's love. There is a brief thunderstorm. Marnie has a fugue episode that sucks her back to the past, the past in which as a little girl she took extraordinary measures to protect this mother she loved from brutal male violence, and when it climaxes and her emotions subside she comes face to face with a mother now completely transformed. Faced with the unimpeachable finality of her daughter's collapse and her new son-in-law's firm and accepting gaze, Mrs. Edgar recounts the tale of how it was that Marnie came to be:

> *There was this boy, Billy, and I wanted Billy's basketball sweater. I was fifteen. And Billy said if I'd let him, I could have the sweater. So I let him. And then, later on, when you got started, he run away. I still got that old sweater. And I got you, Marnie. Then*

> *after the accident, when I was in the hospital, they tried to make me let you be adopted. I wouldn't. I wanted you. (Qtd. in Auiler 524)*[25]

And then she offers her daughter what is for her an extraordinarily genuine, unaffected, undefended, and feelingful admission: "You're the only thing in this world I ever did love." Richard Allen asked screenwriter Jay Presson Allen about the feelingfulness of this scene:

> *RA: In your adaptation, you develop the relation between Marnie and her mother much more fully, and I wonder whether that was a way, again, of trying to make the character Marnie more sympathetic, engaging to the audience.*
>
> *JPA: I'm sure it was. I don't have any memory of deliberately doing that, but I'm sure it was. I mean, I like Marnie. I felt sorry for her. ("Interview" 12–13)*

What makes this story importantly different from the one we are given in *Shadow* is that unlike Emma Newton, Bernice Edgar has now – just as in her problematic past – no protecting presence, save Divinity, to whom she prayed uneventfully that if Marnie could only lose her memory she would make everything right for the child. That memory – of a frightening murder – Marnie does not forget but only represses, only tucks away into a dark cabinet of the memory where it can do the most harm. Was she, in this, like Hitchcock? "He was a very Edwardian fellow," Jay

---

[25] Auiler notes how Universal was nervous about some of the dialogue in this speech. Hitchcock agreed that prints could be reedited with the necessary cut, but this was achieved with only some of the circulating prints. The DVD, made from original materials, includes the full speech (see Auiler 523–4).

Presson Allen is quoted by Spoto. "He put lids on himself. To work out his repressions he created a framework – his art" (500). Bernice's domestic space is not ensured by male privilege, even though her daughter was born as a direct result of her systematic capitulation to male pressure and demand. Used and abused by men, Bernice never had the opportunity to develop the tender feelings – and a rhetoric for expressing them – that we see springing so naturally from Emma Newton's similarly frail frame. Bernice has been locked up inside herself, and so has Marnie. If Billy taught her that through sexual favors she could come to possess a world, he also showed her the central importance for females of buying into the structuring rhetoric of male desire, male satisfaction, and male power. Marnie, then, became not the "only person" Bernice ever did love but the "only thing," yet one more possession and culmination, one more product of the capitulating interaction that dominated her life.

Louise Latham as Bernice Edgar in Marnie: "Too blonde hair always looks like a woman's trying to attract the men. Men and a good name don't go together." Digital frame enlargement.

Diva

The most powerfully expressive woman in Hitchcock's American work is Jo McKenna in *The Man Who Knew Too Much*. We learn early in the film that her present circumstance of being the wife of a Midwestern general practitioner and the mother of a precocious ten-year-old boy represents a kind of fall, since earlier in her life she was an internationally celebrated star of the stage. As Jo Conway, our heroine made so many recordings, these merchandised so successfully both in and out of America, that people on the other side of the world recognize her face: this is the meaning of the strange look of recognition that the Draytons cast at Jo as with the rest of her family she moves from a *calèche* into the Mamounia Hotel. She is indeed – in her innermost self – the "famous Jo Conway," as the Draytons put it at dinner, a figure of more enchantment perhaps for the adoring Lucy Drayton than for the stodgier husband who "doesn't go in for all this bee bop stuff."

As a star, Jo has had plenty of opportunity to look out on the gazes of others, to identify people by their behavior, to see what the world offers: the stage, after all, is a vantage point, and she has been occupying it – Bill Krohn makes this explicit – as a diva (*Work* 177). She catches the Frenchman Louis Bernard's attachment to an Arab who had exploded in anger at her son on the Casablanca–Marrakech bus, and realizes that if Bernard had been behaving toward the man as a stranger he wasn't one in fact. She catches Lucy Drayton spying on them at the restaurant as she prepares for an exotic dinner with her husband. Moreover, she demonstrates a remarkably broad and remarkably trained vocal range, first as she sings "Que Sera, Sera" with her son at the Mamounia room (in a sequence charmingly choreographed by Nick Castle); later when she engages in friendly chatter with the Draytons at dinner; the next morning when she speaks persuasively to Ben about wanting another child. All of Jo's articulations are shaped, phrased, sung. If we have come to see Jo's vocal power in but a few scenes early in the film, Ben has been living with it for years and recognizes far more than we do the extremes to which Jo might stretch that voice in the event that her very deepest emotional fibers are torn. When he learns that their child has been kidnapped – kidnapped, indeed, by the homely Draytons! – he is not so naïve as to believe that he can merely report this to his wife. He knows as a husband, friend, *and medical practitioner* that a sedative will be required, and makes sure she takes one before he confides the secret. Even now, Jo's expressive power is operatic: we can perhaps imagine that any realistic performance from Jo Conway without the prop of the medication would have been off the charts, and so the sedative also performs a diegetic function for Hitchcock, allows for the presentation and development of a character fundamentally sprung from emotion and the singing voice without faltering into a too believable excess that would ruin the acoustic balance of the picture. Krohn reports Hitchcock's claim that in the scene "the actress got away from him" (*Work* 162), yet her dramatization of helplessness and grief, a kind of *récitatif pathétique*, works very strongly.

"Were you on the New York stage, Mrs. McKenna?" Bernard asks over martinis. "Yes, Mr. Bernard. I was on the New York stage, and the London stage and the Paris stage." Is Jo, we may ask ourselves, always on some kind of stage? By her four friends and former associates from the London theater world who come to visit the McKennas at the Savoy, no less than by the appreciative fans who gathered at the airport to see her de-plane, Jo is positioned as a continuing star, a person elevated above the normal and worth special attention. It is through not only fervent will but also the artful staging of the character of the purposive and unyielding American victim that she persuades officers of the London police to surround and investigate Ambrose Chapel. When the doors are found locked there, she again uses persuasive rhetoric to obtain a ride to the Albert Hall, where Inspector Buchanan has gone for a concert.

At the Hall, and in a sequence that has become iconic of Hitchcock's mise-en-scène, she agonizes through a performance of Arthur Benjamin's *Storm Clouds* cantata, both identifying with the soloist and fellow performer whose every syllable is felt with quintessential directness by Jo (clasping her diaphragm); and dreading some real "storm" that threatens to break in this daunting place even as the choir repetitively chants, "The storm clouds broke / And drowned the dying moon."[26] With a piercing scream this woman interrupts, destroys, vitiates, and transmogrifies the performance of Benjamin's composition: who is she as she screams, the mother Josephine McKenna, past the point of containing her anxiety about a missing child; or the singer Jo Conway, swept away at this horrible moment in her life by a piece of music that seems itself to be pathetic fallacy, a perfect mirror of her human condition? At any rate, she is hardly demure or modest, and it is the character of Jo's scream *as music*, its modern directness and syncopation, its approximation to the natural expression of feeling, its extension of the voice as apparatus, that comes forth to qualify her presence in the auditorium as that of a vocalist who is a mother, not a mother who is a vocalist.

Again we hear "Que Sera, Sera" at the embassy after the concert, but this time in a plaintive and fully amplified cabaret

---

[26] For a very detailed analysis of the music, cinematography, and narrative in this sequence see Pomerance, "Finding Release" and Krohn, *Work* 166ff.

As Jo Conway McKenna, Doris Day belts out Jay Livingston and Ray Evans's "Que Sera, Sera (What Will Be, Will Be)" at the embassy in The Man Who Knew Too Much. *Day was not fond of the song when first she recorded it, but it changed her career. Digital frame enlargement.*

performance style, with Jo crooning from a grand piano in an elegant salon peopled with strangers who listen to her at first only out of politeness. The voice carries out of the room, across the marbled foyer, up the marbled and red-carpeted staircases. . . .[27]

In the end, it is not that the mother finds her child but that the mother's voice does, with the father trailing deftly behind. Or: the voice *is* the mother. If Ben McKenna is a bumbling and humble character, Jo is anything but (notwithstanding at least one critic's observation that the film "meshed the gender characteristics of the couple [Cohen, "Revised" 156]). Perhaps she is the final unrestrained embodiment in Hitchcock of the Daisy Miller who could talk "as if she had

---

[27] Krohn believes this sequence was inspired by a legend about Richard the Lionheart (see *Work* 158).

known [you] a long time. . . . Her lips and her eyes were constantly moving" (56). As to the world of people with whom one might interact – although the American males portrayed in Hitchcock tend to be too diffident, or too confused, to be good company – Jo had the power to speak for herself, just as Daisy did: "I'm very fond of society, and I have always had a great deal of it" (57).

The Dark Souls

"The world of *The Birds* is not loveless, like the world of *Psycho*," William Rothman observes. "Nor does love fall victim, as in *Vertigo*, to a villain's sinister machinations. In *The Birds*, there are no villains. All the characters are presented with sympathy. The birds kill, but they are not murderers" (351). Having no villains makes *The Birds* anomalous in Hitchcock, as indeed the so-called Hitchcockian villain is one of his distinctive trademarks. He recognized that all of America was not fair, nor every American the epitome of nobility and optimism. What of the American villain, except that for Hitchcock he is sometimes not, in his deepest soul, American at all? Vandamm in *North by Northwest* is European (and in his performance there James Mason gives full expression to his half-stuttering, half-whispered Yorkshire burr). All the evil in *Foreign Correspondent*, *Lifeboat*, *The Man Who Knew Too Much*, and *Torn Curtain* is basically foreign. Dr. Murchison in *Spellbound* comes close to being American, so long has he labored there, yet he is British in origin. The purebreds include *Saboteur*'s Fry, Tobin, and Mrs. Sutton, *Rope*'s Phillip and Brandon, *Stranger on a Train*'s Bruno, *Rear Window*'s Thorwald, *Vertigo*'s Elster, and *Family Plot*'s Adamson. In some passages, writes William Rothman,

> *Hitchcock declares the camera to be an instrument of villainy by asserting a link between a villain's gesture and a gesture of the camera. In other passages, he has the camera assume the villain's point of view, or frames a villain staring into the depths of the frame in a way that makes of him a veritable stand-in for the camera. In these cases, it is the camera's passive aspect, not its agency, that is associated with villainy. ("Villain" 218)*

– yet in his analysis the American villain is not expressly identified or examined.

Seen through American eyes, Britain is the birthplace of considerable evil. In the aftermath of World War II and perceiving itself threatened by communism, writes Gael Sweeney, America re-identified itself with "the colonial, the repressed, the noble underdog who desires freedom, and with spectacles of struggle against imperialism," while Britain's imperial ideology was "reviled by emerging nationalisms in the third world"; one effect was a slew of British actors "seen in roles that walk the line between sophisticated, cultured heroism and treacherous, sexually deviant villainy" (217). Even in Hitchcock's American villainy, however, we can find warpings, deviations, perturbations of character that suggest the malsocialized outsider. The murderous lovers in *Rope*, American-born both, are effete, pseudo-aristocratic, homosexual, and, as if all these were not enough, students of philosophy, so that they "lack" the red-blooded vivacity we find in the characterizations of Cary Grant or the red-blooded and bucolic grass-roots ethic that we find in those of James Stewart.[28] In order to be both American and bad, Phillip and Brandon must be alienated as marginal, in terms

---

[28] When, working for Anthony Mann in *Bend of the River* and *The Naked Spur* (1952; 1953), Stewart does have moments of vileness, we see him straining to get dirty through grimaces and broad physical gestures.

Three questionable types: Phillip (Farley Granger, l.), Brandon (John Dall, r.), and the tutor who helped make them who they are, Rupert Cadell (James Stewart) in Rope. *The problem, again, is language – Rupert has been trying to teach, but are the students really understanding? Courtesy Academy of Motion Picture Arts and Sciences.*

of class, proclivity, and frame of mind. Bruno Antony is a similar model, alienated through hatred of the father and effeteness of manner.[29]

There is a tiny scene in which Bruno actually addresses his father (Jonathan Hale) face-on, and rather than the monster Bruno thinks him the man is shown to be a rather ordinary

---

[29] Robert Walker was playing this role because Hitchcock had been "anxious for an off-beat casting" and "could think of no other performer but Walker when it came to the selection of his villain who suggests the weird bargain in crime." Walker had been contracted to MGM but was lent out for the film (Production Notes).

tycoon, one of the robber barons who made America and retreated to a pastoral fortress, having produced an aesthete for a son, a boy doted upon by a frenzied, almost mindless, mother (Marion Lorne). Lars Thorwald is friendless and out of place in his apartment complex, distanced from a nagging wife, finally revealed as optically disabled (his spectacles are loaded with very thick lenses). Perhaps in *The Wrong Man* (1956) the true criminal (Richard Robbins), he in whose place the hero suffers the torments of a jurisprudential inferno, is also an immigrant – he looks as Italian as Manny Balestrero does and we never hear him speak – yet he is nevertheless a cipher, appearing out of the distance like a looming spirit and then vanishing into the police machine. Vandamm's "associate" Leonard (Martin Landau) has suffered the same alienating gesture as Hitchcock's other effete gays (see, on these types, Wood; Barton; and Knapp). *Family Plot* boasts still another effete type, Anthony Adamson (William Devane), a man with a twisted psychology, a repressed history, and a bloated sense of privilege.

The most American of Hitchcock's villains inhabits *Psycho* (I will work to avoid giving the story away). Here is a figure borrowed at once from the good-natured naturalism of James Stewart and the slick commercialized bonhomie of Cary Grant, not to say the demure good looks of Eva Marie Saint and Teresa Wright. In this character we find charm, simplicity of manner, directness, sharp intelligence, sweet tenderness, and delicate dexterity; but also stammering vulnerability, anxiety, entrenched respect for traditional authority, honesty, and cunning. There is a conventional fondness for clean American youth, a healthy love of country and fresh air that far surpasses any greed for money, an observant care for nature, and, undeniably, great interpersonal charm. What might have created this monster, except America itself? – the same richly energized, well-organized social forces that made a trustworthy mother of Collinge, a vulnerable and well-meaning secret agent of Saint, a perfect gentleman of Grant[30] (who could rescue Alicia Huberman from a nest of Nazis or woo the ephemeral Francie Stevens by the Baie des Anges), or of Stewart a stalwart Everyman (able to preach common human feeling to the snobbish Brandon and Phillip, scout out the clues of a murder while trapped in a wheelchair, reunite his torn family in *The Man Who Knew Too Much*, and plunge into the very depths of love in *Vertigo*)? The lush farmland, the exploding city, the vibrant mix of immigrants, the unabated passion for movement, the cherished technological talisman, the pervasive commercial riddle, the belief that tomorrow can be better than yesterday – all these American truisms that Hitchcock both knew enough to see through and deeply believed: this was the ground in which American evil grew side by side with the flowers of dignity, capability, hope, and trust.

The soil in *Psycho* is the rich and conflicting tradition of American promise. What grows out of it might be as desirable and desiring as Marion Crane, as earnest as the detective Arbogast, as principled as the boyfriend Sam ... or else a dark soul, very very dark, and hungry not for symbols and principles, not for possibilities and freedoms, but for flesh.

---

[30] Born in 1904 in Bristol, Archibald Leach came to the United States in July 1920 as a stilt walker in a stage troupe. Deciding to stay on, he went to Hollywood in 1931, signed with Paramount, and became Cary Grant. On June 26, 1942, he became a naturalized American citizen.

3

HITCHCOCK AND AMERICAN VALUES

Readers of these pages live and work in a very different environment than the one in which Hitchcock's narratives were set. Ours is a world filled with explosive violence and tension, rampant secrecy, problems of knowledge and ignorance, public eruptions of feeling both repressed and ingenuous, and the widespread diminishment of human experience. "Already today," writes Slavoj Žižek about the twenty-first century as we know it, "there are more connections between computers themselves than between computers and their human users – one could apply Marx's formula here also, insofar as relations between computer-things are replacing relations between persons" (342). "Relations between persons" are the meat and potatoes of the Hitchcock film no matter its content. The American values that Hitchcock highlighted and examined are all person-centered, and the scale of his drama is always the human scale. The community as he depicted it, whether it is local (*Shadow of a Doubt* [1943], *Rear Window* [1954], *The Trouble with Harry* [1955]), institutional (*The Wrong Man* [1956], *North by Northwest* [1959], *Marnie* [1964]), or global (*Lifeboat* [1944], *Torn Curtain* [1966], *Topaz* [1969]), was built of and for fundamentally human connections and problems. After all, it was in the 1920s that Hitchcock had come of age and begun his career, admiring America and things American from afar. When he imagined the United States, and then brought his family to live and work there, it was still a country that inspired romantic dreams of fabulous possibilities. "The men and women of the 1920s," writes Ann Douglas, "were the first to ride in airplanes, and they took them to every part of the globe.... They installed electric service in their part of the American continent; they lit up and cleaned out and looked hard at its dark places" (53). Hitchcock was part of that world.

Hunger for Practice: *Torn Curtain*

A concise and lambent account of the initiation of the Cold War is given by David Halberstam when he writes of the 1945 armistice that "an unwanted war had not brought a true peace" (9). With a fragile domestic coalition fostering American engagement in Europe, a Soviet hegemony over Eastern Europe at war's end, a concomitant anticommunist fever building in largely Republican America, and Russia's explosion of an atomic device in 1949, a line was being drawn, as it were, in the sand. American political and economic activities were more and more being designed and framed to combat an unseen, lethal, and formally undeclared enemy that, if it could find the way, would control the world. In an astute cultural analysis of that time, Robert J. Corber notes how many aspects of Hitchcock's films of the late 1940s and 1950s were orientations, subtle or not, to the idea of communism as a blinding threat, but this does not alter the fact that Hitchcock generally forbore to make any explicit reference to Cold War politics that could overshadow the dramatic content of his stories. If, for example, in real life the physicist Klaus Fuchs made an admission on January 13, 1950, that he had "passed atomic secrets to the Soviets" (Halberstam 45), the closest reference Hitchcock made to such blatant and unambiguous treachery was with Philip Vandamm securing and preparing to flee South Dakota with military-industrial secrets of some kind intended for an enemy off in the great anywhere. Vandamm's nefariousness is never spelled out as Soviet-based, nor is any other character in Hitchcock's films from 1948 through 1964 indicated directly as an enemy agent whose planned initiatives might imperil American economic, nationalist, military, or scientific imperatives. Even in *The Man Who Knew Too Much*, which posits a group of definitive agents from a definitive enemy state, we never learn the name or nature of the state and never guess at its deepest purposes.

In virtually every case Hitchcock's postwar films do not depend on the viewer's acknowledgment of an aggravated detente outside the theater, a conflict of suspense in which nuclear bombast weighed both public, professional, and casual engagements. The sole reference to nuclear possibility is Sebastian's secret behavior in *Notorious*. No Hitchcockian character (beside the sailors in *Lifeboat* [1944] and the ex-soldier Ben McKenna) recollects having done war service (and Ben's recollections are dismissed as soon as he expresses them); none makes explicit reference to the fraught politics of the Marshall Plan, the Truman legacy, the Eisenhower rapprochements, or the Nixon promise.

Until, that is, *Torn Curtain* (1966), when the East–West divide and the global political scene are infused directly into a plot that makes open reference to the Cold War stalemate and the espionage associated with it. Krohn calls the film "a poetic vision of the communist world" (*Work* 268). But this film also says and shows something important about a value system deeply entrenched in American cultural life.

Upon landing in East Berlin (with his graduate student/ fiancée Sarah Sherman [Julie Andrews] secretly on his tail), Michael Armstrong (Paul Newman) is formally welcomed by the East German government, and he and Sarah are escorted into the offices of the Minister of Security, Gerhard (Hansjörg Felmy). Arrangements will be made for both of them to live happily in the East. Michael will be conducted forthwith to Leipzig, where he can engage in high-level theoretical work in physics with the esteemed, if also hilariously egotistical, Dr. Gustav Lindt (Ludwig Donath).[1] In the meantime, he is assigned as bodyguard a hulking and "oddly likeable" gunsel named Gromek (Wolfgang Kieling), who lived once, deliriously, in New York. Not so stupid and rather gracious in his manner, for all his gum-chewing entrenchment in a black leather macintosh,[2] Gromek clearly finds Michael and his girlfriend fascinating beyond the fact that they must be the targets of his surveillance.

One morning he tracks Michael skipping out of the hotel and, after eluding him in a sequence at the Old National

---

[1] Who graciously wrote Hitchcock to say, "It didn't take more than a day and I felt that I belonged to a family. And then the work on the set with you is so much to the point and without any trimmings, that for any real actor it is sheer pleasure" (Donath to Hitchcock).

[2] Hitchcock caused to be written, and filmed in its entirety, a factory sequence where Armstrong has the opportunity to meet Gromek's twin brother (also played by Kieling, with his hair white – although he had agreed by contract to shave his head), and here the moral virtues of the bodyguard are spelled out explicitly. But the scene was finally not used, and Hitchcock made the decision to send it as a gift to François Truffaut, who planned to deposit it with the Cinémathèque Française (see Truffaut 313). That Kieling pleased Hitchcock enormously is evident from a dictation of thanks, in which the filmmaker calls him "one of the finest actors I have ever had" (Hitchcock Sketch).

Gallery ("The museum sequence is the height of artifice," writes Brigitte Peucker [207]), paying a clandestine visit to a local farmhouse.[3] Gromek the trusty bloodhound has caught on that Michael is meeting with agents of a tabooed underground group, Pi, and thus that his defection was nothing but a staged operation of the CIA. Confronted and provoked by Gromek, Michael has no choice but to kill the man – by forcing his head into the farmwife's gas oven (a far from oblique reference to Nazi extermination techniques).[4] Back in Leipzig soon later, Michael is facing an inquisitory board of professors, tasked with determining whether he is sufficiently advanced to gain exposure to the elite Lindt, when he finds his seminar presentation suddenly interrupted by a security agent who wants to know if he visited a certain farmhouse outside Berlin. His defenses mobilized as the session is put on hold, Michael confides to Sarah what is really happening. The remainder of the film consists of his insinuating himself into Lindt's confidence under pressure of time – since Gerhard's forces are now hot on his tail; securing the arcane mathematical secret from Lindt's beartrap mind; and then managing along with Sarah to get back to Berlin and flee the country in the costume baskets of a visiting Danish ballet company who have been performing *Francesca da Rimini*.[5]

---

[3] Michael is driven to the farmhouse in a taxi driven by Peter Lorre, Jr.
[4] "I thought it was time to show that it was very difficult, very painful, and it takes a very long time to kill a man," Hitchcock told Truffaut (311).
[5] By Peter Ilyitch Tchaikowsky (1876) and selected rather than Ravel's *Daphnis and Chloe* after discussions with Stanley Wilson and Hein Heckroth (Heckroth to Hitchcock). Also considered were other ballets, like *Francesca*, including "fires": *El Amor Brujo*, *La Gitana*, *The Fountain of Bakhchisarai*, *Walpurgis Nights*, *The Firebird*, and *Gayane* (Robertson to Herrmann). The scene shown in the film was choreographed by Michel Panaieff. Hitchcock arranged for the theatrical pandemonium scene (after Michael screams "Feuer!") to be filmed with hand-held, as well as standard, camera equipment (Robertson memorandum).

Tamara Toumanova (1919–1996) was one of Georges Balanchine's stars of the ballet, and she also worked closely with Léonide Massine. In Torn Curtain *she dances the lead in* Francesca da Rimini *and has key scenes with Paul Newman and Julie Andrews. On December 16, 1965, she wired Hitchcock, "Accept my deep and humble gratitude for giving me a new light in my life and a step forward in my career" (Toumanova to Hitchcock). Courtesy Academy of Motion Picture Arts and Sciences.*

The surface plot of *Torn Curtain* – American agent creeps into communist territory, steals military secret, and gets back home alive – is hardly the most interesting thing about this far too underrated film, and it certainly doesn't reveal Armstrong's quintessentially American values in his relationship with Lindt. This German intellectual is, of all possible creatures, a *theoretical* physicist, a man who operates through the language of mathematics to suggest possibilities, affinities, constructions, and problems that are not manifested objectively in a laboratory context. His orientation is entirely abstract. Indeed, it is because his thought is so rarefied that his private classroom is a space in which he can openly inscribe his formulae: they are legible only to him and his closest acolytes. As Norman O. Brown wrote of Ficino's fifteenth-century academy in Florence, so it can be said of Lindt's exclusive society:

> *The point is first of all to find again the mysteries. By which I do not mean simply the sense of wonder – that sense of wonder which is indeed the source of all true philosophy – by mystery I mean secret and occult; therefore unpublishable; therefore outside the university as we know it. (3)*

In order to get at the thoughts beneath his thoughts, Michael must convincingly assure venerable old Lindt that he *is* one of those adoring acolytes, a scholar of such esteemed merit that he deserves the right to verbal intercourse with one of the greatest brains of the century. Thus it is that Michael must *act* to learn by *performing* that he already knows: he must be a doer, yet also a faker. The film consistently gives us a picture of Michael as not only a man with a high-powered intellect in his own right but also an actor, in both key senses of the word: a person who wears a false identity for dramatic purposes; and a person who can mobilize doings. If he performs fakery with elegance and precision he also engages himself from start to finish in getting things done, moving from point to point, facing challenges, achieving, making things happen. Even the conversational strategy he uses in the climactic moments in Lindt's classroom to seduce information from the professor mirrors Michael's active status: he speaks of having actually built the Gamma-5 engine, "but it didn't work."

"It works! It works!" gleams Lindt, in a purely theoretical manner, since he doesn't claim to have built anything. Further, with his Midwest twang,[6] Michael can be nothing but indisputably American: Hitchcock's casting of Paul Newman in the mid-1960s for this role is a real statement about finding and using a quintessentially American personality to embody a quintessentially American personality. Lindt, by contrast, with his garrulousness, his cigar, his twinkle, his effete mannerisms and courtly etiquette is nothing if not the epitome of old European style and culture. The conversation in Room 29 is thus not only between agents of the Western and Eastern sides of the Iron Curtain, but also between an American practical man and a European formalist, a dynamo and a bonfire.

Some appreciation of Hitchcock's way of constructing such a conversation can open us to a greater respect for his technique in other films, since Hitchcockian filming is never only a matter of what characters onscreen say and do to further a diegesis. Dramatic actions must be appropriate to, and characters' language precisely descriptive of, the situated moment, which is invariably visual, so that casting and performance, mise-en-scène, lighting, camera angle, construction of setting, and music must all be woven into the director's "action" as he makes a scene. We need to note that Room 29 isn't an American-style flat classroom but a steep vertical lecture theater. That it is not particularly large suggests that at this university even medium-sized classes are given in a formal setting, where the professor stands as the center of attention upon a kind of stage and the

---

[6] Having been born and raised in a suburb of Cleveland, Newman had no trouble relying on Midwestern vocalization patterns, although in numerous other films, such as *Cool Hand Luke* (1967), he shows that other styles were available to him.

students cluster around for the best possible vantage points.[7] Implicit in the setting itself, then, is the vertical hierarchy that underpins the classical European teacher–student relationship, a hierarchy reflected in the content of Lindt's many comments to Michael as well as in Michael's adoring attentiveness, his open-eyed concentration on every syllable the professor utters. This is a double attentiveness, of course: it reflects what any proper student would demonstrate through deference to such an august personage as Lindt, thus adding to Michael's performance as the dutiful and eager acolyte who would kneel at the feet of his master; but it also demonstrates to us (while not to Lindt) the rapt concentration with which Michael the spy is focusing upon his target as a data source.

On top of the setting, we have the fresh-faced openness of Armstrong and the wrinkled, suspiciously wry maturity of Lindt. We have Lindt's gabbling impatience with elementary formulae, and Michael's no-nonsense changes of pace and direction to keep up. We have the New World devouring the Old World in the name of progress. The European in all his mannerisms and general style looks backward to history. The American looks to the future. The film is built, writes Robin Wood, "on strong foundations that have something of the essential simplicity of myth. But what gives it its particular pungent flavor – what acts as a veritable principle of composition, common to almost every episode – is Hitchcock's sense of the necessary moral impurity of action in an imperfect world" (*Films* 201).

The dichotomy between reflection and action isn't new. "In America," wrote Alexis de Tocqueville in 1840,

---

[7] See, for another case of action in this kind of place, Fritz Lang's *Das Testament des Dr. Mabuse* (1933).

> the purely practical part of science is admirably understood, and careful attention is paid to the theoretical portion which is immediately requisite to application. On this head the Americans always display a clear, free, original, and inventive power of mind. But hardly any one in the United States devotes himself to the essentially theoretical and abstract portion of human knowledge. In this respect the Americans carry to excess a tendency which is, I think, discernible, though in a less degree, amongst all democratic nations.
>
> Nothing is more necessary to the culture of the higher sciences, or of the more elevated departments of science, than meditation; and nothing is less suited to meditation than the structure of democratic society. (48)

For all his garrulous boasting and expressive conceit, Lindt is the model of a meditative theorist. The mind is always turning, and when he stands at his blackboard to scribble, formulae trip from his fingers like fluent streams of thought. Michael, however, has the cutting, clear, targeting eyes of the man who only searches for what he can use. He is interested in practice and committed to the practical world. Intentionality, productivity, achievement, and onward progression are painted on the hungry canvas of his face. He's going somewhere; he's going to make something of himself. He's in that limitless crowd on the plains of Howdehow at the finale of Carl Sandburg's "The People, Yes," shouting at the top of his lungs, "Where to? What next?" And where, one might wonder, was Hitchcock in all this, the European man turned American, the traveler, the trans-Atlantic soul? McGilligan recounts how Hitchcock was immediately put off when Newman, a dinner guest at his house, stripped off his jacket before sitting, asked for beer instead of the wine he was offered, and then got up to fetch it for himself out of the kitchen (664): old-fashioned *gemutlichkeit* offended by brash, jazzy, casual sensibility. Yet Dan Auiler says that "Hitchcock took enormous exception to

Newman's detailed notes on the script and to the lengthy time the actor required to get into character . . . those long moments on the set while he tried to work out why his character would walk through a room" (525; 545): a filmmaker's American zest for speed and efficiency balking at an actor's surprisingly archaic, meditative personality!

Charms of Duplicity: *North by Northwest* and *Psycho*

A completely different kind of performative intelligence, reflecting an altogether different set of prerogatives and values, is demonstrated by Roger O. Thornhill in *North by Northwest* (1959) – Roger, that is, not the actor Cary Grant who is embodying him, since even at the level of the narrative the problem of putting on a face is pervasive and central. In every trace of his manner and speech there is a distinct yet subtle tincture of British heritage, evident in his scrupulous grammaticism (Eve: "Is that a proposition?" Roger: "It's a proposal, sweetie") or his reliance upon a sense of gamesmanship and fair play, not to say his monarchical bearing leavened with a healthy ounce of British working-class scampishness (trademarked by Cary Grant). Roger is something of an alien presence deposited inexplicably on the American scene (a reflection of all those "originary" British immigrants); his attitudes and assumptions are betrayed as relatively recent additions to, rather than intrinsic elements of, the American character type. Michael Armstrong and Gustav Lindt were obsessed about theoretical possibility and practical fact, but Roger's professional life, to which his privacy is apparently seamlessly adjoined, is based on what he himself calls the "expedient exaggeration." He is, in fact, little more than a professional liar, kingpin of a major Madison Avenue advertising agency in an era – the late 1950s – when advertising has expanded rapidly to command attention and devotion in a newly burgeoning consumer culture.

Stuart Ewen notes, for instance, how the postwar era was "one in which mass consumption erupted, for increasing numbers, into a full-blown style of life. ... The suburbs were a contained representation of open space – there was little reality within which yeoman self-sufficiency could grow" (208). First with big producers working to empty their postwar warehouses on an unassuming public; then with the expansion of the workforce and the profusion of television and magazines ("There was little room in these [television] shows for the industrial hardship or social radicalism that had actually characterized the immigrant experience in America for many" [210]); and then with the expansion of the big-city department stores (Edward Filene, a Boston department store magnate, "developed an international reputation as 'the mouthpiece of industrial America'" [54]), the late 1950s represent a time when shopping was a central economic piety. The modern transformation of American society, from one in which people made what they needed to one in which they bought virtually everything from dedicated manufacturers, was virtually complete. In such a world, the forked-tongued man was king.

A number of times in *North by Northwest* we see Roger's entirely amicable duplicity, his effortless double-speak, and his personal alienation from an economy he shapes and manipulates.[8] He gets embedded in a web of lies, either

[8] A combination of qualities that only Cary Grant could possess and deliver. Also considered at one point or another for this role, and clearly less than desirable, were John Wayne, Jimmy Stewart, William Holden, Rock Hudson, Kirk Douglas, Gregory Peck, Glenn Ford, Frank Sinatra, Dean Martin, Ray Milland, Joel McCrea, and Jeff Chandler (Hitchcock list). Herbert Coleman, who produced the film for Hitchcock, tells of a meeting with MGM head Sol Siegel in which Siegel said, "Cary Grant seemed right for the part" but offered a rather meager budget (278). Coleman goes on to report that near the end of shooting, Grant became peckish about money and a special side deal had to be struck with him (284–5).

mistruths of his own knowing construction (ordering his secretary to dissemble to a woman while sending her expensive chocolates); or mistruths he is forced to utter in order to save himself or redeem a situation (his pretenses to the housekeeping staff at the Plaza). Perhaps most fascinating are statements and postures that are taken by others as mistruths even when, as far as we can see, they are not, his telling an abject truth but being deemed to be lying, since his listeners have always taken (or expected) Roger to be a liar and see no reason to change their estimations now. At the Townsend estate, for example, he is confronted by a man who takes him to be an American spy, Mr. George Kaplan. As a spy, Kaplan would of course not be expected to tell the truth, so that when Roger demurs and insists that he is not Kaplan – the truth as he sees it at the moment – his interlocutor automatically refuses to believe him.

He escapes from this encounter with his life, but manages – in a state of complete intoxication – to drive into a police car, with the effect that he is arrested and brought to Glen Cove station. Claiming that he was kidnapped, he is taken by detectives to the estate he had visited the evening before, with his lawyer and mother in tow, but now a cover-up is in full swing and there is no evidence at all. No matter how much Roger protests that he was forced to drink a bottle of bourbon there and then placed behind the wheel of a stolen car, no one will believe him. His mother caps the scene by sighing, "Roger, pay the two dollars!"

The film also insightfully plays upon the fact that journalism and the media in general are structurally engaged in producing mistruth since the construction of consumable stories depends on information that is at best partial (for a full account of this problem see Epstein). At the United Nations, Roger inadvertently becomes party to the murder of an innocent diplomat, whose Long Island property, it turns out, was being used without his knowledge by foreign agents. As Roger crouches over the man's corpse, holding the dagger that killed him in wide-eyed astonishment, a bystander who has been taking press photographs of dignitaries swivels around and snaps his picture, this image immediately appearing on the front page of the *New York Times*. Now, Roger's every proclamation of innocence is degraded into a lie by the power of the press – the national press to boot. Not long later, his "criminality" still unimpeded and unpunished, he finds himself trapped by the villain and his henchmen within a smug middle-class crowd of culturati grasping for what they take to be sophisticated works of art and furniture in a fashionable Chicago auction house. His only way out is to mobilize this sedate and far too complacent crowd to physical action, to create a melée in exactly the social class where such a thing is least likely to exist; so he fabricates bidding – tells a chain of lies, in order to appear to be competing for objects he does not want. Eventually he goes too far (as he knows he will) and provokes a fistfight; this a cue for the auctioneer to call for the police, the escorts Roger has been hoping for.[9]

Our hero's lies are sometimes intended only to be beneficent.[10] At the Mount Rushmore monument, where the

---

[9] Robin Wood comments on the similarity of *Torn Curtain* to *North by Northwest* (*Films* 201–2), although he does not adduce the link between this auction scene and the ballet sequence in *Curtain*, where Armstrong stages his escape with Sarah by creating pandemonium during the performance in a kind of echo of Roger's disruption at Shaw & Oppenheim. (See note 5.)

[10] Although not quite as beneficent as Hitchcock's. The entire Mount Rushmore sequence was filmed not on location but in Stage 27 at MGM, using technical processes and photographs made by Robert Boyle on location. Hitchcock was especially fond of special effects constructions (such as rear-projection composites), and so it could be argued that, even beyond the fact that all films are not in actuality the situations they depict, the typical Hitchcock film, and especially this one, is built out of artful and wholly well-meaning lies. For more on Mount Rushmore see Pomerance, *Horse* ch. 3.

film climaxes – Richard Millington observes that "the testing of Roger Thornhill's character unfolds as a series of ordeals in places that trace out the mythological history of American individualism" (137–8), and thinking in particular about this place Stanley Cavell sees that Roger and Eve there "are crawling between heaven and earth, a metaphysical accomplishment, as if becoming children again" (171) – Roger agrees with the Professor to go through with a masquerade whereby Eve, a closeted American agent posing as the villain's girl, will brazenly shoot him "dead" in front of her boyfriend. In this way, she will guarantee that any and all doubt of authenticity will be removed from herself. There follows something of a reprise of the United Nations murder, since like it the present act takes place in a lounge associated with a famous architectural monument and within eyesight of numerous potential witnesses all drawn from the class of "everyday residents" in the scene.[11] Roger does a brilliant job of playing dead, equipped as he is, in his advertiser's persona, to pretend to almost anything that will persuade almost anybody to a point of view or a cause.

He is soon in a hospital room "recovering," yet at the same time eager to get away and find Eve, with whom he has fallen in love. The Professor has him locked in, since the CIA plan, which must not be interrupted, is that she will fly off with the wicked Vandamm to Europe. Roger asks if his jailer might go out and buy some bourbon – another deception, since he doesn't want a drink at all – and then quickly takes off through the window.

Indeed, *North by Northwest* repeatedly shows Roger coming into possession of, or attempting to acquire, what he does

---

[11] Both scenes, too, are set in amazingly realistic studio reproductions of real settings.

not want.¹² He does not deeply and sincerely wish to be labeled with the identity of George Kaplan, or to drink the liquor poured down his throat in Long Island, or to wear the suits in the closet of Room 796 of the Plaza (Kaplan's room, that he cannot stop himself from sneaking into and peeking around in), or to glow through the noxious publicity in the *Times*, or to secrete himself in the Pullman conductor's uniform in Chicago (his only means of getting through the police cordon there), or to own any of the articles he bids for at the auction, or to revel in the tourist view of Mount Rushmore (an experience dictated by the Professor); nor to swig that bourbon he asks for in the hospital, or even, and most particularly, to possess the quaint Asian sculpture (containing the secret microfilms that the villain plans to export) that he manages to find in his hands before being trapped with Eve at the top of the monument. While the millions of addicted consumers Roger plays to in his everyday life, those whose purchasing bolsters American culture, experience interminable want – a want and willingness to shop; shopping with a fever to buy – Roger himself appears to want nothing but to be left to his own devices.

The story of the film, a mobile thrust in which he is deeply and complexly engaged, falls upon him, encircles him, entraps him, even provokes him, but is hardly a structure he willingly enters, rationally proceeds through, and resolves by gracefully leaving behind – this in the face of the fact that his final gestures *are* graceful, his actions rational, and his entrance to the complexity, at gunpoint, more willing than not. All this being true, we can never quite believe this is the story Roger

---

[12] Millington notes that at Mount Rushmore he "takes possession . . . of a newly defined capacity for action" (147), but I think we can see by his trepidation and general discomfort there that this capacity isn't something he particularly wants, either.

Eva Marie Saint, Cary Grant, and James Mason amicably posing for fan photographs at the Mount Rushmore monument. Courtesy Academy of Motion Picture Arts and Sciences.

would wish to be in, except that in it he finds Eve. At film's end, as the two of them are on board an eastbound train heading into a very dark tunnel, we have to wonder whether they will ever come out.[13]

Beyond its virtually ceaseless invocation of consumer culture, and its constant suggestion of the role of advertising and "expedient exaggeration" as pointers to contemporary economic participation, *North by Northwest* is a stunning and

---

[13] One viewer who was so enchanted he didn't care was the screenwriter Ernest Lehman, who wrote to Eva Marie Saint, "What a superb, miraculous performance you gave, in an impossibly difficult role, and made the whole movie *work*! (For the first time, I cried a little while watching the film. Don't know why)" (Lehman to Saint).

challenging display of American opulence: as if to say, here is the world that stands outside and above middle-class consumerism, the world all the purchasing on earth cannot possibly buy unless you already have it; yet also, and at the same time, the goal every red-blooded consumer aspires to, the Dream. Given Hitchcock's notable perspicacity in matters of social observation and criticism, a display like this was a way of cultivating a monstrously large (international) audience by pandering to viewers' blind cupidity rather than their observant thoughts. He knew well enough of America what Richard Hofstadter observed, that "both our religion and our business have been touched by the pervasive and aggressive egalitarianism of American life.... What we loosely call Jacksonian democracy completed the disestablishment of a patrician leadership that had been losing its grip for some time" (50–1). The super-rich were hidden in enclaves. What the public saw was a second America.

Richard Allen suggests that the film evokes "a monumental sterility" (*Romantic* 152), as any paean to objects, acquisition, and domination might ultimately do. Commencing, for example, at the brand new C.I.T. building at 650 Madison Avenue,[14] unavowed monument to fiscal prudence and capitalist reverie, we are soon taxied over to the Oak Bar of the Plaza, an oasis where the controllers of American business and media meet for after-work cocktails, where unfold the conversations that shape the culture as a whole.[15] Sedate,

---

[14] Of which photographs were taken of the lobby and, in color, of the elevator starters (two each for six self-service elevators) (Falconer wire). C.I.T. was, and is, a hugely successful financial holding company founded by Henry Ittleson in 1908. It had moved to its new headquarters at this address just prior to the Hitchcock shoot.
[15] Research photography was done of the Oak Bar and Restaurant, noting uniforms of bellboys, waiters, room captain, etc. (Falconer wire). Unaccompanied women were not seated in the bar at this time.

woody, lush, well serviced, this is a kind of sanctum of the real America, a place the multitudes who read advertisements do not have the privilege to see (because the advertising magnates are drinking there, and taking telephone calls). Then we move to the Old Westbury estate of Lester Townsend, bounded by immense and tidily kept swathes of verdure, elaborate gardens.[16] The study there (a studio set designed by Robert Boyle, like all the interiors in the film) is furnished in leather, lined with framed landscapes and leather-bound books, and laid with a rich and immense Persian carpet. Every nuance of the house bespeaks wealth and seclusion, secure distance from the huddled masses yearning to breathe free: the valued treasures of American royalty. Checking out Room 796 at the Plaza, we are visiting a national historic landmark facility and experiencing hostelry of the highest elegance. Soon later we are at the members' lounge of the United Nations, marbled and tranquil, functionally furnished[17] but designed in the modern international style with vast picture windows overlooking the Triboro Bridge;[18] here sit and confabulate the agents of international power, the representatives of the planet in meditative assembly. Then we are on the dining car of the Twentieth Century Limited bound for Chicago, ordering brook trout to be served upon a white tablecloth with silverware as the curling Hudson trickles by outside at sunset.[19] In Chicago we visit not just any hotel but the lush and very exclusive

[16] The exteriors were photographed at the Phipps Estate house in Old Westbury, Long Island, designed by George A. Crawley and opened in 1906.
[17] In reality by Vladimir Kagan, in the film by the MGM properties department under the supervision of decorator Frank McKelvey.
[18] Now the Robert F. Kennedy Bridge.
[19] Research photography was done of the platform at Grand Central Station with the train on the track, but all the train interiors were studio sets photographed in composites with rear-projection of the passing terrain.

The Frank Lloyd Wright–style Vandamm house jutting out of the rocks above Mount Rushmore, in North by Northwest. *This image is one of a set of painted mattes by Matthew Yuricich (b. 1923). Digital frame enlargement.*

Ambassador East. The auction takes place at the Shaw & Oppenheim Gallery,[20] a fictitious location but one commanding our imagination of a high-end house catering to only the wealthiest consumers for whom purchase is a sport. The film concludes in Vandamm's Frank Lloyd Wright–styled aerie in Rapid City, a house jutting out into the twilit cliffs from cantilevered redwood supports and faced over with twinkling glass trapezoids reflecting the night.[21]

---

[20] Through Herbert Coleman, Hitchcock learned the preciosities of auction practice at the Parke-Bernet Galleries, where "there was absolutely nothing to photograph with motion pictures since the people sit in a very sedate manner and make no movement. As a matter of fact it is almost impossible for the uninitiated to see when they are bidding, and it is only the experience of the Galleries' uniformed observer, who stands at the front of each section, which enables him to repeat the bids to the auctioneer" (Falconer to Coleman).

[21] In fact a 30 × 24 inch matte painting by Matthew Yuricich. Sections of the wooden cantilevering and veranda were built on the soundstage, along with the interior.

In all of this, Hitchcock is showing us an America of the nouveau riche. When this film was made there was little in the United States more than about three hundred years old, but New York and Chicago were full of significant architectural works that suggested age and European style. The Plaza, as we see, is faced with gargoyles and gilded statues, its interiors marbled and wooded as in an ancient castle. In Old Westbury and later in South Dakota we are looking at residential styles of the American financial elite. If through his suave manner and because of the intricacies of the plot Roger is able to weave a path in and out of such territories, he commands our attention less than the territory he visits. The film is a travelogue into the space of the controlling class, a vision of the principles of acquisition and mobility that structure and shape economic behavior in America, where everyone can be presumed to cherish a dream of being where he is not, of climbing a magical ladder to get there. Roger knows this and makes his living by fostering the dreaming and the climbing. So it is that in the film's finale, upon the face of Mount Rushmore, he finds himself in the not only unenviable but also profoundly ironic position of not climbing at all; not climbing because of having nothing but air above him, and trying hard not to plummet. If Alice discovered in Wonderland that you had to run just as fast as you could to stay where you were, Roger learns something morally analogous: that you have to struggle with all your might not to fall lower than you are. He has been persuading his fellow citizens to reach for what they haven't got, spending money they only wish they could earn.

In *Psycho* (1960) we meet one of these brainwashed citizens. Marion Crane (Janet Leigh) is a hungry young woman who has no doubt been reading Roger's ads. She harbors a perfectly "respectable" vision of married life, wanting to

One of many camera positions for the Mount Rushmore chase sequence, one of the true legends of Hitchcock's filmmaking. The "rocky" formations under the feet of Grant and Saint as well as behind their backs are made of painted foam material and erected on Stage 27 at MGM. In the rear is suspended on a curved batten a large painted backing (by John Coakley and associated artists), this lit by skypans. Filtration at the camera would produce a twilight effect. Courtesy Academy of Motion Picture Arts and Sciences.

meet her boyfriend Sam Loomis (John Gavin) in her house, "with [her] mother's picture on the mantle, and [her] sister helping [her] broil a big steak for three" instead of in the lurid shadows of a Phoenix hotel room where they are trysting as the film begins. "Sexually, Marion may be calculating (affectionately)," writes Jean Douchet, "but she doesn't seem repressed; ... No doubt her sexuality is often frustrated, as she seems to live alone, but frustration and repression are entirely different things. Equally frustrated are her other female desires: to enjoy her sexuality respectably and with assured companionship" (*Long Hard Look* 33). Sam Loomis, for his part, is caught up in a treadmill, sweating to pay off other people's debts and send his wife alimony, though "she is living on the other side of the world somewhere." Sam cannot face bringing Marion to his storeroom behind a hardware store in Fairvale; in order to run away with him she needs to help by finding some money.

The central idea of getting money that one doesn't already have thus comes to Marion as a fundamental philosophy of life. She is working for a real estate broker who has just made a big sale. He's got forty thousand dollars in cash and needs her to hold it until Monday morning. Who will follow if she merely and innocently disappears with it into the sunset? On her journey she is beset by a highway patrol officer who wants to make sure that, sleeping by the side of the road, she's all right. Now she becomes utterly paranoid and her deeper values kick in: she isn't by nature a thief, and she knows better than to take what isn't hers. To flee successfully she must sell her car and buy another, and this takes up seven hundred dollars. But after this transaction, she is resolute on resting through a stormy night at the Bates Motel, then returning to Phoenix the next day with the remaining money intact. It can hardly be her fault that this plan doesn't come off. One never knows whom one might meet on the road. But her intention had been to revert to traditional American values, a focus on what Ewen called yeoman self-reliance, honesty, privacy, keeping up fences to esteem one's neighbors. The lapse occurred back in the city, a place full of strangers with strange values, where too much cash floats around unattached and too many dreams collide.

There is a thin line between taking something that is not yours and possessing something by persuading an innocent

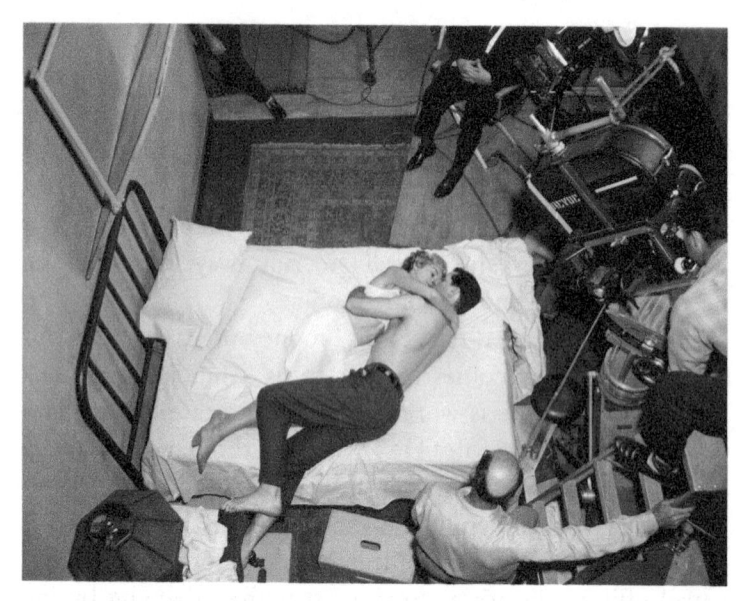

Marion Crane and Sam Loomis at lunchtime. Janet Leigh and John Gavin with the Hitchcock crew for a shot from Psycho. *Courtesy Academy of Motion Picture Arts and Sciences.*

to hand it over to you. Roger Thornhill is an expert in the latter technique, not quite a thief, to be sure, but also not a man whose life is based on encouraging those around him to be happy with their lot. Marion is a child of the consumer age, imperiled because a prize came too close for her to neglect it. Without that money, she would have had no compulsion to flee Phoenix, no need to be on the road, no need for a warm room in a cozy motel.

Plain Conviction: *The Wrong Man*

No adherent of Roger Thornhill's advertising and a moral antithesis of Marion Crane – no coin he does not possess

A view taken across the street from the actual home of Christopher Emmanuel Balestrero on Seventy-Third Street, Queens. A number of photographs taken of homes in this area were used in the preparatory research for The Wrong Man, *and Hitchcock strove to make all his shots on the actual locations involved in the case. Courtesy Academy of Motion Picture Arts and Sciences.*

would ever fall into his pockets – is Christopher Emmanuel Balestrero (Henry Fonda), Jacksonian protagonist of *The Wrong Man* (1956). This "wrong man" was intended by Hitchcock from the start to be a fully typical, real, down-to-earth American, not an idealization. "For the sake of authenticity," the filmmaker told Truffaut, everything was minutely reconstructed with the people who were actually involved in that real-life drama. "We even used some of them in some of the episodes and, wherever possible, relatively unknown actors" (237).

Manny is one of two children of an aging Italian widow, not quite as devoutly Catholic as his mother but as honorable, trustworthy, reliable, and competent as an honest man could be, and a loving husband and father. He lives in a tiny bungalow in the Jackson Heights section of Queens – as solidly lower middle-class as one can be.[22] This is a man who works loyally for his paycheck. He plays double bass in a band that has been engaged at Sherman Billingsley's Stork Club,[23] and puts most of what he earns into a savings account. He is struggling to make ends meet, and one has the impression that, as with most Americans in this supposed age of prosperity, life has always been this way for him. His wife, Rose (Vera Miles), is in need of some dental work. To get the few hundred dollars for this, he must borrow against her life insurance.

A man of impeccable routine, he leaves work in the small hours each morning, descending into the underworld of the subway, catching the "E" train to Queens,[24] sitting for his toast and coffee in a tiny snack bar where he plays at betting using his Racing Form, walking quietly home. Manny

---

[22] The Balestrero family actually lived on the second floor of the house, while Manny's sister-in-law Rose had the main floor; the film cedes him the whole space. Hitchcock originally asked his researchers whether Manny would take off his coat in the hall downstairs and hang it up or would take it upstairs, a question obviated by the restructuring of space in the film (Questions on Script).

[23] Hitchcock had thirteen meticulous questions about Billingsley's operation, including where the musicians kept their instrument covers and whether the doorman would lock the musicians' entrance after Manny left (Questions on Script). In the early 1950s, Billingsley had been subjected to a chain of hate mail threatening that the club would be destroyed, demanding unionization, or predicting that the owner himself would be harmed or killed. In 1954, Billingsley suffered a seizure there and "accused the union of slipping knockout powder into his tranquilizers" (Blumenthal 175ff.; 227).

[24] What would have been advertised on the posters on the platform at Fifth Avenue?, Hitchcock wanted to know. How many people would be on the platform? What would be advertised on the subway car? And all of this, also, for Roosevelt Station in Queens, where Manny would exit (Questions on Script).

exemplifies all the finest and simplest American virtues: quietness, good manners, politeness to strangers, affection for his sons, loving duteousness toward his wife, respect for his mother. He is a gentile Bontzye Schweig, unprepossessing, demanding nothing. In his travails, very soon to come, it is impossible not to see in him, too, a reflection of Job.

As he stands at the insurance company wicket asking to borrow that money, the clerks look at him suspiciously, tell him they'll need a little time to make the arrangements. After he leaves they swiftly contact the police, who stalk outside his house and pick him up. He has been identified as the perpetrator of a chain of local robberies. Escorted to the station, he is compelled to offer a handwriting sample and informed that things do not look good. Detectives drive him to a number of commercial locations where he is asked to stroll in and then out again. Soon enough, he has been rigorously identified by a number of well-meaning shopkeepers and is formally charged.

The police fingerprint him, arraign him, lodge him in a cell. By the time he gets out on bail, he is already grayed with despair and weariness, already ground down. Things get much worse, of course. As he and his wife try to remember where they were when the robberies took place, the names of two witnesses come to mind, but when he tries to find these men he learns that one is dead and the other has disappeared. In the court trial, the insurance company clerks who identified him are adamant and definitive, well rehearsed. Manny's wife has been losing her grip day by day, and the agonizing procedure of the trial brings her to the edge.[25] One

---

[25] The real trial lawyer, Frank D. O'Connor (played in the film by Anthony Quayle), informed Hitchcock's researchers in a January 26, 1956, meeting that Mrs. Balestrero's decline was "rather rapid. The first meeting with the Balestreros was on Sunday, January 18th. He noticed a decided change in Mrs. Balestrero by Thursday, January 22th, and on the following Monday, January 26th, she was in a very bad way. . . . Mrs. Balestrero, at no time, became violent – only deeply depressed" (Points to Be Checked Out).

night she lashes out at him, striking his face with her hairbrush, then lapses into a kind of catatonia, for which she must be hospitalized. But then suddenly, and out of nowhere, the real thief is found and Manny is exonerated. He moves with his family to Florida and we learn in a screen credit that some time later the wife was healed.[26]

In his moment of deepest despair, Manny confronts his mother and begs to know, "What should I do?" She tells him quietly, confidently, but perhaps with too old-fashioned a conviction, "Pray." Manny has never been under any delusions about the structure of the world in which he lives: it is, for him as for others in modern life, hopelessly secular, and the path he must tread in it, as David Sterritt notes, "straight and narrow" (69). The music he plays to earn his bread is, after all, not Bach's cantatas but jazz (specifically swing, which uses a percussion-bass ground with brass melody), that quintessence of American culture sprung from the lyric of hope within the darkness of slavery and despair.[27] Bernard Herrmann's "Prelude" (the main credit theme) "accurately represents the dour Manny Balestrero, whose drearily regimented lower-middle-class existence in the 1950s is anything but jazzy," writes Jack Sullivan. "At the end of the main title, Manny appears on the left of the screen standing rigidly, like

---

[26] An establishing shot of Manny and his wife walking down a Floridian street was made with doubles (and by Howard Winters Associates in Coral Gables), so that Henry Fonda could leave the country (Krohn, *Work* 180; Bolton to Screen Actors Guild).
[27] And he is playing swing rather than serious music, no doubt, because work is hard to get, as was the case with so many well-trained professionals after the 1910s. Alex Ross points out the example of Fletcher Henderson, "[Duke] Ellington's future rival for the crown of king of swing," who "started out as a classical piano prodigy; when he went to work with Ethel Waters in New York, he had to learn jazz piano by listening to James P. Johnson piano rolls" (140). In his home, we see that Manny has been coaching his young sons in classical piano music.

Henry Fonda as Manny Balestrero. Note how the lighting by Robert Burks works to highlight the star without compromising the "documentary" flavor of the scene. Courtesy Academy of Motion Picture Arts and Sciences.

a marionette, a striking contrast to the festive balloons floating above" (211).

Following his mother's advice, he stares at the image of Jesus on his wall. Hitchcock's camera glides in to frame that sanctified face. And within the face, doubly exposed beneath it, we see another man approaching us, step by step, until the eyes meet and dislocate Jesus' eyes, and this is the face of the real thief, a tall and slender man with a relaxed and unexpressive visage, more or less a body double for Manny. "I tried to dramatize the discovery of the real culprit," said Hitchcock, and this because "my picture is made from the viewpoint of the prisoner himself" (Truffaut 239).

It is possible to read this moment as a revelation. This transparency of faces, this juxtaposition, is a directorial penetration of the character's tenacious hold on traditional values regardless of the secular modernity he has had to embrace: in the swirl of the modern world with its vast uncaring circulation and anxiety-ridden disconnection from the past, tradition and faith are left as the only perduring and stable resources. If the film had had a happy ending (an impossibility for Hitchcock), such a reading might make sense. But *The Wrong Man* leaves us with a different tonality altogether. Manny and his family have been subjected to the tortures of living hell not by an evil presence or embodied malevolence but by an impartial, thoroughly democratic, and intensively streamlined system. Like Chaplin's Tramp sucked into the machine in *Modern Times* (1936) and twisting around its gears, Manny is inside the social machine that is modern urban America. And since he is a working man, not a member of the cultural and economic elite, the machine is not lubricated for him. Therefore, even when the *right* "wrong man" is found, Manny never quite becomes truly right – truly a wrong "wrong man" – but disappears into the matrix again, his tortures still fresh and his wounds still open.[28]

The Wrong Man is one of Hitchcock's most astute depictions of modern life, and much of its profound beauty lies in

---

[28] On page 173 of his masterfully informative book *Hitchcock at Work*, Bill Krohn publishes an astonishingly prescient photograph (made during the filming of *The Man Who Knew Too Much*, which preceded *The Wrong Man*): Hitchcock sits with twisted posture in a chair, gazing off-camera left with an expression of tough resignation, even bitterness, or else great weariness; his hands hang limply from the wrists, his bottom lip is turned down. But in the extreme foreground, right, we see the arm and equipment of a double bass player, the instrument itself dominating the photograph just as Manny's will at the very beginning of *The Wrong Man*, and the hand poised upon the strings as though to pluck them in Bernard Herrmann's musical cue.

the simple depiction of Manny's vulnerabilities as a citizen of the country's greatest city in a time when appearances, performances, stagings, and presentations dominate morals, feelings, biographies, commitments, and memories (on modernity and performance see Douglas 55ff.). Truth is in surfaces, largely because the rapid motion of modern enterprise and the rapid and shocking collisions of strangers afford opportunities for only the most superficial contacts and understandings. As Manny finds out, one's experience is defined and controlled by strangers who estimate events and outcomes from a distance, using imprecise descriptions and measurements and only indirect knowledge. Even the most sensitive and empathetic viewer must admit by film's end that Manny does look very much like the man who committed the robberies. One can be arrested and convicted merely because one looks as though one should be. As a culminating gesture to indicate the precariousness of our positions in modernity, Hitchcock shows us how even Manny's wife can come to suspect that he must be guilty, since no witness can be found to claim otherwise and since all the available evidence tends to point in that direction. Even Rose, whose link to him is presumably spiritual and inviolate!

He prays to Jesus, yes, but what if the robber does not choose at the same moment to venture out for another attempt? What if the robber has left town? Must we figure to ourselves that Jesus saves Manny by inspiring the thief toward another robbery, the act that will betray him? Or, in a city filled to the limit of every dimension with actions and reactions, is Manny's act nothing more than a man looking at a picture on a wall, and the thief's act nothing more than a man once again going for a walk to snatch at somebody's money?

In appreciating *The Wrong Man* it is crucial to attend to the sonic tone, because this is a direct sign of the director's intent: to render modern urban life in its quotidianness, its plainness, its ultimate truth. With the sole exception of Rose's outburst at Manny – an outburst provoked by her entire loss of self – there is no moment in the film in which we hear anyone speak other than quietly and directly. Manny, the detectives, the defense attorney, the witnesses, the legion police officers and court attendees – not one of these persons ever raises a voice, dramatizes, exaggerates, or melodizes. In structuring the sound this way Hitchcock presents a picture of a world that is deeply and thoroughly systematized, a rational-legal empire in which authorized definition puts closure to event, and verifiable weight and calibration characterize motive and intent. The film thus relentlessly depicts objectification and impression control, all of this, it need be said, styled as casual, personal, and thus civil rather than scientific. By virtue of one's presence in a scene one is taken to have a legitimate view, in this way it being possible for the clerks to not only point Manny out as a likely suspect but definitively pinion him against the wall of justice. The identity of a citizen can depend on judicial practice. And a citizen's innocence, if he can claim any, flows merely from the fact that no one has yet mobilized the machine of justice against him.

This is why one of the most profound shocks in Hitchcock is made possible by a simple and unremarkable diegetic transition: as Manny goes innocently to the insurance office to see if he can borrow some money legally, unbeknownst to himself he is instantly regarded by a nondescript clerk as though not long ago, at the same wicket, he used a weapon to get money by force. The stunning effect takes its place when we recall this scene later on, as Manny's eyes circle around and around his cell. This man now enchained in the dungeon of justice was at one point just a loyal husband trying to help his wife, a man who not only had done no robbery but who had no idea robbery had been committed. We must go back to *The Count of Monte Cristo* to find a similarly abrupt and magnificent transition: the innocent and unsuspecting Dantès shows the prosecutor Villefort a letter the danger of which he does not recognize, and soon finds himself locked in the Château d'If – locked away in darkness, and forgotten.

The Right Kind of Girl: *Rear Window*

If Michael Armstrong demonstrates the solid efficacy of American ingenuity; and Roger Thornhill brazen insouciance and personal charm; if Manny Balestrero points to humility and temperate balance as strengths, a vital sequence in *Rear Window* gives a picture of pluck and self-confidence carried to heroic extremes. Plucky courage was well known in America, and well known to Hitchcock. It was plucky courage that American fighting men had showed the world in two world wars, and that Hitchcock could appreciate in a personal way since until 1955 he was a British citizen living in Hollywood with close relatives in the United Kingdom. As a mythmaking structure, Hollywood cinema had long trafficked in the dramatic display of bravado as a signal feature of the American character. Swashbuckling buccaneers (Douglas Fairbanks Jr., Jeff Chandler, Burt Lancaster), hard-riding cowboys (John Wayne, Hopalong Cassidy, Tom Mix, Randolph Scott), insouciant and daring gangsters with impeccable polish and charm (James Cagney, Edward G. Robinson, Lawrence Tierney), melodramatic lotharios (Melvyn Douglas, Clark Gable, William Powell, Cary Grant): all these types were rationalized in their storylines through some narratively central, keenly focused display of moral strength. But what we typically did not see in genre films was courage of the everyday sort, what might be called small courage. The ability to overcome one's personal fears in order to save a situation, redeem a wound, make things right. The ability to stand up for a principle, even if standing up made one vulnerable to pain or death.

Making a crucial statement about what he believed the fount of the American character to be, and of his views regarding personal strength regardless of gender, Hitchcock arranges *Rear Window* (1954) so that pluck and courage are infused in the character of a stunningly beautiful, fashion conscious, smart and witty, polished, gracious, and cultivated woman. In the role, he cast (even without notifying her [Spoto 369]) Grace Kelly, a "cool, elegant beauty," who with "her suggestion of inner passion, her flashes of congenial wit – and her willing submission to his mentorship" was for the filmmaker "the answer to his professional fancy and personal fancy" (372).

Kelly's Lisa Carol Fremont has been dating our professional photographer-adventurer hero, Jeff Jefferies (James Stewart), for some considerable time when the film begins. He has sustained severe leg fractures on a job. Now, wheelchair-bound in a full-leg cast, he uses his binoculars and telephoto lens for peering at the day-to-day routines of his many neighbors across the courtyard. Lisa, an independent young woman of substantial means, entertains herself by working in an expensive dress salon (from which she can clothe herself rather lavishly as she pleases, and with a sense of occupational duty).[29] She has been bringing Jeff

[29] "There was a reason for every color, every style," said Edith Head to Donald Spoto, "and he was absolutely certain about everything he settled on. For one scene, he saw her in pale green, for another in white chiffon, for another in gold. He was really putting a dream together in the studio" (qtd. on 372). "Hitchcock," she said on another occasion, "is the only person who writes a script to such detail that you could go ahead and make the clothes without discussing them" (McBride 167).

fancy meals, keeping his spirits up, teasing him with kisses, and in general trying to convince him that a long-term relationship culminating in marriage is the prescription for his full return to health. In the early 1950s, even if the divorce rate was climbing, heteronormative marriage was rigorously upheld in popular culture and mythology as the key to spiritual, financial, and psychological success.[30] As Elaine Tyler May notes, "The vast changes in gender arrangements that some feared and others hoped for never fully materialized" (75).

But Jeff is skeptical, uneager to exchange his liberty of movement (ironically lacking throughout this film) for legal and loving bondage. Beautiful as Lisa may be – and it cannot be more evident that he is stricken by affection for her, or that in her appearance in this film Kelly apotheosizes the stunning radiance of the fresh American girl – she isn't the right type for a man who has to "eat fish heads and rice ... try to keep warm in a C54 at 15,000 feet, twenty degrees below zero ... get shot at ... get run over ... get sandbagged at night because somebody got unfavorable publicity from [his] camera." "Those high heels," he jibes, "they'll be great in the jungle, and the nylons."[31] The

---

[30] Bill Krohn notices that "career-marriage conflicts seem to have interested [screenwriter John Michael] Hayes, who would later try to smuggle one into *The Man Who Knew Too Much*, but in the treatment for *Rear Window* the subject is given a very 1950s twist: because of her profession (model turned fashion buyer), but also by the mere fact of *having* a profession, Lisa 'has suppressed those spontaneous female responses sought by the normal man who wants his woman to be a lady in the drawing room and a minx in the bedroom'" (*Work* 138).
[31] Commenting on a very tricky set-up for a shot of Lisa's feet in high heels, Hitchcock admitted to a shoe fetish. "Looking at her admiringly after her first adventure in the lion's den, Jeff glances down at her shoes, which hardly seem appropriate for high-risk activities," writes Krohn (*Work* 144–5).

lingerie "will make a big hit in Finland, just before you freeze to death."

Jeff has been fishing among his neighbors for telltale demonstrations, a man acting with all the vital impulse of the cinemagoer; and among other clues he has caught what seems to be evidence of a murder across the courtyard. A traveling salesman, Lars Thorwald (Raymond Burr), subject to a nagging and bedridden wife, appears to have done away with her; at least she has disappeared without a trace, and Jeff catches the burly man tinkering with a set of heavy-duty knives and with his wife's purse.[32] At first put off by Jeff's nosiness about his neighbors – as a matter of daily routine it seems beneath her class – Lisa is finally convinced to join in with his observations when she realizes that if Mrs. Thorwald is gone (for a visit in the country), her purse is not. From her point of view, no woman going off on any sort of journey would leave her purse behind, unless it were a journey from which the traveler did not intend to return. When Thorwald briefly leaves his apartment, she descends with Jeff's nurse Stella (Thelma Ritter) into the garden, where Thorwald would appear to have buried something in his "pet flowerbed," but then on an impulse she points up at the Thorwald windows and begins, of all adventures, and in her party dress and heels, to climb up the fire escape in the direction of this forbidden territory. "Lisa!" Jeff whispers frantically (on this hot summer's night the voice will carry; if he's been careful

---

[32] A foreshadowing, perhaps, of the relevant purses in *Marnie* (1964). The theme of the curious man itching to probe inside a woman's purse may have been gathered from Sam Fuller's *Pickup on South Street* (1953 – one of two films Thelma Ritter made just before coming to *Rear Window*), in which Richard Widmark fingers a woman's purse on a New York subway car at rush hour (this scene reprised by Martin Scorsese in *The King of Comedy* [1983] as it plays silently on television late one night with the famous comedian Jerry Langford [Jerry Lewis] attentively watching).

Thelma Ritter (l.) with Grace Kelly, both in gowns by Edith Head. Kelly's dress has more fabric and reveals the arms, thus establishing her relative youth and wealth. Ritter (1902–1969), one of Hollywood's principal character players, had just made Pickup on South Street *for Samuel Fuller and was on her way to* Daddy Long Legs *for Jean Negulesco. Courtesy Academy of Motion Picture Arts and Sciences.*

up until now not to let Thorwald know of his surveillance by stifling sound, here in reflex, even with Thorwald away, he continues to restrain his voice: "*Lisa!*"), but Stella is already rushing in to say he is to telephone Thorwald's number the moment he sees the man returning.

Lisa, meanwhile, is still scaling the fire escape across the way, clinging to the balcony next door to Thorwald's, then in a deft athletic maneuver sidling across in her heels to his windowsill, holding on to the window frame for dear life, and then dipping inside. "It's at the moment when Lisa . . . involves herself in the murder story Jefferies believes he's been watching that she finally succeeds in capturing his interest," writes one observer (Peucker 210). Swiftly marauding through the apartment as we watch, along with the paralyzed Jeff and with suspended breath, she manages to . . . find the purse! But during this escapade, certainly one of the most daunting acts performed in any Hitchcock film, Jeff and Stella have been distracted at their guard post by Miss Lonelyhearts in her ground-level apartment beneath. The pathetic spinster has been rejected by a man she picked up at a nearby bar and has now downed a bottle full of pills. By the time Jeff's eyes come back to the hallway outside Thorwald's door, the brute is already returned, ready to turn his key, with Lisa still inside.

Thorwald comes upon her. She remonstrates through pantomime that she's in the wrong apartment by mistake. He doesn't buy it, becomes brutal, taking her in his hands. Jeff is beside himself, paralyzed with anxiety and helplessness. Somehow he manages to phone for the police. And now Lisa, a trooper if ever there was one, goes beyond the bravery that led her to climb into that place, beyond the curiosity-driven audacity that led her to search it, beyond the classy aplomb that moves her to confront Thorwald even in his own lair with a brazen mistruth, and, turning her body slightly, opens her hands behind her back to flash the wedding ring in Jeff's face. This, for Lisa, is a moment of paramilitary triumph, since she has worked her way into foreign territory, dug for the hidden treasure, and now delivered its essence – the fact that it exists – by clandestine communication back to her team member who, she is very well aware, will be watching the tiny glimmering object through his telephoto lens.

Thorwald, however, also has eyes. He notices her pose, turns his gaze out the window to follow the line of her performance, and finds the audience! Yes, there, across the courtyard! In that apartment, where in shadows a man is watching all this! (And we with him.)

While numberless students and critics of Hitchcock have zeroed in on this sequence (much as Thorwald zeroes in on Jeff) to reveal the Master's adeptness at staging and also to highlight the link between what Jeff is doing watching Thorwald and what we are doing watching Jeff watching, what remains utterly remarkable as a portrait of the American personality is the filmmaker's treatment of Lisa, the girl from uptown, the one who has to have lobster thermidor delivered from West Fifty-Second Street, the one who wears gowns fresh off the plane from Paris and whose life is a living embodiment of *Vogue* magazine. There she is now, scampering up a fire escape, sliding onto a window ledge in her high heels, invading a presumed murderer's cave, finding irrefutable evidence that something dark and unthinkable has undeniably been happening there, and transmitting that evidence back home. On the most superficial level – which is the diegetic level where this has received its most frequent address – Lisa is showing Jeff that she certainly *can* become the sort of girl he needs; that marriage between them is possible. But while she is doing this she is also showing the viewing audience that women can have power, agency, activity, and adventurous triumph within their grasp. Indeed, there is no character in *Rear Window* with the derring-do, the prowess, or the skill that Lisa shows in this scene.

Who, then, is this all-American girl and how does she epitomize the culture in which she lives?[33] The European beauty (for example, Carlotta Valdes, subject of a portrait in *Vertigo*) is withdrawn and refined, a cultivated bloom, an

[33] George W. S. Trow could remember "being confused" about Lisa Fremont: "The world was supposed to be about all of us as, on the one hand, completely powerful, functional people, and, on the other hand, we were supposed to be working from a clean slate on the deepest and most serious problems confronting the world. Yet . . . when you got to the top or toward the top of things, you found, indeed, very flawed but glamorous people" (118–19).

object, as John Berger showed, for the dominating prerogative of the male gaze (47). Not only does she suffer reduction by being subjected to appraisal in general, but she is primped and tailored, adjusted and clipped, colored and smoothed and bedecked all to make for "beauty," which can be regarded as a central value of Old Europe. America has much in it that is surely beautiful, but American culture does not regard beauty as a principal value. Beauty, it is insisted, must be connected to function, to practicality, to movement. If the American can admire European beauty it is only with respect to the foreign – as when Mark Twain admires the youth of Genoa:

> We went to the park on Sunday evening. Two thousand persons were present, chiefly young ladies and gentlemen. The gentlemen were dressed in the very latest Paris fashions, and the robes of the ladies glinted among the trees like so many snowflakes. The multitude moved round and round the park in a great procession. The bands played, and so did the fountains; the moon and the gas lamps lit up the scene, and altogether it was a brilliant and an animated picture. I scanned every female face that passed, and it seemed to me that all were handsome. I never saw such a freshet of loveliness before. I do not see how a man of only ordinary decision of character could marry here, because, before he could get his mind made up he would fall in love with somebody else. (160–1)

– only, that is, when he does not have some vibrantly active American female to admire back at home.

What supersedes beauty for the American is effort and accomplishment, the ability to make and do and the success that comes when objects and situations are put together, produced, effected, and charged with the power of function. And, Hitchcock is saying here, one doesn't need males for this triumph. Here is the case of one magnate overshadowed by his canny partner: "By the turn of the [twentieth] century, to live on Potter Palmer's Gold Coast . . . was to reside at the center of Chicago elegance and social power. Potter Palmer had bought this stretch of dune and marsh in the early 1880s, pumped in clean sand from the lake bottom as fill, strong-armed the city to build a through street – later called Lake Shore Drive – and invited a group of his friends to form with him "a community where there had been wilderness" (Miller, *City* 414). His wife "set out to remake the city socially" (415), but was also "a dauntless do-gooder, and a feminist as well. She held meetings for female factory workers and women activists in her French parlor" (416). Lisa Fremont, for her part, is the all-American girl not because she is good to look at, although she is, but because, in the tradition of Mrs. Palmer, she unfailingly comes through in a pinch, saves her man's honor while simultaneously bringing moral balance to a disrupted community and loving harmony to a relationship that had foundered in doubt.

As to saving Jeff physically: she is no more capable of this than anyone. Thorwald barges into the photographer's apartment (his *camera obscura*) and finally drops him out the window. At film's end Jeff is beatifically reposing with *two* full-leg casts, and Lisa, still an epitome of practicality and enchantment, is ensconced on a divan beside him, reading *Beyond the High Himalayas*. Or not quite. Seeing that he is sweetly sleeping, she puts the book down and picks up the beauty issue of *Harper's Bazaar!*

The Loyal Bergman: *Notorious* and *Spellbound*

Similarly fixated on accomplishment, yet accomplishment of a very different sort, is Alicia Huberman (Ingrid Bergman) in *Notorious* (1946). Her father having been arrested, tried, convicted, and imprisoned in Miami for being a Nazi spy, she escapes from a life led under his wing by joining in partnership (at once romantic and chaste) with Devlin (Cary Grant), an American intelligence operative. He flies her to Rio de Janeiro in order that they may infiltrate a Nazi ring there. Alicia has fallen in love with Dev, but the job he has in mind for her is to marry an effete mother's boy, Alexander Sebastian (Claude Rains), penetrate the Nazi meetings he hosts in the sanctum of his "Italianate villa, situated at the curving coastline in the outskirts of Rio" (Jacobs 225), and finally discover the secret hidden in his wine cellar. Sebastian's mother is a daunting old martinet, who suspects Alicia of disloyalty and arranges for her to be slowly poisoned. As her "old friend," Devlin manages to invade the house just in time, mount to her bedroom, see that she is in peril of her life, take her up in his arms, and carry her out to safety while the immaculately proper Sebastian, surrounded by his Nazi cronies but unable to prevent them from seeing all this, can do nothing but watch and anticipate his own doom.

Much of Hitchcock's work in the 1940s is scathingly critical of social proprieties and bourgeois sensibilities, a pattern that would soften as in the 1950s he worked for the big studios exclusively and set his mind to fat profits and a brand of entertainment that showed a glossier surface (while retaining critical, philosophical power). Here in *Notorious*, for example, is an outright critique of the bourgeois marriage, since with Alicia and Sebastian we know from the outset that their union is not based on mutual affection and that her part in it, at least, is a staged production: marriage may be a performance.[34] As the tension mounts scene by scene, we are

---

[34] "Claude Rains and Ingrid Bergman made a nice couple," Hitchcock told Truffaut, "but in the close shots the difference between them was so marked that if I wanted them both in a frame, I had to stand Claude Rains on a box" (172).

explicitly treated to Alicia's difficulties in concocting and sustaining an image of marital coupling in the face of her own emotional disconnection and her anger at Devlin for "deserting" her: the story of an actress, then, as we find again in *Vertigo* (1958). In going along with Devlin's project and allowing Sebastian to meet her again (he was a chum of her father's when she was a child); in acquiescing while the effete Nazi courts her, indeed in permitting herself to come close enough to him that intimacy might ensue; in going through with the wedding; and in undertaking married life in a household controlled by the dominatrix mother, Alicia performs a kind of athletic trick, surely puts herself on the ledge in a foreshadowing of Lisa's accomplishments in *Rear Window*.

Ingrid Bergman and Cary Grant as Alicia and Devlin in Notorious *(Vanguard/RKO, 1946), at the beginning of a notably long kiss that has them traveling across the space of a room. (Hitchcock was flying in the face of the Production Code with this protraction of physical contact.) Digital frame enlargement.*

With Alicia, too, we have an American girl of noticeable beauty. In the mid-1940s, Bergman was one of the great figures of the American screen. Seen in retrospect, as Robin Blaetz notes, "the professionalism, the generosity, the simplicity, and the all-important wholesomeness have proven to be real" (52). Yet in *Notorious* Bergman's regard is only for action, for the truth of a fulfilled commitment, and for the triumph of stealing a secret from those who would use it for monstrous ill. At a grand soirée to which Devlin has wangled an invitation, she manages to obtain the key to the shadowy Sebastian wine cellar and passes it to him;[35] together they descend into the shadows and reveal the horrible, chemical truth: a number of the bottles contain uranium for making a bomb.[36]

---

[35] The key is revealed very close up at the end of a long boom shot that commences with a high angle from the Sebastian balcony and slowly descends through the airy space of the foyer to land in macro-close-shot on Alicia's folded hand. (Alicia palms the object to Devlin as soon as he arrives at the party, a few shots later.) A special wooden moveable platform was constructed to house the camera for this tour de force (Krohn notes that Robert Capa photographed the shooting [98]), and Hitchcock reprised the effect, but with different support equipment and in color, for *Marnie*.

[36] "We develop the story," Hitchcock told his original producer, "and now I introduce the MacGuffin: four or five samples of uranium concealed in wine bottles."
"The producer said, 'What in the name of goodness is that?'
"I said, 'This is uranium; it's the thing they're going to make an atom bomb with.'
"And he asked, 'What atom bomb?'
"This, you must remember, was in 1944, a year before Hiroshima. I had only one clue. A writer friend of mine had told me that scientists were working on a secret project some place in New Mexico. It was so secret that once they went into the plant, they never emerged again. I was also aware that the Germans were conducting experiments with heavy water in Norway. So these clues brought me to the uranium MacGuffin. . . .
"Finally, I said, 'Look, if you don't like uranium, let's make it industrial diamonds . . .'
"Well, I failed to convince the producers, and a few weeks later the whole project was sold to RKO" (Truffaut 168).

If, as we see through Lisa Fremont and Alicia Huberman, female practicality is seriously valued in American culture, practicality over maternity, practicality over glamour, practicality over charm (the trooper practicality of Eve Kendall scampering over the faces of the presidents on Mount Rushmore, even with a broken heel, a spirit that endears her to Roger Thornhill more than any other quality does), it is a value trumped in Hitchcock's portrayals only by loyalty. Loyalty: the fierce insistence on staying by a person who needs you, the belief that transcends both circumstance and contingency, that survives the collapse of personality and agency, that faces the threat of death. Rose Balestrero is able to be loyal *up to a point*, but no further – yet neither she nor Manny is ever posed as a superhuman or heroic type. In *Spellbound* (1945), however, Bergman plays an epitome of loyalty, thus centering our attention on a rather spectacular form of sanity. The virtue of loyalty, in the end, requires that we trust to our perceptions and convictions against all doubt and double thinking, that we believe in our understanding and our purpose unshakeably, no matter the obstacles to orientation, to action, or to life. To be loyal is to affirm that one has come to a knowledge of the world, a knowledge that is immutable and impregnable – not because it is one's own, and one takes oneself as important, but because the world is knowable in its foundations, because the eye can see, because one must take seriously what has been handed over in this life.

The story of *Spellbound* is taken from *The House of Dr. Edwardes* by Hilary St. George Saunders and John Palmer (writing collaboratively under the pseudonym Francis Beeding). As produced by David O. Selznick, a devotee of psychoanalysis taking sessions with Dr. May Romm, the film evoked (serious analysts might say, toyed with) Freudian ideas at a time when the Viennese practitioner and his theories were extraordinarily popular in America. According to Jonathan Freedman, "Popular acceptance of an Americanized psychoanalysis inflected by practical, self-help, social engineering ideologies was enhanced by the Hollywood films of the postwar period" (82). Even with a visually stunning dream sequence involving sets based on paintings by the surrealist Salvador Dalí – "structurally films are dreams" (Pomerance, *Eye* 73) – the film had a mediocre reception in previews, "due to its heaviness" (Bradley). Yet Bergman brings to it a natural radiance and simplicity of performance that are swiftly attractive.

She is Dr. Constance Petersen, a young psychiatrist at the Green Manors retreat. As the film begins, the staff is celebrating the retirement of the chief of staff, Dr. Murchison (Leo G. Carroll) and the arrival of his successor, Dr. Anthony Edwardes. Constance has studied Edwardes's writings and fallen in love with him in advance: his is a brilliant intellect and his voice on the page a shining and persuasive one, and she is an avid student susceptible to intellectuality and the charms of the articulate voice.

In the flesh, the man (Gregory Peck, for Truffaut not a Hitchcockian actor [167]) turns out also to be tall, dark, and handsome; and to have a fire in his eyes just for her. But as the two share a tryst late at night in the library soon after his arrival, it becomes evident to Constance that this Dr. Edwardes is an impostor – and more than that, an amnesiac. There is fear that he murdered the real Edwardes, and with no delay he flees. Following him to the city, Constance commits herself in two ways at once. First, she remains the person who has been struck by love, and will not yield her impressions to any new information presented by anyone about this man. Secondly, she insists that she will bear the responsibility for treating him, will help him recover the lost memory and the self that has been locked up with it.

Bergman as Dr. Constance Petersen, "analyzing" one of her most obnoxious patients, her colleague Dr. Fleurot (John Emery), who refuses to stop trying to seduce her in Spellbound *(Selznick International, 1945). Courtesy Academy of Motion Picture Arts and Sciences.*

As a central feature of her therapeutic program, and also in order to help him evade the police, Constance brings "John," as he now calls himself, to visit her own mentor, Dr. Brulov (Michael Chekhov), a brilliant and penetratingly analytical immigrant with no fondness for "police tactics" or "the third degree," both of which he presumably experienced to satisfaction in the homeland. Fiercely independent and committed to the liberty of personality and endeavor, Brulov is an echo of Phillip Martin, the hermit from *Saboteur*. Neither man has implicit faith in the police, Brulov especially (and with a bitter panache). One of the side effects of the couple's visit is that they witness him in vituperative discussion with two detectives, observing an unmistakable and direct demonstration of his own staunch loyalty to his principles, his patients, and his freedom to think for himself. Clearly, John is one who cannot think for himself – does not even recognize that self – and so the encounter with Brulov is invigorating and also challenging for him.

It is in Brulov's house that we are party to a strange little bedroom scene.

Constance is asleep; John is shaving in the bathroom. Suddenly he takes up the razor and, mysteriously caught up by the repetitive jacquard pattern on the bedspread, moves to slay her. But then, changing direction, he creeps downstairs to find the old man, a better target. We see close shots of him descending, the open straight razor gleaming in his hand. With all innocence, old Brulov walks out of the kitchen to offer a tall glass of milk, and as John drinks it – Hitchcock arranges for the camera to "drink" it – the scene fades to darkness. Brulov had put a bromide in the milk. But the lesson to him, to Constance, and to us is that John is perhaps a dangerous man, far more so than we had suspected. Still, however, in the face of this knowledge and without the least hesitation, indeed with a flaring of commitment and passion, Constance declares loyalty to the man she believes she most deeply knows. When he awakes, she encourages him to tell Brulov and her about his dream, and from its mystery a truly dark and chilling possibility arises.

It is again necessary to reflect that in order to grasp Hitchcock's method, one must see beyond the story. On its surface, *Spellbound* is a love story set in the world of psychiatric therapy; its chase element – the real Dr. Edwardes has been found murdered and John is suspected by the police – was added by Hitchcock on screenwriter Ben Hecht's suggestion because "it would be impossible for an imposter who was not a psychiatrist to remain in the sanitarium very long" (Hitchcock to MacPhail). But the film does not actually turn upon psychoanalysis – only its plot does. The movement of the film itself turns upon Constance's deep loyalty and trust, so much so that it is impossible to watch *Spellbound* without a conviction in her conviction that John is tender and good. The film is an invocation to us to allay our fear, be courageous in our perception and analysis, take ourselves seriously when we see something of character and disposition, and not be persuaded by institutional forces (the police, the news) that we should renege on our affections or loyalties because it might serve someone else's ends that we do. There was a message here about America's obligations to Europe in a time of war; and about Americans' obligations to one another in a time of hardship, strain, and exhaustion.

Hanging On

In Hitchcock's American films we see this fundamental "yeoman" strength and fidelity evidenced in every direction, among both noble and ignoble characters. In *Saboteur*, the manipulative operator Fry (Norman Lloyd), an unctuous and remorseless villain if ever there was one, is held tenaciously by the hero's hand from the torch of the Statue of Liberty. We look down into his livid, desperate face, the face of a man at his very limit. Barry Kane has a grasp upon his sleeve, loyal and true, but in a macro-close shot we suddenly see that the stitching of the jacket is coming undone at the shoulder. "I'll cling!" Fry gasps, but pathetically – because he is too poor to have afforded himself decent tailoring; in the end it isn't his resolve, it's the fabric, that gives way. A side effect of mass production.

In *Marnie*, we have the assiduous if uninspired office manager at Rutlands, Mr. Ward (John Launder), a mugwump who can never seem to remember the combination to the safe. This arcane spell is written on a little card stuck inside the top drawer of his desk. Again and again, Ward needs that combination, and again and again he must open his drawer to find it. Of memorizing it Ward seems terminally incapable; yet at the same time his is a dogged routine, systematized, loyal to his own precautions, and reliable. He never gives up on that system; and the system never gives up on him. In *Rope* (1948), the nefarious killer duo is visited for dinner by their victim's father, Henry Kentley (Cedric Hardwicke), who "forever cataloguing his library" seems lost in an endless, though absolutely refreshing, labor. Rather dour in spirit, he is a fierce believer in liberty, indeed one of the true democratic stalwarts in the whole Hitchcock oeuvre, rising into heat at the slightest provocation that his hosts might be a pair of insouciant fascists frothing over with ignoble Nietzscheanism. Kentley is all the sadder a figure because of the distressing irony that his son lies murdered, but hidden, only footsteps away. (He can preach, but he can't protect.)

A particularly telling character, and this because he so strictly inhabits the wings of a scene, is the composer in *Rear Window* (Ross Bagdasarian). Trying vainly to write a popular song, he has diddled out a few phrases on the piano (with Hitchcock tuning his mantle clock behind his back). The ditty seems professional enough, if also entirely undistinctive, and he cannot, at any rate, proceed far before falling into a funk. Something is standing in the way of his hearing a harmonic resolution, much as for Jeff Jefferies (and us) something is continually standing in the way of our seeing the full meaning of the actions played out before us. As the film progresses, we drop in on this composer several times, always a little casually, and each time he has added something, a note or a phrase, tinkered a little with the tempo; still, however, stretch the muscles of inspiration as he might, he cannot "reach" the song. At the film's climax, however, and in a moment given emphasis by Jeff's repose in his twin casts and Lisa's contentful posture upon his divan, the composer is suddenly again the focus of our attention. He has company now, Miss Lonelyhearts. She has also been listening to his work; perhaps it has given her a reason to live.

Now the song is finished, has been recorded, and is in his hands. "I hope it's gonna be a hit. This is the first release," says he with promise. And sitting with him, she responds, "I can't tell you what this music has meant to me." He bends to his record player to give her the first listen, and we hear it, too, a glorious, fully orchestrated melody that ascends to a heavenly peak. The camera pans left across the chain of apartments we have been spying upon. Thorwald's is being repainted. The couple who lost their little dog to the murderer's vengeful cruelty have a new puppy now, and are teaching it to sit patiently in their little basket and be lowered into the garden.[37] The dancer Miss Torso, who has been entertaining flocks of "gentlemen," goes to the door and receives Stanley, her true love: "Boy, it's good to be home!" Down in the garden the sculptor, exhausted from her labors in clay, has fallen asleep in her lawn chair. And next door the newlyweds are settling into their first argument.

"Dreaming," croons the singer on the recording, "I thought I'd never wake" (an homage to Caliban's song in *The Tempest*), and after passing over Jeff and settling upon her with her magazines, the song resolves upon the final word, a kind of cadence: "Lisa!" The point of all the earlier scenes, as the composer kept being stymied in his creativity, was that we might see this little demonstration at the end, a mini-sermon that said, "Don't give up."

---

[37] Hitchcock shot a version of this with a Great Dane, but discarded it (Krohn, *Work* 145).

Perseverance is perhaps the primary American value expressed through Hitchcock's work. Miss Lonelyhearts didn't give up, the composer didn't give up, Lisa didn't give up on Jeff, Jeff didn't give up on Lisa. Jeff "caught" Thorwald, we now surmise, only because he didn't give up trying. In *Marnie*, Mark Rutland does not give up on the woman he loves, though she is voyaging through hell. In *The Man Who Knew Too Much* (1956) Jo McKenna does not give up singing, and because she does not give up she is reunited with her kidnapped son. In *The Wrong Man*, Manny does not give up on himself or, as we finally learn, on Rose, who simply didn't have the strength to cling to him. In *The Trouble with Harry* (1955), the painter Sam Marlowe (John Forsythe) doesn't

The finale of Alfred Hitchcock's filmmaking career. In Family Plot *(Universal, 1976), George (Bruce Dern) and Blanche (Barbara Harris) slowly mount the carpeted stairway of Adamson's San Francisco home, searching for the glittering truth. Courtesy Academy of Motion Picture Arts and Sciences.*

give up on his painting, no matter that nobody has ever bought any of it yet. In *Vertigo*, Scottie Ferguson won't give up on bringing Madeleine back to life. In *The Birds* (1963), with the earth seeming to shudder beneath them and the heavens to open, Mitch Brenner won't give up on protecting his family.

And in *Family Plot* (1976), the goofy taxi driver/actor George Lumley and his giddy spiritualist girlfriend Blanche Tyler (Bruce Dern, Barbara Harris), hunting for Eddie Shoebridge, don't give up, nor does Blanche give up in searching out the massive Rainbird diamond. That diamond, big as a bird, shiny as pure light, is the last object she sees in the film; and also the last object any viewer sees in the films of Alfred Hitchcock. Perhaps he was saying, through that stone winking at us playfully upon the giant screen, "Don't give up your journey. Follow the path all the way to the end."

4

HITCHCOCK AND AMERICAN SOCIAL FORM

As Alfred Hitchcock's fans and scholarly devotees have long appreciated, no filmmaker is more adept at putting the elements of a story into pictures, at mastering the mise-en-scène of cinema. Not only the central persons and objects in a scene but everything that surrounds them, and the precise angle from which one sees it; the distance – emotional and spatial – between us and the seen world; the modulation of a body's expression, posture, illumination as it moves in the light – all of this is decidedly felt and arranged by a masterly talent. It would not be unfair to say of Hitchcock that even though he was fascinated by telling stories, he was more interested still in the problem of picturing.[1] I have looked at some of his casual sketches: they have a distinct power of

---

[1] Spoto notes how in the early 1920s, working with and watching the German expressionists, he "came to understand the nature and power of an unstable and distorted image" (77). For C. A. Lejeune, writing in *World Film News* (May 1936), "Hitch's genius is for draftsmanship" (qtd. in Spoto 173).

line and balance, a sense of remove, a palpable weight. It is at every moment vital and worthwhile to open one's eyes in experiencing Hitchcock's work: further, since the sound track of any of these pictures is a rich delight, one should link what one hears to what one sees (that is, one should hear through the picture). If one surrenders the obsession with following plot points that afflicts so many filmgoers, one can discover in Hitchcock's American films a deeply engaged and critical discernment of social form. Hitchcock is a storyteller, to be sure, but even more he is a visionary who reveals the social world through pertinent detail organized with exceptional cogency and cleanliness, that is, in an eloquent grammar.

Further, the Hitchcockian camera rests upon, rather than rambling through, its observations, points toward and lingers with a fragment of space and time or nuance of fictive experience established in dramatic optical space. Hitchcock meditates upon form rather than racing across events pall mall to rush a story onward with rhythmic and addictive jolts. The Hitchcockian camera never – even in diegetically perilous circumstances – wishes to be anywhere but where it is. This tends to mean that the Hitchcockian story unfolds at a reasonable, leisurely pace, and in this respect it could be argued that for all his passionate interest in American life and notwithstanding his eventual American citizenship Hitchcock was most deeply a European filmmaker, at least a filmmaker with a deep regard for an important aspect of European experience. "Just in this one matter lies the main charm of life in Europe – comfort," writes the voyaging Mark Twain:

> *In America, we hurry – which is well; but when the day's work is done, we go on thinking of losses and gains, we plan for the morrow, we even carry our business cares to bed with us, and toss*

and worry over them when we ought to be restoring our racked bodies and brains with sleep. . . .
I do envy these Europeans the comfort they take. When the work of the day is done, they forget it. (186, 187)

Hitchcock's work is always comfortable, even when morbid or anxiety-provoking. And comfort was important to him as he worked. Tea was served twice a day on his set.[2] That set was quiet, and Hitchcock entirely and completely prepared:

> *He was so prepared because his work had already been done. Every shot had been thought out. He knew exactly where the camera was going to be, where the people were going to move, so that he wasn't a director that, on set, went, "Oh, God, now where are we going to put the camera? Let's see, over there. Or no, a moving shot." It was all done, so that he could be perfectly relaxed, and you felt that.* . . . *Between scenes he was very relaxed and he would regale us with these wonderful stories. It was just a wonderful, wonderful experience professionally because of the talent and the respect he deserved and then just socially because he was so pleasant. (Janet Leigh, qtd. in Raubicheck 33–4)*

Even in the 125-degree heat of Marrakech, shooting the market scenes of *The Man Who Knew Too Much* (1956), he placed himself tranquilly inside an air-conditioned Chevrolet (Bumstead to Pomerance). Each shot was a perfect composition for him, and when it was done, no residue of it was left to stain the shots to come.

---

[2] Margaret Lockwood told Spoto, "He never altered one custom, the idiosyncrasy, during morning and afternoon tea break, of throwing the crockery over his shoulder and smashing it on the floor with airy nonchalance" (192).

Because there is a poise in his examination of American life, Hitchcock's frame reveals myriad details in its composition. It's worth examining a few cases in point, keeping in mind that whether he was shooting on location or through a detailed scenic replication on a soundstage, Hitchcock's abiding interest was in accuracy of representation, fullness of frame, precision of acoustic and dialogic sound, and – as was the case with Henry James, too – the revealing social detail.

A Sophisticated Scene

The opening sequence of *North by Northwest* (1959) (which I have mentioned briefly in these pages) is set at the end of a working day when the white-collar army of business executives and creative geniuses is on the way home from Madison Avenue. The gist of the plot here is that our hero, Roger Thornhill, is proceeding from his advertising company offices to a cocktail session with business associates in the Oak Bar of the Plaza Hotel. Because of a conversational ambiguity during that session, and through no fault of his own, he will be mistaken for another man (a man, by the way, whom many people think non-existent [see Pomerance, *Eye* 52ff.]), kidnapped by a pair of unamiable thugs, and spirited out to Long Island – the beginning of a substantial – as Roger would have it, "sentimental" – adventure. On his way to the Plaza, he chit-chats non-stop with his secretary, Maggie (Doris Lang), bequeathing her a to-do list involving memos that need to be written and chocolates that are to be ordered and sent, etc. What is required by the script, then, is a chain of abrupt conversations at a certain time of day in the middle of a great city.

However, Hitchcock's mise-en-scène, elaborated with his screenwriter Ernest Lehman, fills the screen both optically and acoustically with informative detail about the social position of people like Roger, the cultural environment in which advertising executives work, and midtown life in New York at the time. We begin inside the C.I.T. Financial Building, as elevator doors open into a marbled lobby and a bevy of executives, secretaries, and consultants issue forth at once. Roger is in mid-conversation as he strides forward toward the camera (which dollies backward to let him move), and Maggie is copying his every syllable reliably into her shorthand notebook. He does not look at her in order to show concern for her ability to write while moving – presumably this is a trick the two of them perform on a daily basis – but he does glance at the notebook to be sure she is getting down his dictation. A uniformed lobby attendant says hello to Roger by name (he is a known face in the building, a commanding citizen of the working population there) and they have an extremely brief one-to-one that Roger glides through and abruptly leaves behind.

The space in which this happens, with workers moving through it in all directions dressed formally for serious business encounters, is a cool, sedate atrium with mid-level fluorescent lighting and expensive facing on the floor and walls (a studio replication). High-powered, dignified, and relatively wealthy persons mingle and move here in order to fulfill commercial transactions with others of their sort. Roger stops at a news kiosk, deposits a coin, and picks up a *World Telegram* as he leads Maggie past a trough of gleaming rubber plants and toward the sunlit doorways. While we can listen to the conversation the two are having, the many others passing them in this lobby are paying no attention. This kind of business talk is routine here. All of what happens in this place involves men giving dictations, transmitting important information, heading to important rendezvous. It is not difficult to presume that virtually every stranger we see wandering past Maggie and Roger is heading to some tactfully scheduled late-afternoon meeting at some important and artfully secluded bar. "You'd better walk me to the Plaza," he tells her, and she protests that she doesn't have a coat on – a reference not to the temperature (it is sunny outside) but to the fancy style of dress that will be on show at, and around, the Plaza, since the Plaza is a temple of class but here on Madison Avenue, in the thick crowd now swarming around them, almost all the women are dressed in short-sleeved frocks as Maggie is.

Thomas Hemmeter suggests that Roger's life before this film begins is unstable. "The film's opening scenes show that Thornhill had lived his New York life in a state of temporal stasis, having retreated into an illusory time defined by his relationship with his mother, a woman who performs both as a sexless wife and a maternal refuge for this aging adolescent fearful of adult relationships" (70). Caught up listening to Roger's drone of dramatic dictation in counterpoint with the click of footsteps upon the pavement, we may note, too, how he glides through this throng as though lubricated with his own self-esteem, seems to reign over it as an important member of the executive class. Even at the end of this long day his haircut is immaculate, his shirt unruffled, his sleek steel-gray suit perfectly tailored and perfectly napped. About navigating through this throng he finds nothing strange or taxing, and manages deftly to keep Maggie in tow.

"Can we take a cab, Mr. Thornhill?" she begs.

"What, for two blocks?"

"You're late, and I'm tired." She does seem weary, a case study for a broader structural situation in which hardworking (and relatively powerless) women are disregarded by the men who shape their working days, depend desperately upon them, but do not recognize or openly admit this dependence.

Roger doesn't seem tired at all, so we may easily imagine the absence of workaday stresses falling upon him. All around, as his eyes begin to search for a cab, the other pedestrians are targeting, too, each bustling worker with eyes upon the next step that can take him somewhere. Thus, Manhattan is depicted as a community of exceptionally driven, purposive, motile people sharing a limited space. The sidewalk is crowded only because it cannot be broader (and, on Madison Avenue in the East Sixties, it is already rather broad). This is an epitome of the urban setting in an intensive business climate, a place where there are few interpersonal collisions principally because no one takes eyes off the "road," loses sight of a private destination as he shuffles ahead. We may recall Walter Benjamin's observation that "the sidewalk which is reserved for the pedestrian, runs along the roadway. Thus, the city dweller in the course of his most ordinary affairs, if he is on foot, has constantly before his eyes the image of the competitor who overtakes him in a vehicle" (*Arcades* M14, 6).

At the corner of Sixtieth Street, Roger does plunge into the vehicular world, managing to steal a cab from a man who was just about to open its door, on the grounds that he has "a very sick woman here. You don't mind, do you?" The man, a little nonplussed, is also more than accommodating: "Well, no, it's perfectly all right!" The cab drives off and we cut to an interior shot that is made with a rear projection of the street traffic outside the rear window, not a bad example of Hitchcock's frequent yen to jump out of location shooting into the comforts of the studio. "Poor man!" sympathizes Maggie, but Roger, opening his newspaper, isn't concerned about the fellow at all: "Oh, come, come, come! I made him a happy man! I made him feel like a good Samaritan!"

She frowns, "He knew you were lying."

"Ah, Maggie," Roger lectures, "in the world of advertising there's no such thing as a lie; there's only the expedient exaggeration; you ought to know that." This stance of Roger's has fed a great number of critical evaluations that labor to set him up as a sort of charlatan. Indeed the purloining of the taxi comes into that analysis as prima facie evidence of Roger's ability to justify his action any way he pleases, but he is even more generally regarded as a suspicious personality, a con man who needs his comeuppance, a symptom of urban fragmentation or disorganization, a troubling speck in an otherwise pristine surface.[3] True, Maggie is not sick at all, thus certainly not "very sick," so that the victimized pedestrian is done out of his rightful ride on entirely bogus grounds. Presumably this is the sort of act Roger is accustomed always to perform: take something from someone on false pretenses, that is, through the deceitful medium of advertising. But this street-corner interaction also – or instead – reveals a feature of New York life that

---

[3] "He is brash," writes Robin Wood, for example, "fast-talking, overconfident on the surface; entirely irresponsible and inconsiderate of others (he cheats two people out of their taxi by pretending his secretary is ill . . .)" (133). Writes Jean Douchet: "The audience must always somehow identify with the central character. But especially here, simply because Roger Thornhill, a representative type of the average modern man, is much more conditioned (thus made passive) by advertising . . ." (55; my translation). And Robert Corber is utterly unforgiving. For him, Roger's "erratic behavior and disjointed conversation with his secretary only add to the confusion. For example, when he sees a taxi pull up to the sidewalk, he rushes for it, pushing aside the man who has hailed it. Once inside he glances at a newspaper, interrupts his secretary, who is repeating his dictation, and asks her if he has put on weight. . . . The opening sequence suggests that he is a typical product of New York's crowded pavements and bustling traffic. Like the crowds of workers who come and go in the opening shots, he seems to lack direction. His life is disorganized and chaotic and seems to be made up of purely random events that bear no relation to one another" (194–5).

might well have taken Hitchcock by surprise the first time he encountered it as a foreign tourist but that by the late 1950s was something he knew to expect and value: fundamental civility. While for outsiders New York is easily regarded as an exorbitantly expensive, rude, aggressive, even violent den of iniquity where one must continually be on guard to protect one's self and valuables from the grasp of the incessantly hungry, such a view overdramatizes the real conditions of life in the big city. New Yorkers, perhaps especially those who work on the Upper East Side, are as unfailingly polite as people anywhere else, not predictably rude and aggressive at all. Roger's statement to the pedestrian was an indication of courtesy, not aggression; and the stranger's articulate reply to him indicated sweet good-tempered civility and courteous responsiveness. As to taxis, another will come by in a moment.

That urban crowd is a deeply civil one. Roger has learned his manners and ruffles no feathers as he strides through it. We will later discover that everyone in this film has done the same, even the villains. Hitchcock's New York is thus entirely *une ville embourgeoisée*, the rancid darkness of film noir being plainly absent from his constructions and his vision of urban life there.

The cab traverses the block between Madison and Fifth on Sixtieth Street, then proceeds around the curve of Grand Army Plaza toward the hotel's front door, but Roger wants the Fifty-Ninth Street entrance, so the driver, himself wearing a sports coat, swings right at the corner and then makes a U-turn on the wide street to halt at the proper door. So crisp and beautifully exposed is the rear projection plate for this sequence, with its faithful rendition of late-afternoon westbound traffic and the taxis lined up at the Plaza, that our attention is evenly divided between listening to Roger and Maggie's chatter and watching the busy cars (and horse buggy) in the rear with the calm security of those who (like Roger) do not have to drive. Roger pays off the driver, leaves his paper with Maggie, and gets out of the cab, which we can now discover as belonging to (the delightfully fictitious) KIND TAXI INC. Every commercial vehicle belongs to someone somewhere every driver has his decorum to keep up and his responsibilities to carry out. This city, in short, is meticulously organized, even if to the stranger it seems a weltering hubbub of movement and formlessness.

Social organization and hierarchy are part of this. Roger crosses through a line of pedestrians on the sidewalk – mostly women (and only one of them, Maggie might notice, with a coat!) – and finds himself in the hotel's richly marbled

To be this crisp and bright, the process plate (showing everything outside the rear window of the cab) would have been developed in triplicate, with all three strips of film projected simultaneously in a triple-head projector originated in 1938 at Paramount by Farciot Edouart but also used in the 1950s at MGM under the direction of A. Arnold Gillespie. Crucial to a shot like this is balancing the foreground lighting (used on a vehicle mock-up on a soundstage) with that in the plate. Digital frame enlargement.

lobby. Ferns perch on top of the polished brass revolving door, one side of which is locked in the open position (as a sign of gracious welcome), and as Roger paces across the lobby he hears a string quartet bouncing through Harold Adamson and Jimmy McHugh's "It's a Most Unusual Day" (a 1948 hit in *A Date with Judy* and suffering renewed popularity in the late 1950s thanks to a 1957 recording by June Christy).[4] The lobby is high-ceilinged, capacious, elegant, reposeful, dignified, and lush. This is where the uppers take themselves for a fortified sojourn or a few five o'clock martinis. With surety, Roger knows, one will meet here only others of one's class. (But of course, he is momentarily to be shown otherwise.)

The Oak Bar is on the west side of the lobby, decorated as per its name with dark wall panels, wooded columns, dark curtains, and drawn bamboo blinds. Victor, the waiter captain (Harry Seymour), knows Roger as a habitué of the spot and directs him quickly to his trio of "friends." A mural on the wall behind their table signifies Victorian London, artfully dressed socialites having trouble crossing a muddy carriage-trodden road. The martinis are sparkling, amber with vermouth, and expensive-looking. As he speaks about trying to send a cable to his mother, who is playing bridge in an apartment that has "all paint and no telephone yet," we focus on the three attentive faces of his drinking partners, one of whom, Fanning Nelson (Carleton Young), cannot hear very well and is raising a hand to an ear, one of whom, Herman Weltner (Frank Wilcox), knows Roger well enough to be

---

[4] This is not the only popular melody to garnish Bernard Herrmann's galvanizing score. The celebrated fandango theme (that begins with the main titles) is a reference to Leonard Bernstein's "America," from *West Side Story*, a show Roger is on his way to see the night he is kidnapped; and he makes reference to "I've Grown Accustomed to Her Face" from *My Fair Lady* (see Krohn, *Work* 205, 210; and Pomerance, *Eye* 51–2).

actually listening to him, and the third, Larry Wade (Robert Shayne), with one of those false masks of attention, as if to say, "I am overwhelmed with interest by everything that comes out of your mouth." We are being cued to listen to Roger with only half attention, yet also to be attuned acoustically, also optically, to the entire dramatic space that extends beyond this table.

In the corridor outside the bar we can see that two men have moved into place and are looking our way, men dressed in suits that are not expensive enough, who do not "belong" in the Oak Bar in the way that the familiar Roger does. And we can hear a young male voice moving around out of view, calling for "Mr. Kaplan, Mr. George Kaplan." This turns out to be a bellboy (Ralph Reed), to whom Roger is hardly listening but whom Roger now signals in order to send off that telegram. The men outside see his signal as a response to the bellboy's call, and this misalignment of perceptions leads to the turnaround that kicks the film's plot into action. We have diegetic reason, then, to be attending and following the signaling established by Hitchcock's careful design.[5]

But there is more. The henchmen have not made an entrance to the Oak Bar, while, physically speaking, they could have. The positioning of the men in a secondary space makes it evident that this sanctum to which Roger has gained easy entry is in point of fact a very exclusive little gathering

---

[5] "That Roger is taken for [George] Kaplan (literally) by the men who initiated the bellboy's page is itself a social nicety (although not a nice nicety) since he made a signal and the signal was enthusiastically read. What more need ever be accomplished beyond making a sign that is read? That he did not intend to make the sign is surely immaterial, for what is an intention to an audience but a sign of an intention, and he has made a sign!" (Pomerance, *Eye* 17). One might add that Roger takes the bellboy to be his bellboy, that is, the bellboy whose attention he wants; but he does not know (and cannot, as we can see by the choreography) that the bellboy is already someone else's.

place, especially on a late weekday afternoon when the business crowd is looking for a watering hole. While the story of *North by Northwest* is all about action, transformation, danger, and redemption, the subtext is an essay on class formation and distinction, exclusivity, and social alienation. If Fanning Nelson is cut off from Roger because of his partial deafness, he is also a signal to us, by way of that deafness, that being "cut off" or "removed" is of central structural importance in the film. Roger is "removed" from him as from everybody by virtue of his incapacity for loving commitment, an incapacity that will be ameliorated by film's end.

There is nothing in *North by Northwest* that is less replete and meaningful than this sequence, and a patient examination reveals layer upon layer of interpretable meaning connected with the context of the tale. The film's surface gives us a spy story with love woven in, but the structure of the pictorialism reveals an elite urban civilization, a mass culture, a topography of remove and solitude, an embedding in chains of mass communication and advertisement, a solicitude for street etiquette, a pulsing circulation. We are seeing a picture of modern life, with its concentration on motion, change, representation, duplicity, and performance, and the spy and love stories that are told by means of this structure are of only passing interest when compared with it. Marshall Berman comments on how for Baudelaire the fashionable world "in a decidedly nonpastoral form" is "linked with the underworld" (143): an unwitting and revealing illumination of this scene and this film.

On the Road

In *Marnie* (1964), we find a curious affection that has formed between Mark Rutland (Sean Connery) and the heroine

('Tippi' Hedren) – the wounded heroine – of the tale. In one after another job, and across a number of states, she has been committing robberies and disappearing. Now having fled to Philadelphia and taken up the false identity of Mary Taylor, Marnie – as we will come to know her – has infiltrated the premises of Rutland and Co., publishers, become useful to the boss for overtime work, and struck some tendrils in his heart. But her deep purpose, here as it was through her youth, is penetration, extraction, and possession.

She wangles her way into the company safe one day, snatches a pile of cash, and is gone. We pick her up at a stable in nearby Virginia, riding her pet beauty Forio with ecstatic abandon. But as she gallops toward the camera in fully throbbing engagement, Marnie must suddenly draw to a halt because Mark Rutland is waiting upon the grass, an ominous frown etched into his patrician face.

He confronts her with his knowledge of the theft, escorts her back to her rooms at a local lodge, watches her pack up,[6] and drives her into the future along a perfectly typical Pennsylvania interstate with low manicured hillocks by the sides and a gentle flow of mid-day traffic. With calm self-assurance and in a quiet voice he interrogates her about her past: she bids a pack of lies, then lays out more genuine patter (still almost entirely fabricated). That she has intrigued him he makes very plain. She counters that she hated her former employer, Strutt (Martin Gabel: a man we glimpsed early in the film, porcine, beady-eyed, cupidinous, vengeful). "The way you hate me?" says Mark, with a tone that perfectly balances etiquette and profound desire. "Oh no," says Marnie.

[6] According to Tony Lee Moral, just before filming Marnie packing up in front of Mark's supervision, "Hitchcock walked up to Hedren and said something that made her so mad and irate that for the first time she could hardly remember her lines. The fact that Hitchcock may have done it deliberately didn't occur to Hedren until she had time to reflect on his directing methods" (Moral 111).

"Not you." A profound and touching conversation, given its highway setting, a sleekly engineered, high-investment social infrastructure in as public a space as one can find. They pull off the road into a Howard Johnson's restaurant, one of more than six hundred such operations – some franchised, some not – in existence across America by the early 1960s. This is a scene lifted directly from the real experience of contemporary American road culture, a meticulous depiction of the era's promising designs, capaciousness, and plenitudes. Mark's car snuggles directly up to the building (a whitewashed bunker pricked out with neon and polished metal, for modernism), smartly depositing our couple at the simple and welcoming glass-paneled doors. "Come in –" the entrance seems to beckon, "But . . . you are already in." As they sit in a booth upholstered in rust-brown Naugahyde, a pleasant (and not especially young) hostess gives them menus and good-afternoon wishes while in the deep background we see one of her co-workers, dressed in a hospital-green and white uniform and with her hair piled up in a tidy ziggurat, dutifully tending the cash (a standard arrangement in HoJos at the time). The ambience is tidy, airy, modern, yet without flash. Another waitress now approaches the table with ice water and printed paper placemats. Marnie and Mark talk confidentially in the quiet atmosphere: Howard Johnson's didn't have cover music playing all the time, wasn't trying to crowd customers out onto the road or make for high turnover as much as to seem hospitable and comfortable for those who were strained by traveling.[7] Marnie's desire is that Mark

[7] The company was founded in 1925, then expanded through the 1930s and 1940s. One early accommodation to the pleasure of customers was production of ice cream (in twenty-eight flavors) with an increased butterfat content. In 1961, the celebrated Pierre Franey and Jacques Pépin were hired as "executive chefs" to oversee production, at a central facility, of the numerous food items that would be flash-frozen and shipped to local franchises around America.

will permit her to escape apprehension by the police, but he demurs – impossible: he'd be an accomplice; and besides, he's covered the loss, figured what she'd stolen and replaced the money in Ward's safe. She is distinctly uncomfortable, yet struck by his genuine concern, a cat without pedigree who yearns to prowl but likes the sense of this tom's purr. She knows there isn't anywhere for her to go. Frankfurters and coffee are ordered, then more or less abandoned on the table.

The waitress has swung back like a pendulum, this time with the bill and a little regulation salutation, "You folks be sure and come back, now." In road culture, this mantra is always translated as a general, not a personal, invocation, as in, "Come back to the company, not necessarily this branch. The company wants your affiliation wherever you go, and wherever you go Howard Johnson's will be there to serve you at the side of your road." Howard Johnson's didn't yet have significant competition as a roadside hospitality business, so that anyone using the expressways of America was bound to turn up at one or another of the company's franchises sooner or later – McDonald's had only a few hundred franchises by this point, and they were not typically situated beside highways (Halberstam 170) – but nevertheless the service was impeccably friendly, polite, and genuine, not as a commercial ploy but as an unreflected outgrowth of interactional habits at the time.

Americans were less curt in 1963 than they are today, more generally civil.[8] The world wasn't yet filled with people disattending one another to fixate on computers and palm devices,

---

[8] Things darkened with the assassination of John F. Kennedy, which occurred, in fact, while the shooting script for *Marnie* was being finalized (Pomerance, *Eye* 134). The fox hunt, scheduled for November 25, 1963, was postponed because of the national day of mourning (Moral 102, 103).

or to dote on themselves through the rationale of cynical individualism. American geography was being developed for the first time in many places, forests replaced with subdivisions and malls, the downtown core of many cities falling into deterioration,[9] the interstate system put in place, automobile sales skyrocketing. Marnie assures Mark that she has no romantic connections, and never had: "No lovers, no steadies, no beaus, no gentleman callers, nothing."[10]

The diegetic road trip on which Mark is taking Marnie, an interval of which is spent at this accommodating Howard Johnson's restaurant, is likely along Interstate 95, the Delaware Turnpike, heading from the D.C. area northbound toward Philadelphia (Mark says explicitly he intends to bring her back there).[11] Middlebury, Virginia, the site of Garrod's farm where Mark intercepts her, is slightly west of Washington. It was in 1957 that I-95 formally opened.[12] Only shortly before this time in American history, with superhighways nothing but dreams or long stands of dugout, "tourism was a far smaller industry than it is today," writes David Halberstam. "Air travel was prohibitively expensive, and the railroads were in decline. The family car was becoming the key

---

[9] On one particularly troubling case, see Hersey.
[10] The phrase "gentleman caller" refers to Tennessee Williams's *The Glass Menagerie* (1944). The play, originally titled *The Gentleman Caller*, opened with Laurette Taylor starring in a performance noted by numerous actors who watched it as the experience that changed their lives. The Amanda Wingfield character originated by Taylor, then later played by such actors as Gertrude Lawrence, Joanne Woodward, Katharine Hepburn, Shirley Douglas, Shirley Booth, Jessica Tandy, Julie Harris, and Jessica Lange, is an overprotective mother, here ironized by Marnie who feels throughout most of the film that her mother's love was always utterly unavailable to her.
[11] Background plates and establishing shots for the sequence were made on Highway 1, the Baltimore Turnpike, in West Chester, Pennsylvania (Moral 102).
[12] When around 2017 a section near Philadelphia is completed, it will be the longest unbroken interstate road in America.

to the new tourism. ... [It] experienced far fewer flat tires and mechanical mishaps than prewar cars but with all the rest and bathroom stops required ... it was hard to make more than three hundred miles a day" (173). Families were always on the lookout for a hotel.[13] As Hitchcock shows it, the highway is hardly the site of bumper-to-bumper traffic, potholes, and untended, overgrown shoulders that it would eventually become when expressway travel was a fundamental American way of life. Through the windows of Mark's car, we see the road still pristine and shining, the vehicles cruising it agleam, the sense of space catered by its lilting topography limitless and provocative.

This highway was in every sense a public achievement, aiming to imitate the German Autobahn, where "amenities such as access roads, visitors' centers, reception halls, observation platforms, and spectators' galleries were part of the facilities' overall design. These were so well integrated that it was difficult to distinguish where technology ended and propaganda began" (Schivelbusch, *Three* 168). The shots of the highway preceding Mark and Marnie's automobile conversation and their visit to HoJo's show a river of gray purity flowing smoothly across the gently rolling landscape, and recall posters for the German Reichsautobahnen. In an extended essay comparing massive prewar American public works with those of Italy and Germany, Wolfgang Schivelbusch quotes Fritz Todt's adage that the highways "should be a tightly drawn, indestructible band connecting technology

---

[13] And not only families. Production designer Robert Boyle told an American Film Institute seminar in 1977 that he did his own location scouting for the film, and generally preferred to do so. "A location manager or production manager is liable to be thinking about it in terms of how close it is to the nearest Holiday Inn where he can put the troops up and things like that.... They will select locations that are convenient, whereas an art director is probably more apt to think of it in terms of its particular value to the film" (qtd. in Moral 64).

and nature" (*Three* 174) and notes (in what seems a stunningly prescient reflection on these Hitchcockian shots) that the Autobahn was built so that it should offer a pathway dignified by its sublimity (175).

Many of Hitchcock's shots leading to the Howard Johnson's sequence are made – through the rear projection technique – of Mark and Marnie driving along exactly such a "sublime" pathway. Since we see very little traffic heading in either direction, we get the clear impression that Mark is one of those men who live at the crest of the cultural wave. He is piloting a Lincoln Continental, no less – one of the most expensive General Motors products, and distinctly more futuristic than the top-of-the-line Cadillac – and navigating through a new road system with assurance and calm, all the while performing his interrogation. As to the car, we see it from above when Mark parks it at HoJo. A fountainhead of streamlined prowess, it is another hallmark of sublimity. Like the other vehicles designed at General Motors by Harley Earl, the Continental was possessed of "the look of motion, even while [it was] at rest" (Halberstam 124). These cars "were longer, lower, ever sleeker, ... and even when they were standing still, they were to give the impression of power and motion" (123).

Thus, in this sequence we see Hitchcock attending to a distinctly mobile American culture, a culture of rolling highways and sleek automobiles, the latter of which are themselves dramatic locales. People not only ate, camped, watched movies, and made love in their vehicles; they thought of automobile transit as a natural way of being and of the highway system as a kind of national park, bringing into material existence grounds for displacement and motion that had "always" seemed necessary, wonderful, and inevitable. People "went for rides" as a way of passing leisure time.

Yet it's not only narrative action that Mark is demonstrating by driving with Marnie by his side. That so much of the long sequence takes place either inside the moving vehicle or inside the HoJo facility (built expressly to accommodate vehicle traffic) indicates mobility in a more general and diffuse way as a dominant cultural form. Already a significant segment of the American economy was devoted to moving people, things, and information, and within a decade every *Fortune* 500 company was aimed this way. Mark is a mover, leaving one identity and way of life and gathering up another, as a result of his encounter with Marnie. And, very unlike the typical employer she has met and robbed over the past few years, he has already seduced Marnie into her own transformative voyage, back to the past, as we shall see, and then forward to a wholly new kind of future. These two are prototypical Americans, experiencing their meeting, their strained interaction, their negotiation and renegotiation of status vis-à-vis one another, and their emotional commitments as well, purely and plainly in terms of the highway of life.[14]

When Mark tells Marnie frankly that he has found her interesting, he could be quoting one of the great American philosophers of the road, Jack Kerouac: "I shambled after as

---

[14] As central elements in film, automobiles and the road proliferated at this time: Edgar G. Ulmer's *Detour* (1945), Nicholas Ray's pioneering *They Live by Night* (1948), and Douglas Sirk's *Written on the Wind* (1956) reflected the trend. Hitchcock had a central highway sequence in *Psycho* (1960); John Frankenheimer had included a significant (and beautiful) highway sequence in *All Fall Down* (1962); Frank Tashlin culminated *The Disorderly Orderly* (1964) with a spectacular road ballet; and road culture and driving were powerfully evoked in Howard Hawks's *Red Line 7000* (1965), Guy Hamilton's *Goldfinger* (1964), Frankenheimer's *Grand Prix* (1966), and Stanley Donen's *Two for the Road* (1967), not to mention obsessive road treatments in such French adorations of American road culture as Jean-Luc Godard's *Bande à part* (1964) and Jacques Tati's *Trafic* (1971).

Mad to be saved. Digital frame enlargement.

I've been doing all my life after people who interest me, because the only people for me are the mad ones, the ones who are mad to live, mad to talk, mad to be saved" (5).

A Tunnel of Love

In *Strangers on a Train* (1951) Guy Haines (Farley Granger) is a famous tennis professional. Working-class by birth, he dated, then married Miriam, a girl of his own station and a case study of lumpen resentment and moral laxity. Now, and very badly, he wants a divorce, part of a strategy for moving up in the world. Guy shows telltale signs of Robert K. Merton's anticipatory socialization, behaving in advance as though he is already a member of the elite group he desires to join, since he has been hobnobbing in the social circle of Senator Morton (Leo G. Carroll) and eager to make the senator's daughter Ann (Ruth Roman) his wife. One day, on a train trip from Washington, D.C., he is picked up by Bruno Antony (Robert Walker), exceedingly spoiled, rather bored, with a deep-seated resentment against his father and a narcissistic susceptibility to celebrity. Bruno is crème de la crème in East Coast society, living with his parents in a gargantuan Virginia palace that floats upon extensive manicured lawns. He's been reading all about Guy in the papers, that Bruno: specifically about the delicious Ann Morton, and about the lowly wife refusing to go along with the divorce: too bad! Smarmily he proposes to Guy that each of them has someone he would like to get rid of – Guy his clinging wife and Bruno his detested father.[15] Guy's inability to directly and bluntly reject Bruno – insecure to the hilt in his position as climber, he cannot permit himself to be unfriendly to even a cur – leads him to shrug the fellow off obliquely: "Sure, Bruno, sure." Guy means only sarcasm, linguistic alienation, but the slightly demented Bruno takes him with point-blank seriousness. He proceeds unilaterally to frame a murder plan, killing Miriam and expecting Guy to reciprocate. We have the feeling, suggests George Toles, that "the two men belong together" (536).

The challenge of dispensing with Miriam Haines Bruno undertakes by making his way to Metcalf, the small town where she lives, finding her address in the local phone book, then following her one evening as she takes a bus to the amusement park at the edge of town.[16] Douglas Gomery

---

[15] Considerable critical literature is devoted to Bruno's ostensible homosexuality. See for examples Wood, "Murderous Gays" and *Films* 336–57; Doty 486ff.; and Corber "Washington." Doty observes that the idea of playing Bruno as homosexual came from Robert Walker and was worked out with Hitchcock (486), but of course the source novel for the film was authored by Patricia Highsmith, a writer with keen sensibilities toward homoeroticism.
[16] "A huge amusement park was sprawled over ten acres of Rowland V. Lee's ranch near Chatsworth where the troupe worked for ten night sessions. The park, a glittering sight with its runway of freak shows and games of chance, merry-go-round and various amusement concessions, attracted hundreds of sight-seers during the shooting hours of from sunset to dawn. Among the more famous visitors were Ida Lupino, Shelley Winters, and Robert Cummings" (Production Notes).

comments, "Late in the nineteenth century, amusement parks were built at the end of trolley lines in major cities in the United States to encourage riders to journey through the entire system. Amusement park entrepreneurs presented a variety of acts to attract audiences in the hot summer months" (8; see also Waller). Miriam is in the company of two boys (Tommy Farrell, Roland Morris), flirting with each of them in turn and stringing both along, as Bruno coolly surveys. At the test-of-strength game he gives a brave display, knowing that she cannot take her eyes off him, hammering down so hard that the weight flies all the way to the top and almost shatters the bell. But now the little romantic trio is heading

Miriam Haines's (Laura Elliott) craft disappears into the *Tunnel of Love* in Strangers on a Train *(Warner Bros., 1951)*. Bruno is a few yards behind her, gliding silently in a craft named Pluto. Digital frame enlargement.

for the Tunnel of Love and Bruno is right behind them. A small rental boat. The three young people embark, giggling and jostling. Bruno sits contented, nibbling his popcorn, in a craft named Pluto, silently slithering across the darkened lagoon toward the ersatz mountain with the tunnel at its base. As the first boat makes its way through, we watch the looming young shadows at play upon the grotto wall. Then, a few seconds behind, the solitary, dedicated figure of Bruno.

Unrepentant giggles.

Lingering on the waters near the exit, we hear a girl's scream from inside the tunnel – he has somehow done it!

But no, one of the boys has just been fresh with her.

They are still giggling as they head for a little island, permit their boat to skid onto the shore, hop out, and race off. The camera doesn't move, and in a moment the prow of Bruno's craft slides in, a perfect companion. He gets out and paces after them, discovers Miriam alone in a coppice, asks her name. When she replies, he raises his hands swiftly to her throat. Her thick eyeglasses fall into the grass and the camera drops to watch the reflection of the scene in her lenses, as Bruno finishes her and drops the body down.[17] He

---

[17] For the shot in which the strangulation is seen reflected in the dropped eyeglasses, a set of gigantic glasses was manufactured; this shot was cut from prints exhibited in Baltimore, Ohio, and Milwaukee (*Strangers on a Train* legal file). "When he was pursuing Laura Elliott all over the amusement park ... Robert Walker declared it was a case of the blind leading the blind. In the picture, Miss Elliott wore glasses with diminishing lens in order to give her eyes an evil, slit-like appearance. Being of normal vision, the actress couldn't see a thing through the thick lens. Blocks of wood had to be placed for her to stumble against, so she would know where to stop in the scene. As for Walker, he is near-sighted, and wears glasses constantly *off* screen. So Miss Elliott with her glasses *on* and Walker with his glasses *off* had to carefully rehearse which way they were going in order to avoid falling on their respective faces" (Production Notes).

goes back to his boat, puts it in reverse, and slides into the black lagoon, as the boys' voices call out in the night, "Miriam? Miriam? ..."

But that Tunnel of Love: Is it entirely a space for joy and abandonment, or do its dark shadows, its thickly veined walls, the torpid waters through which the little boats sluggishly move, and those self-guided boats themselves that wallow through here without concern or interest, without involvement in the hot affairs of their inhabitants, signify something more malevolent and more furious than simple affection or passion? Implied for the typical customer here is a romantic encounter real or presumptive, a sexual bonding that carries with it dramatic emotional and social implications. This tunnel, perhaps something of a fallopian tube, is ultimately the site of a birth, after all – the birth of a social contract, a wedding. (The Tunnel of Love is designed as an accoutrement and aid to courting rituals, and was especially functional in a time when the physical aspects of wooing were socially repressed and before sexual expression in public gained popular currency.) In its deepest aspect, then, it is a technology of melodrama, embodying melodrama's "pure and polar concepts of darkness and light" (Brooks 4). Woody Register notes melodrama's "narrow escapes, fortuitous meetings, misunderstood communications, peerless heroes, angelic heroines, and diabolical villains," all appertaining to an entertainment form that constituted an "unsophisticated, anti-intellectual pandering to popular emotions" (198). Register goes further, quoting Porter Browne to the effect that melodramatic constructions are an "antidote to urban ennui" (347, qtd. in Register 199); audiences for melodrama are reduced to childlike status, seeking thrill but not the invocation to thought.

Inside the tunnel, we are in a territory where the deep-seated but socially contained hunger for pleasure might find expression: the open-mouthed kiss, the squeal of touch, the yearning to enter or otherwise experience the body of the other. This is the substrate locked away in Victorian culture, a culture even in the United States and even in the high modernity of the early 1950s not truly liberated and replaced by open passion, the images and beckonings of advertising notwithstanding. The Tunnel of Love exists because what happens inside its grotto cannot be seen to occur in the light of day (yet must happen). If Laura's very presence here is a transgression, her deviance is doubled because she has two lovers in her boat, twice the sanctified portion; and, further, because she is sought after in two different ways in two boats, a double doubling. As a form, the shadowy grotto is intrinsically reflective of alienation from – ascension above – working-class society. By 1886, at his Schloss Linderhof, Ludwig II had constructed a fully operational grotto with dynamos powering gelled lighting that would play color effects through a watery chamber where he could ride a Wagnerian swan boat across a greeny lake. This fantasy he intended as a personal interpretation, and acquisition, of the celebrated blue grotto in Capri, dating to Roman times and written of effusively since the mid-1820s. In the grotto one escaped to another world of unconscionable desire and fulfillment, a dream reality that at once negated, and leashed the participant to, the humdrum of daily life.

In going to the park, Laura is already distancing herself from the imposing constraints of small-town society – the constraints, too, of her marriage to Guy – and by opting to visit the Tunnel of Love she is margining herself off yet again, beyond the periphery of the town to the periphery of the park itself. "Miriam," writes Corber, "represents the sexually 'deviant' woman demonized by cold-war political discourse because she refuses to restrict her sexuality to the privatized space of the nuclear family. The subject of her own desire, she circulates freely among men. ... The scenes in which Bruno follows her at the amusement park are constructed in such a way as to excuse her murder" (Corber, "Washington" 115).

It is a sharply divided culture that Hitchcock is reflecting in this amusement park sequence. In the film's daylight scenes, epitomized by the stylish etiquette when Bruno meets Guy on the train or during the tennis match; or by Guy's visit to the record store in Metcalf, where he has a spat with Miriam ("Aw, skip it, Miriam. It's pretty late to start flirting with a discarded husband, especially when you're going to have another man's baby"),[18] what predominates is a carefully balanced play of moral propriety, clean appearances, wholesome intentionalities, and, above all, interpersonal decorum. No matter what people are engaged in doing, they are polite and relatively restrained, primly courteous, quietly self-conscious, these attitudes constituting a social lubrication that makes possible the intensive circulation of modern life without concomitant collisions and accidents. If from senators to baggage handlers the population is committed to role-playing, the performances are given with polish and grace, quite as though performers really believe in the principles they openly demonstrate. The early 1950s was a sincere time by day.[19] At night, however, one could retire to an

---

[18] A line cut from prints exhibited in Massachusetts, Toronto, and the Province of Ontario generally (Strangers on a Train legal file).

[19] Erving Goffman writes, "The performer can be fully taken in by his own act; he can be sincerely convinced that the impression of reality which he stages is the real reality" (17).

electrified phantasmagoria like the park,[20] sail out on the dark lagoon, and touch upon deep passions locked away from everyday life.

David Nye observes,

> *The amusement park temporarily overturned and rewrote the social order. It inverted central values of American society – thrift, sobriety, restraint, order, and work – and exploited technology for pleasure. It temporarily overcame the separation between social classes, ethnic tensions, the difference between country and city, and the segmentation of the city itself into suburbs. It transformed the public into a crowd to be manipulated into spending money for momentary pleasures and gaudy visions of self-transformation.*
> *(129)*

Nocturnal sex was furtive, but rich; indeed the furtiveness made it rich. Using Miriam's jaunt through the Tunnel of Love as an icon, one may see throughout *Strangers on a Train* characters whose polite facades cover seething darker formations – Krohn sees a "strange mood of melancholy" that Robert Walker "casts over the film" (*Work* 118) – characters committed to the burial of those shadowy formations and the relentless display of shining, garrulous facades.

Barbara Morton (Patricia Hitchcock), Ann's younger sister, is one example, on the face of it a deliciously charming debutante. As she watches Bruno demonstrate strangling at the senator's soirée she is capable of actually imagining that he intended to kill *her*, that is, not only imagining him as a

---

[20] David Kyvig notes one of the boons of electrification, "bright light able to banish the night's darkness and lengthen the day" (44; qtd. in Fischer, "Shock" 22), but the intense illumination left around it pools and alleys of intense darkness, beautifully rendered by Robert Burks's high-key black-and-white cinematography in the park sequence. Electricity augmented light and darkness equally.

murderer but dreaming of herself as his victim. She notices him staring in her direction as his hands close on the tender neck of vapid Mrs. Cunningham (Norma Varden).[21] This is certainly an interesting sight taken in by an interesting young person, but more galvanizing still is the macabre frame of mind Barbara has kept hidden behind her elite prurience. Her sister Ann is not different. Discovering that there is some bizarre "relationship" between her fiancé Guy and this strange man Bruno, she actually voyages into an episode of wonder as to what kind of (filthy) connection the two might "really" have: in short, for all her ostensible grace and charm she is capable of fantasizing a scenario that is unnamable, sinister, out of key: again, this occurs nocturnally, as the chatty soirée swirls around her.

The senator himself is – can only be – a veritable model of public decorum, so much on guard in every situation he cannot possibly be taken as fully present. But always there is a slightly shady modesty to him, betraying that, like other politicians in Washington, he guards secrets which, revealed, would damage him. Bruno's forgetful, apparently harmless mother (Marion Lorne) – "just as crazy as her son" (Truffaut 198) – seems entirely lacking in malevolence until, with

---

[21] A veteran of considerable screen work (*Stormy Weather* [1935], *Waterloo Bridge* [1940], *Random Harvest* [1942], *The Secret Garden* [1949], *Gentlemen Prefer Blondes* [1953], *Elephant Walk* [1954], *Three Coins in the Fountain* [1954], *Witness for the Prosecution* [1957], *The Sound of Music* [1965], among 153 film and television roles), Varden (1898–1989) was profoundly enthused working with Hitchcock and more than once sent him handwritten notes (in purple ink, on lavender paper) begging for more work. On August 13, 1958, she invoked *North by Northwest*: "I called you this morning, but you were busy with 'interviews,' which worries me very much for fear you should cast someone in *my* part, by mistake of course" (Varden to Hitchcock). On November 27, 1959, she tried again, regarding *Psycho*: "Dear, dear Mr Hitchcock, Am I going to be with you this time? I do hope so –," to which he replied, "Dear, dear Miss Varden: I am afraid not. What a pity" (Varden to Hitchcock; Hitchcock to Varden).

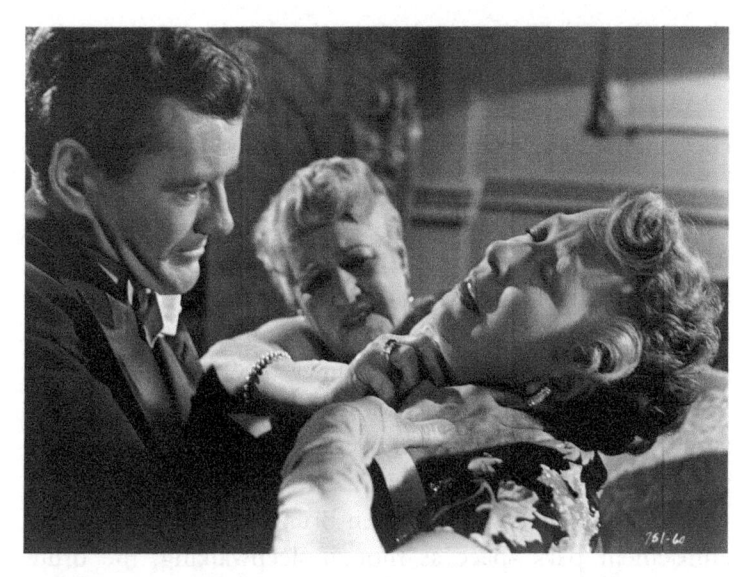

Bruno Antony (Robert Walker) "demonstrating" strangling. Mrs. Cunningham (Norma Varden, r.) was having such a good time. Courtesy Academy of Motion Picture Arts and Sciences.

Bruno, we see the painting of St. Francis she has been working on: diabolical and deeply grotesque, whether or not it represents – as Bruno laughingly avers – her husband, it is a blatant shock to the eye.[22] Guy's legalistic, demanding wife is an itching nymphomaniac in disguise. All these characters are at their liveliest in obscurity, in a metaphorical dark interior grotto, or tunnel of love, that twists both

---

[22] Production designer Ted Haworth was responsible for finding this painting. Hitchcock wanted it modeled on the work of Abraham Rattner (1893–1978), an abstract expressionist who had done work as a camouflage artist for the U.S. Army during World War I. Krohn notes how a claw is featured in place of the right hand (and also draws a connection between a "huge misshapen claw" in the foreground of the image of Bruno laying Miriam's dead body in the grass, and the lobsters in Bruno's necktie) (*Work* 118–19).

alluringly and frighteningly into depths that everyday life does not reveal.

Also implicit in the twentieth-century America that Hitchcock adopted and reflected was a pervasive sense of the banal everyday, what the founder of Coney Island's Steeplechase Park George Tilyou saw as "the ordinary person's body and its connection to the machine" (Lukas 46). In the entire amusement park sequence, there is something at once garish and ebullient – the electric lights, the repetitive hawking of Charles B. Ward and John F. Palmer's 1895 hit "The Band Played On" on the public address, the sparkling, nervous smiles of the customers – but overriding it, and founding the structure, a tedium both routinized and machinic: the way Miriam and her boyfriends, then Bruno, trudge through the amusement park space as though sleepwalking, the brute mechanism of the show-your-strength machine, the routine of lining up for the dream boats, the silent and subtly controlled motion of those boats on the lagoon, the straightforward procedure through the Tunnel of Love, and finally, as a culmination, Bruno's stolid, unreflective, almost robotic movements following Laura and putting her through the death procedure step by step. Not only is the body's organicism submitted to the brutality of machine discipline in the tunnel, but, writes Scott Lukas,

> the ride is heightened by the separation that occurs shortly after boarding: one is removed by the darkness from the space of the living, symbolized by light. The darkness takes hold of the rider, and around each turn . . . is an unexpected occurrence. Such a ride attempts to build on both expectation and surprise, capturing the rider in a simulated space of terror. (125)

Beyond its shining possibilities and boundless promise, then, and even in its normality; beyond its prosperity and optimism, beyond its slick technological wonders, America was itself an amusement park, a hiding place of forbidden obscurities, thrilling fears, and a horribly anti-social impulse.

A General Store

Having bought her pair of lovebirds and driven them up to Bodega Bay as a sly little gift for Mitch Brenner, Melanie Daniels pulls her sports car into a freed-up parking spot in front of Brinkmayer's General Store, a clapboard structure advertising U.S. Post Office, Hardware, and Groceries and manned by a caged and elderly clerk who is sorting mail (John McGovern). Fred Brinkmayer is purposeful, quiet, and efficient, a civilian gentleman holding a sinecure. In her full-length mink ("With her lavish fur coat, she's like a dream vision, a golden goddess who has descended in her sky-blue chariot to earth" [Paglia 30]), Melanie makes something of a picture for him, standing out distinctively as a city person and thus one of those "foreign" types whom locals both denigrate and depend upon, at least during the summer season. More than a stranger, however, Melanie is also one who doesn't mind displaying her wealth, perhaps even taking advantage of it, although her presence doesn't occasion noticeable reaction from this or any other of the polite citizens of the town. One lady, for example, accoutered with much less flamboyance, merely excuses her way out of the store and makes no eye contact with, or judgment upon, our Melanie as the store's doorbell chirrups behind her.

To Brinkmayer, "first gruff and laconic, then slowly, bashfully bewitched, gazing at her like the elders of Troy thunderstruck by matchless Helen, for whom they think the city well lost" (Paglia 30), Melanie offers a pleasant "Good morning!" and says she is looking for a man named Mitchell Brenner.

BRINKMAYER: Yeahuh.
MELANIE (with eagerness): Do you know him?
BRINKMAYER: Yeahuh.
MELANIE: Where does he live?
BRINKMAYER: Right here. Bodega Bay.

Mr. Brinkmayer has a tone, if not exactly of reserve then of parsimony. He wouldn't lie, wouldn't be evasive, but also wouldn't tell any more than he was being asked to tell, a characteristic of those who, not exactly wishing to keep their lives a secret, nevertheless do not intend to open the privacy of their neighbors to curious outside eyes. Max Lerner notes "the two goods that Americans have always seen in [the small town] – the friendliness of face-to-face relations and the concern about the town's affairs felt by all its citizens" (148–9). Brinkmayer must live in close harmony with Mitch and his family, after all; but not with this stranger from the city.

"Yes, I know, but where?" she presses, and he is again polite but diffident. Nodding: "Right across the bay there." A local would know how swiftly to follow the line of that gaze – would not, indeed, need to be told where Mitch lives – but an outsider would see only a stretch of water, only a vague hint of direction. So she must press again, "Where?" and now, a little chafed that he has been led this far, irritated to be putting down his routine work, Brinkmayer exits his cage and, with a neighborly smile, leads her to the door. Having remembered his manners, he becomes avuncular, a little sheepish, and also charming, since she is, after all, a pretty lady and she wants the town beau: "Now. See where I'm pointin'?" He stretches his left arm out and indicates what he is squinting at – namely, the camera. "See them two big trees 'cross there?" We cut to a shot across the bay. Storm clouds brewing. Cars parked on the little fishing wharf. The masts of boats.

> MELANIE: You mean on the other side of the bay?
> BRINKMAYER: The white house?
> MELANIE: Yes.
> BRINKMAYER: That's where the Brenners live.

Thanks to Brinkmayer, Melanie the stalker has located Mitch the evasive stag in this bucolic wilderness, and has acquired the means to connect with him. But why, we may ask, should she have needed to converse with this elderly man in order to do it? Now she wants to know if by "the Brenners" he means Mitch and his wife, but the answer is straightforward and plain: "No, just Lydia and the two kids. . . . Mitch and the little girl." "The 'kids' are Mitch and his sister: though nearly a generation apart, they are locally collapsed together, suggesting that Mitch, tied to his mother, is still partly trapped in childhood" (Paglia 31). When she asks if there is a back road she can take, rather than driving around the bay, she must confess that she wants to surprise them, doesn't want them to see her arrive. "Oh," says he, his poker face revealing absolutely no attitude, no curiosity, no approval, no concern. She could get a boat – she assures him she's handled one before: he amicably asks if he can order one for her. As he dials a number, she interrupts. "I wonder if you can tell me the little girl's name."

> BRINKMAYER: Little Brenner girl? . . . Alice, I think. Harry, what's the little Brenner girl's name?
> HARRY (off-camera): Lois.
> BRINKMAYER: Alice, ain't it?

Harry's voice, a little gruff, came from some undefined location in the back of the store. The camera shows shelves piled full of Campbell's soup and candies and peanuts, and the pale green walls of the shop, a domain of magical spirits, potions, incantations, and sacred publicity.

HARRY (off-camera): No, it's Lois.

We cut back to the clerk, standing with some children's puzzles on a rack in the foreground. "It's Alice." With a feminist stretch, Paglia notices that "both shop scenes, in San Francisco and Bodega Bay, contain misidentifications of birds or women, which the film often ominously treats as a single category of capricious being" (31).

Melanie needs to know the girl's exact name. And now, some ancient barrier having melted, the old man eases to her and opens up. After all, by now she is a local, having drawn him away from the envelope of his taciturnity and responded to his warm smiles and engaged in the proper minimum of conversation.

BRINKMAYER: In that case, I'll tell you what you do: You go straight through town 'til you see a little hotel on your left. Then you turn right there. Now you got that? Near the top of the hill you'll see the school and just beyond, a little house with a red mailbox. That's where Annie Hayworth the schoolteacher lives. (*A smile.*) You ask her about the little Brenner girl. Save yourself a lot of trouble. Name's Alice, for sure.

Melanie has undoubtedly now secured to herself a particular, comforting feeling that might come to any outsider faced with the secretive complexity of a wholly unknown community when a sort of map has been provided. She has learned the names and locations of some key players on the scene. Further, she is standing in the shop that can provide everything one needs, and has befriended the proprietor. It would be easy for her to relax into the assurance that the "map" really does reveal the "territory," although it certainly doesn't. Who, after all, *is* Lydia Brenner or Annie Hayworth? What are their histories, their interconnections, and their experiences in these precisely indicated places in and around the town? It will not be until the very end of the film, after destruction, terror, death, and displacement, that Melanie begins to be adopted as an honorary citizen of Bodega Bay, adopted and taken into the family yet at the point of leaving forever.[23]

It is certainly true that the scene in the general store authenticates the setting of the story as a whole – a small town remote from the protective shell of advanced civilization, this transposed by Hitchcock from Daphne du Maurier's Cornwall. And it is true, further, that as a stranger to the town, Melanie could not possibly have access to any of the primary characters of the film without being the beneficiary of direction from *some* local citizen who knows everybody and everything that is going on. But our vision of that store from within strikes, I think, yet another more elegiac chord. This general store represents the agrarian America now in decline. "Everywhere," Lerner tells us,

---

[23] Regarding the suspended ending of the film ("the kind of open ending the director had always preferred" [McGilligan 628]), with Mitch, Lydia, Cathy, Melanie, and the two lovebirds driving away toward the horizon and the entire landscape filled with birds, Hitchcock told Arthur Knight, "One had to leave it to the imagination of the audience that this bird attack was a local thing. Otherwise, where do you stop next? The Golden Gate Bridge? Then you're on a whole new theme. You're on the theme that Daphne du Maurier had in her short story – that the world was being taken over by birds. Well, that's too far to go in a film" (163).

> even in the most prosperous areas, the small town was undercut by the big changes in American life – the auto and superhighway, the supermarket and the market center, the mail-order house, the radio and TV, the growth of national advertising, the mechanization of farming – so that it turned its face directly to the centers of technology. It was the city and the suburb – the cluster-city complex – that became the focus of working and living, consuming and leisure. "None of the kids ever come back here to live after they've gone away to school," said an older man from Shannon Center, Iowa, which had lost almost half its population in the 1940s. (149–50)

Mitch Brenner, being just a little more old-fashioned than most ambitious young people his age (but not Annie Hayworth), has not quite left Bodega Bay. He has an aging widowed mother to care for and a keen sense of responsibility. Perhaps his young sister will go off to college and be one of those who don't return. We already see a thinning town population, with the streets filled mostly by tourists from the city-suburb complex. The suburbs, particularly, had exploded in the 1950s, when "millions of Americans – particularly young, white couples of the middle class – responded to a severe housing shortage in the cities by fleeing to new mass-produced suburbs" (Spigel 31). A "newly defined aesthetic of prefabrication" characterized the value structure of the new America, with "older people, gay and lesbian people, homeless people, unmarried people, and people of color ... simply written out of [the new] community spaces" (33). Reforming modernizers "continued to advocate assembly-line production as the key to delivering housing for the masses" (Baxandall and Ewen 53). Bodega Bay and other small towns were still holdovers from a nineteenth- and early twentieth-century value structure, places where a predominantly white middle-class population could wait in a presumed safe retreat from the city, the suburb, and modernity.

Hitchcock's problem was always to visualize what was experientially true for his characters and whatever story elements were necessary for provoking the emotional response of his audience. Here, he needed Bodega Bay to be the small-town oasis in a vast and daily growing desert of urbanized, technologized, rationalized, and modernized American culture; but in order to highlight this distinction and framing, *inside* the town itself he needed a space that could be to Bodega Bay just what Bodega Bay was coming to be for America: a bubble of the past. Annie's house couldn't work: as a thinker and teacher, she would have too contemporary a taste. The Brenner house couldn't work: Lydia is originally urban, and Mitch comes up only on weekends, so the place is much more a recent acquisition, a countryseat hideaway.

But the Brinkmayer store could be designed to suggest that it went back generations and generations, that renovation and upgrading were barely thinkable there, that inside these walls the agrarian past still had a pulse. Further, the store setting was not only integral to the story, it was tightly designed as a visual array, all of its parts finely and stably cohering in terms of shape, color, arrangement, and social purpose. In that store, and seeing the world from the veranda outside it, one could sense in Melanie – and thus share – a feeling of constancy, tradition, permanence, gravity, and reality (all of which would be upset by the bird attacks). A thoroughgoing contrast was Hitchcock's frequent use of rear projection, which had the effect, according to Wood, "of giving an air of unreality to [Melanie's] situation, of isolating her from the backgrounds, of stressing her artificiality by making it stand out obtrusively from natural scenery" (*Films* 157).

We can see directly how diversification and topographical spread, two salient characteristics of urban economy and spatial usage in modernity, are contradicted inside the store. Here is sold virtually everything one could possibly need for a multitude of purposes functional, decorative, domestic, technical, private, and public. In dubbing it a "curio-filled cultural institution" (30), Paglia gives only a casual glance at the space as a design and package. Given the range of its merchandise and services, the store not only represents but constitutes the economic locus for the town community, perhaps most centrally for the farmers who depend upon Brinkmayer's for their feed (Lydia is telephoning to check on the feed she's been giving her chickens when Melanie arrives for dinner). Toiletries, toys, tools, and tidbits – they are all here for sale. By the early 1960s, and spreading across the land, mall culture was replacing this kind of localized venue with specialty shops (increasingly franchises) if not with the new mall-based discount department stores K-Mart and Wal-Mart, both founded in the year this motion picture was shot. In community after community in America, "Brinkmayer's" was disappearing.

The urban phenomenon of the department store, originating with La Samaritaine and Printemps in Paris in the 1860s and with such venues as Selfridge's in London as of 1909 (see Rappaport), was part of modern culture and its centralizing thrust, but in American small towns there developed through the nineteenth century and survived well into the twentieth such distinctive merchandising centers as Brinkmayer's, not only warehouses where one could obtain all of one's needs at a reasonable price but territories inhabited by a relatively tiny sales staff who knew the customer by name, by history, and by character. This was a traditional retail shop, where, as Schivelbusch notes, "buyer and purchaser still confronted one another in person: when a customer entered this presaged, if not necessarily a transaction, at least a dialogue between him and the shopkeeper. The department store put an end to this sales conversation" (*Railway* 189).[24]

The Brenners are conversant, familiar, cherished customers in this little store, as is Annie Hayworth and every other resident of Bodega Bay, and as becomes Melanie. The postmaster knows Lydia and her family for the personalities they are, if with a little generational bias that affords less attention to the youngest. Fred Brinkmayer has been meeting their every need for years, was undoubtedly present at Mitch's father's funeral. He controls not only what one can acquire for survival in the town – coffee, biscuits, sugar, eggs, cotton, Band-aids, and probably wine – but also the ease with which, and the extent to which, one can communicate directly with the outside world: his telephone line is the one on which arrangements are made – he knows all the numbers – and his postal wicket is the brain center of town.[25]

But also to be considered is the way merchandise is arranged within the store, since the idea of expansion is not expressed in the small town. Not only is everything available here, everything is crammed into a relatively small space, and we can see this plainly, with the shelves filled to overflowing and packets hanging over them wherever possible, providing for a sense of bounteousness and capacity. The people who live in Bodega Bay, far from that center of American civilization, the city, are not lacking because of their distance. And with the vision of this richly laden, amicable, civil, proper storehold one can have instantly an idea of what resource it

[24] For an interesting play upon the general store and the conversations that might occur there in the last third of the nineteenth century, see George Stevens's *Shane* (1953).
[25] For a beautiful discursion upon the telephone as an agency of modernity, see Gunning.

Research photograph of the actual general store interior in Bodega Bay, California, with proprietor. Hitchcock also had photographed numerous citizens of the town and a few dozen of the children who normally attended the Bodega Bay school, in their everyday school clothing. Courtesy Academy of Motion Picture Arts and Sciences.

is, exactly, that the birds ultimately choose to attack, since this store *isn't* it.

The birds attack: the wharf, center of the fishing business, thus the external economy; The Tides restaurant, center of entertainment and refuge for travelers; the gas station nearby, center of locomotion, since it is the place of rest from, and preparation for, travel. Just out of town is Annie's school, the place where the past becomes the future, the center of time. All these hallmarks of modernity we see attacked and pillaged by the birds, but the general store, that bastion of small-town life, that archaic capital, that pedestal of old American values, is secure. At the end of the film, this general store will remain standing to stock the citizens of tomorrow. To rest here is to suffer the protection of what America can produce, but also to be passed over for "better" things to come.

Brinkmayer's General Store is a bubble of the past. A similar bubble finds indication in *Psycho* (1960), when Marion Crane's sister Lila comes to visit the boyfriend, Sam Loomis, in his hardware store in the town of Fairvale. Here again, but with a little more space, is the tranquil site of old-time value, a place filled with goods for specific needs, a peaceable proprietor (whose personal life is modern if his business life is not). In these precincts, we meet "a gloomy battleaxe-type old lady" (Helen Wallace), as Douchet describes her, looking for an insecticide that will kill painlessly. "I say, insect or man, death should always be painless" (*Psycho* 150). In *Marnie*, the same peaceful, predictable, rhythmic, almost bucolic quality that we find in these stores, that reassurance of the value of times gone by, is detectable in the slow and habitual movements of Rita, the office cleaner, who threatens inadvertently one evening to catch the wily Marnie as she is in train of robbing the company safe. (But Rita is deaf, and does not hear one of Marnie's shoes drop to the floor as she tiptoes out.) It is not the dramatic tension of Marnie's robbery coupled with Rita's incipient detection that offers this study of repose but the simple vision of Rita mopping the floor of the large office space now utterly vacated of workers. The light is clean and bright, the movements of the cleaner regular, almost hypnotic. It is as though time stands still. Very briefly at the Mount Rushmore Visitors' Center, before the melée caused by Eve "shooting" Roger there, we have the same sense of decorous order, the many tables filled with tourists quietly enjoying a little meal or a cup of coffee, the monument with the glaring presidents hovering silently in the sunshine outside the picture windows.

Bickfords after midnight in *The Wrong Man* is another "extraordinary bubble of reposeful solitude and selfness" (Pomerance, "Clean" 117), as is that tiny cart in front of Gump's at 250 Post Street, San Francisco (Kraft and Leventhal 157–9), where Scottie Ferguson buys Judy Barton a bouquet. The whole of the small town in *The Trouble with Harry* (1955), Brulov's study in *Spellbound* (1945), Phillip Martin's house in *Saboteur* (1942), the chummy badinage between Rupert Cadell and Mrs. Wilson the housekeeper in *Rope* (1948), Emma Newton's kitchen in *Shadow of a Doubt* (1943) – all these spaces, topographical spaces and social spaces, indicate a pre-modern time of great civility, innocence, and trust: something fleeting, something Hitchcock could see vanishing before his eyes.

Giants

But what of the American Dream, that belief in the individual's power to change and affect the world, that "dream of possibility – not just of wealth or of prestige or of power but of the manifold possibilities that human existence can hold for the incredible variety of people of the most assorted talents and drives ... the hope for a better world, a new world, free of the ills of the old, existing world" (Lemay 25)? It has declined, of course, become no more than "the American Dream" in the sense supplied parodically by Edward Albee, "a picture of our time" (Canaday 12), personified by a strapping young man, centerpiece of his family, glory to behold, but gelded. What of the blue, blue rivers and the purple-mountained majesty, the vast waving prairies, the metropolis reaching upward to the stars? What of the immensity of the American personality, rhapsodized by Carl Sandburg or morosely critiqued by Fitzgerald in *The Great Gatsby* pointing to the "foul dust [that] floated in the wake of his dreams" (2); what of that figure embodied as Paul Bunyan, the Jolly Green Giant, the great colossus? What of the magnificent giant who peoples the New World? To the swollen pocketbooks, prestige, and aristocratic panache of rich Americans Hitchcock could pointedly allude by having Frederick Devereux (Frederick Stafford) in *Topaz* (1969) come to reside at the St. Regis in New York (the hotel he himself always chose [McGilligan, *Darkness* 203]) and at a swank Georgetown home in Washington,[26] or by having Roger Thornhill knowingly prowl the lush interior of the Plaza,[27] or by having the McKennas inhabit the swank Savoy in London; by playing the obnoxious and tedious *arriviste* Mrs. Van Hopper (Florence Bates) as denizen of a luxurious suite in Monte Carlo in *Rebecca*; by waltzing his camera through the enormous ballroom in the Fifth Avenue palace of the "fascist dowager" Mrs. Sutton (Alma Kruger) in *Saboteur* (Krohn, *Work* 47); or by arranging for the elegant Lisa Fremont to cater dinner to Jeff Jefferies from, of all places, "21."[28]

As to the physical style of architectural greatness, he could acknowledge it in *North by Northwest* with the opening-credit image of a glassy green façade on Madison Avenue,[29] or with

---

[26] Hitchcock used for the Washington residence the home of Jacqueline Kennedy's step-second cousin John W. Auchincloss, at 2818 P Street (*Topaz* locations file).
[27] Grant in fact resided there during the shooting (Taylor 249).
[28] Where Hitchcock adored to dine. He was fêted there shortly upon his arrival in America, while being interviewed by the best-selling author/journalist H. Allen Smith (1907–76) (see Spoto 187 and Pomerance, "Clean" 104).
[29] This sequence designed by Saul Bass was not what Hitchcock originally wanted, but the original idea, a traveling sequence through Roger's advertising offices showing preparatory sketches for ads (that would be the title cards), was rejected as too expensive, even though Grant offered to make the necessary shots without a fee (Krohn, *Work* 213).

the Mondrianesque composition looking down from the top of the United Nations Secretariat as Roger, having been caught with a murderer's dagger in his hand, flees, or the view at twilight of Vandamm's rather sumptuous mountain aerie at the top of the Mount Rushmore monument (where the "presidents" kept their "brains"). In *The Wrong Man* he could show the misted twilight towers of the great George Washington Bridge, a monument to engineering and the age of steel (see Pomerance, "Clean" 115–16), just as in *Vertigo* he showed the engineering triumph of the Golden Gate Bridge from a point of view that would extend and magnify its impressive form,[30] or as in *Saboteur* he paid homage to Hoover Dam and the launching of a great ship from the Brooklyn Navy Yard or to the looming magnificence of the Statue of Liberty, seen up close and from below as well as, climactically, from the lip of its torch overlooking the gateway to the country.[31] America was again and again for him a stage on which big personalities enacted big events in the face of big structures.

Nevertheless, in the Mount Rushmore sequence of *North by Northwest*, we find a direct and altogether more insightful invocation of the American giant. "Every civilization," writes Lerner,

> *has its characteristic flowering in some civilization type, the persona of the social mask on which the ordinary man in the civilization models himself. In the Athenian civilization the persona was the leisure-class citizen with a turn for art and philosophy;*

---

[30] Fort Point, built between 1853 and 1861 "to protect ships carrying Gold Rush-era cargo" (Kraft and Leventhal 121).
[31] Hitchcock had arranged for and, while ultimately changing the action, was inspired by a series of impressive drawings by John de Cuir (see Krohn, *Work* 53).

with the Jews it was the lawgiver-prophet, in the Roman Empire the soldier-administrator, in the Middle Ages the cleric dreaming of sainthood, in the Chinese civilization the mandarin-scholar, in the Indian the ascetic, in the Italian Renaissance the patron-condottiere, at the height of French power the courtier, at the height of British power the merchant-adventurer and empire builder; in German and Japanese history it was the elite soldier of the Junker and samurai classes, with the Communists today it is the worker-commissar.

The persona of the American civilization has been . . .; the "tycoon."

The American president, as ideal type – and even if he is pre-modern – is modeled on this form, a man who makes deals, a man who leads his countrymen not only forward but to greater munificence and glory, a man who makes the arrangements by which there is a chicken in every coop and a car in every garage if not also a sense of independence in every breast, a man who challenges the blood to race with aspirations of national glory, a man whose iconic personality amalgamates and unifies the disparate races and classes on the American scene. And with Mount Rushmore, these tycoon figures – they are at once administrators and negotiators, philosophers and wheeler-dealers – are magnified appropriately, until they become embodiments that would tower four hundred and sixty-five feet in height if fully realized according to the scale of the heads alone (Marling 88). Gutzon Borglum, who made the sculpture, saw the gigantism instantly as part of the project:

> Everything in modern civilization has so expanded that the very scale, the breadth of one's thought, is no longer limited by town, city, county, or state. . . . I believe it was natural and consistent

> with the great modern awakening that I should have turned to the huge cliffs of our land, the lofty granite ledges, and in them carve monuments and there leave records of the founding of our great nation and the development of our civilization. (Borglum 7, qtd. in Marling 87)

Into and upon the four great faces – of Washington, Teddy Roosevelt, Lincoln, and Jefferson – rove the commercial king Roger Thornhill and his secret agent lover, Eve Kendall. As they scramble on these huge faces (see Pomerance, *Horse* 71ff.), they become at once infinitesimal in proportion, mere exemplars of the common man doing what is right in a morally balanced and justified world, and, congruently, enormously important because swollen morally to the size implied by their surround. The heroism of Roger and Eve is magnified by the locale, since they are ordinary people pressed into extraordinary service with no obligation beyond their ethical sense of what is right. True that the government agency pressing Roger and Eve into service is a brutalizing international power struggling for dominance over others of its kind, but still, as Roger lectures the Professor in the pine forest when he is given a last chance to see Eve before she flies off with Vandamm, "Nobody *has* to do anything." Roger enters the fray to save Eve's life, and for no other reason, just as she has entered it earlier not for personal gain but in order to fight what she sees as the good battle for the team to which she has chosen to belong.

If the huge faces of Mount Rushmore extend and accentuate the heroism of our protagonists, and emphasize the mortal danger they face with each step, they also suggest the form in the name of which heroic action is being taken: it is the system of stolid and unfettered capitalist development. Not in full flower, perhaps, nor the exact economy that any of these presidents – other than Roosevelt – presided over yet definitely one that apotheosizes and valorizes the *great* individual, the *leading* personality, the man at the helm or looking down from the top (see Cavell "*North*"; Frye). By setting his most spectacular finale at Mount Rushmore, then, Hitchcock proclaims a critical stance that grasps the magnified personality warping its age.

The big personality also briefly inhabited *Rear Window*. Thorwald saw Jeff watching him and found the way to Jeff's lair. With the apartment in darkness, the man opened the door and let himself in, while poor Jeff, paralyzed in his wheelchair, could only hold his breath. Because the flat is constructed so that the door opens onto a little landing, two or three steps above the floor, one may theatrically "make an entrance" into this space. As Thorwald stands tall in the doorway, glints of light bouncing off his eyeglasses, we are looking at him from Jeff's perspective, which is to say, from beneath. The performer Raymond Burr is already a Paul Bunyanesque figure at 6' 2½" in height and weighing two hundred and ten pounds, with a 48½" chest and a size 17 collar (Richard Gehman, "The Case of the Oversize Actor," *TV Guide*, March 4, 1961), so his image as photographed with a wide-angle lens and from below is not only villainous but towering. As a traveling salesman, he epitomizes both the conviction in economic transaction and the conviction in movement that modernity brings. And it is more than evident that his frustration stems directly from his position in the economic hierarchy not as a giant but as a small man, a figure who can only wish he were the titan he so resembles.

By contrast, Roger and Eve become morally titanic by association with the stone figurations on which they scramble to save themselves. With death above, below, and to the side, and these figures of giants signifying boundless American optimism and capability always touching them, they are raised, even as characters, to a status larger than life. When

Hitchcock compounds this construction by casting Grant and Saint, major stars of the day, he is aggrandizing the already aggrandized, swelling the moment with tension and admiration but also taunting us to have a shrewd gaze and to ask shrewd questions. How big are we, in fact, as compared with our world? Are we important? Are we dominant? Is it true, as William Faulkner suggested when receiving the Nobel Prize, that we would not merely endure but prevail? These were questions deeply troubling the American psyche of the time. Viewers of Hitchcock, emerging from the 1950s with a lingering Cold War fear and now readying for a new age, watched *North by Northwest* with a feeling that he was touching their deepest nerves.

5

HITCHCOCK AND THE AMERICAN MARRIAGE

When Hitchcock came to America he was signed immediately into a "marriage" with the contentious and controlling David Selznick. The one had a vision of how action and reality could be filmed; the other wanted to shape the artists who worked for him, assign them limits, teach them discipline, follow their every move. Perhaps it is this relationship that we find reflected in the years that followed, since the Hitchcock "marriage" is a centerpiece of his American oeuvre.

There are really no Hitchcockian treatments of the American marriage or coupling that lack irony: whether the union is legal but loveless, or loving but illegal, whether the family is fractured, or whether the union, portrayed as conventional and "normal," is caught up in bizarre and wholly unconventional circumstances. In *The Trouble with Harry* (1955) we find a family without a marriage, but a marriage is the fruit of the story (much as in Shakespeare's *The Tempest*). In *Mr. & Mrs. Smith* (1941) there is a marriage that cannot show

Clash of the titans: Hitchcock taking direction from (or magisterially giving direction to) the man who brought him to America, David O. Selznick. Courtesy Academy of Motion Picture Arts and Sciences.

itself as such. In *North by Northwest* (1959) we see the probability of a marriage between two people whose lives are based, more or less, on probability. In *Shadow of a Doubt* (1943) we have a stable marriage riddled with slim fractures, and by film's end, disenchanted. *Psycho* (1960) is rooted in marital trauma and frustrated romance. *Vertigo* (1958) is about three loves, one obstructed, one hopeless, one soured, and perhaps a fourth that is haunted. *The Man Who Knew Too Much* (1956) explores a family strangled by convention. *Rear Window* (1954) is a kind of marriage carnival, with idealism in many forms circling around boredom and loathing. The romance and presumable future marriage that terminates

Foreign Correspondent (1940) are secondary to the protagonists' political and career devotions. In *Lifeboat* (1944), marriage and love are treated as decorations of a world gone by, so persistently are the survivors focused on such matters of survival as trying to catch fish for the water they contain.[1] More than once, for Hitchcock, marriage is openly declared as bondage. More than once, too, a matriarch lords it imperiously over a dutiful son, with her husband out of the picture.

Anthropology teaches us that the pair bond originated in an exchange of sex for food (see Harris 169–78). What we know and practice in contemporary Western society, a form of extended union cultivated and fostered through romantic literature and its outgrowth in Hollywood cinema and advertising, subjugates both sexual impulse and negotiated exchange to a rhetoric that, in his *Love and Death in the American Novel*, Leslie Fiedler termed a "sentimental myth of redemption through marriage" (310), a myth whose origin goes back to the courtly love lyric. In mythic terms, the beautiful but vulnerable, often imprisoned female is pursued, championed by, and finally won by the gallant who openly proclaims his fidelity to her charms and person. In such Hollywood classics as *Tillie's Punctured Romance* (1914), *Love Affair* (1939), *Holiday* (1938), *Meet Me in St. Louis* (1944), and *An American in Paris* (1951), we see this story played out paradigmatically, and it structures and enlivens thousands of other films. Typically, the lover encounters obstacles or challenges that he must meet, showing off his superiority and worth, before the maiden can be his.

---

[1] This "ingenious method ... for obtaining fresh water" was brought to Hitchcock's attention by Marjorie Baron Russell, the British Ministry of Information's representative in Hollywood, on June 25, 1943, after a British Information Services radio broadcast three days earlier (British Information Services Radio Section Release).

It can be seen that Hitchcock is forever squinting at, playing with, undermining, or otherwise artfully critiquing this romantic love myth as the basis of marriage and family, often placing obstacles before the maiden, not the male; or indeed portraying unions, successful and not, where love has nothing to do with it. Eric Rohmer and Claude Chabrol go so far as to suggest that marital disintegration is a subject "dear to" Hitchcock (32). And while, as Patrick McGilligan recounts, "More than one close associate observed that Hitchcock preferred the company of women," nevertheless his own wife, Alma Reville, was "the only critic, he liked to say, whose opinion he feared" (*Darkness* 176). "I know," Jay Presson Allen said, "that Hitch was functionally impotent because of everything he said to me. I don't think it bothered him that much. I think he used it in his work" (qtd. in McGilligan, *Darkness* 177). In a discourse upon St. Bonaventure's *Opera Omnia* (1902), Umberto Eco notes that "pleasure arises when the object is a pleasurable one: 'For delectation results in a conjunction of the delectable and a person who takes delight in it.' There is an element of love in this relation. For the highest pleasure comes not from sense knowledge but from love, and involves an awareness of proportion and reciprocity in the object. In love, subject and object both lend themselves consciously and actively to the relationship" (67). This kind of love we find only in the concluding few breaths of *Marnie*, and perhaps not even there (see Pomerance, *Eye* 162–3). In *Marnie* – a quintessentially American film in a way – knowledge and its attached irony seem to melt away, with the result that finally the central couple is left in a moment of mutual regard to which, properly, we have no access whatever. In much the same way in this film, we never have access to the real Marnie, the person within the person, the acting Marnie who breathes beneath, when her masquerade has fallen away.

Alexandre of Paris sent his assistant Gwendolyn to Hollywood at Peggy Robertson's request to try out hair styles for 'Tippi' Hedren "from Alexandre's new sketches" (Robertson to Ascarelli). The fee was two thousand dollars plus airfare and expenses, and Gwendolyn began work at 9:00 A.M., Monday, November 4, 1963, at the Sportsmen's Lodge Hotel, accompanied by Virginia Darcy, Universal's stylist (Robertson to Donnelly; Robertson to Barron). These three designs were not used in the picture, but they give some idea of the range of possibilities Hitchcock and his team were working through. Courtesy Academy of Motion Picture Arts and Sciences.

If we look briefly at *Shadow of a Doubt*, in many ways Hitchcock's most recognizably American portrait, we find in the Newtons a family that "has not escaped the traps set by the world, and [one that] does not provide safe harbor for true lovers" (Rothman, *Gaze* 184), centered by a marriage that has been stabilized through loyalty and trust but not affection. Emma Oakley Newton appears to have married beneath her. Her visiting brother Charles is callous about money in a way that Emma cannot afford to be, since her husband Joe doesn't earn much of it (while Charles is a free floater). Uncle Charles makes it plain by the smarmy nature of his regard and through his abruptness of tone, even from a first encounter with Joe at the railway terminus, that he doesn't have high regard for him as an upstanding pillar of society. After all, as a mere bank clerk, Joe can do little to assist or gratify Charles in business, beyond introducing him to the manager in whose face Charles makes an embarrassing and insulting comment. The Newton house and the family living in it are rather large for a teller's salary, unless that salary is being augmented by money from Emma. As to Emma, while she has committed herself to the dutiful routines of housekeeping, to having nutritious meals always a-ready at the same hour every day, she seems to take no pleasure at the dining table or anywhere else in the home, save in serving her cherished and long-lost brother now returned for a visit. The love that Emma has stored in her life belongs to her brother, not her husband. Even to her children she is caring, instructive, watchful, and protective, yet not embracing. It is only when Charlie's life seems in danger that Emma reacts with effusive emotion, yet here she is stymied and incapacitated to help.

If in some of his English films Hitchcock had shown not only loyalty but a certain playful amity in his screen marriages, notwithstanding his puckish, critical, distanced ironies – the Buntings of *The Lodger* (1927) are a working team, sharing information and excitement as their lives are intruded upon by an odd, perhaps murderous, stranger; in *The Skin Game* (1931) Mr. and Mrs. Hillcrist (C. V. France and Helen Haye) team up loyally in ferocious battle against an enemy of their class; the coupling in *The Lady Vanishes* (1938) (Margaret Lockwood and Michael Redgrave), charged with petty irritations, nevertheless strives toward a heroic and triumphant unification – still, as often as not, his British family is as plagued by fracture, suspicion, instability, doubt, and lovelessness as his American. In *Blackmail* (1929), Alice and Frank (Anny Ondra and John Longden) will form a marriage once the film ends, but it will be based on a transgressive secret: she is a murderess and he knows it. *Rich and Strange* (1931) details a marriage gone almost entirely dry, with both parties (Henry Kendall and Joan Barry) susceptible to love affairs as they take advantage of an early inheritance to make a long sea voyage. *The 39 Steps* (1935), filled as it is with problematic couples – the suspicious and brutalizing crofter (John Laurie) and his tender wife (Peggy Ashcroft), the bumbling hero Hannay (Robert Donat) and his love interest Pamela, to whom he is handcuffed (Madeleine Carroll) – takes time to depict the deliciously lubricated, conspiratorial, and treasonous marriage between Professor Jordan (Godfrey Tearle) and his wife (Helen Haye). More than his accomplice, Mrs. Jordan is his trusty aide, keeping up the solid social front behind which he can undertake his malevolent life (a relationship that will be reprised in Vandamm and his duplicitous sister [James Mason, Josephine Hutchinson] posing as the Townsends in *North by Northwest*). Early on in *Suspicion* (1941) – a film made in the U.S.A. but exclusively about English society – we have virginal Lina McLaidlaw (Joan Fontaine) and the roué Johnny Aysgarth (Cary Grant) in what promises to be a fun-filled, sporting union, before he begins to "borrow" her money.

What, then, does Hitchcock, by all accounts a very happily married man who had a warm sense of family unity (Taylor 79–81; 178), see generally of American married life, its role, its nature, its fragilities? Surely that marriage and love are neither synonymous nor coextensive, that the socially sanctioned and institutionalized bond on one hand and feelings of admiration and compatibility on the other need have little or nothing to do with one another. Love for Hitchcock is always a possibility, while marriage is always a fact. "Although he was a family man," wrote Frank Nugent, "his pictures would have been no help to a man wondering how to become one" (17).

He was and was not working in a vacuum. Other prominent filmmakers played up the family, too, but never with the archness that could actually question love as a guarantee of marital success. With *The Philadelphia Story* (1940), *The Clock* (1945), *Random Harvest* (1942), *The Quiet Man* (1950), and *Sabrina* (1954), George Cukor, Vincente Minnelli, Mervyn LeRoy, John Ford, and Billy Wilder – all big players in studio filmmaking – turned out stories in which the marriage was always to be admired and respected in the final turn. Even in film noir, where marriages were riddled with deceit and treachery – one particularly interesting example is the infected Nosseross marriage (between Francis L. Sullivan and Googie Withers) in Jules Dassin's *Night and the City* (1950) – some element of the dark melodious tone, some unyielding and plaintive riff, always wished and reached for the happy marriage that had failed to materialize, reached as though such a marriage could be grasped, but pathetically not here, not now. Wilder's *Double Indemnity* (1944) and Nicholas Ray's *In a Lonely Place* (1950) are good examples. Hitchcock's marriages do not typically ring with a hope of purity and transcendental happiness so fundamental to much American film, especially, as Stanley Cavell so brilliantly shows, after marriage has collapsed and been born again (*Pursuits*).

False Marriages: *Notorious, Psycho, The Birds*

Hitchcock was fascinated three times in his American phase with "substitute marriage." Examined from a psychoanalytical perspective this is a union that results in an Oedipal triumph, which is a reversal of the circumstances that occasion the "normal" union. If normally the boy's attraction to his mother is betrayed and blocked by her bond to his father – this by way of a conflict between the younger and the older male that results in the youth's splitting off from the family in a marital bond of his own – in these Hitchcock scenarios the father is only an empty placeholder, a figure whose contest with the younger man is just in the latter's imagination and memory since in the narrative itself he is a lacuna, an absence.

So it is that the bond between the boy and his mother, enriched by her immense residual value, and often perduring long past his own marriage to someone else, is played out through tricks of nostalgia, warped recollection, and loss. Son–mother love in the "Oedipal marriage" extends far beyond the playful and experimental form that we see with Hank and Jo McKenna in *The Man Who Knew Too Much* – "He's gonna be a fine doctor!" Ben chides Jo, as at the Mamounia by twilight she teaches the boy how to sing. In conventional socialization games, the older man signally self-diminishes and withdraws so that the child can have affectionate nourishment from the mother, but then intercedes with his own competitive (and domineering) demands when the child's attachment deepens. In the "Oedipal marriage" the father is not present to gamely withdraw and then seriously return; so that the child has the mother figure all to himself.

In *Strangers on a Train* we find Bruno Antony loathing and resenting his father and attaching himself to his mother, but that attachment does not succeed in an "Oedipal marriage" because the father, for all the negativity that the son can muster in regarding him, is notably *not* absent; he remains to control and shape the incommodious domestic environment. Bruno's mother seems scarcely aware of being there (I read her as terrified, and thus herself abstracted into an abstract expressionist daydream); and the dithering Mrs. Cunningham, something of a mother substitute, becomes the negation of a now unavailable maternal love object at the soirée where Bruno uses her neck to "demonstrate" tough love (through strangling) and comes close to killing her.

In *Notorious* (1946), however, a son–mother partnership festers like an unweeded garden. Here we are introduced to the strangely "wedded" pair of Alex Sebastian (Claude Rains) and his aging mama (Leopoldine Konstantin). While in the outside world it is apparent that Sebastian possesses and exercises poise, personal charm, power, chivalry, and allure – on the riding path, as Devlin prods Alicia's horse to bolt, he races after it in a flash and brings the horse to bay (just as the canny Devlin knew he would) – nevertheless once he is inside his home, where his mother's exceptionally sour, "wicked" presence (Krohn, *Work* 101) is dominant, he is reduced, even physically shrunken, and becomes nothing but her pawn and a shadow of himself.

One beautiful little scene shows the reduction plainly. Recently arrived home with her after their wedding, Alex walks into Alicia's bedroom to deliver the house keys that she has been requesting but that his mother, whose "overprotectiveness fosters his dependence and leads indirectly to the final confrontation" (Leff 181), has been holding back. Bergman stands in the foreground as Rains makes his entrance from the rear of the shot, and it is evident that on the floor between them, between the doorway and the camera, technicians have installed a little ramp. In the door frame he is tiny, a full head shorter than she is, but as he approaches he seems to grow; and then to diminish again as he goes back to his business away from the magnetic draw of his new wife. Hitchcock knows the principles of classical art: Vitruvius, Eco tells us, "distinguished between symmetry and eurhythmy": "the latter was the type of beauty that depends upon the requirements of vision. It was primarily a

The camera placement gives away the deep structure of relations in this scene from Notorious. *Alex Sebastian (Claude Rains, l.) is legally married to Alicia Huberman (Ingrid Bergman, l. rear) but the highlights on his cuffs, collar, and newspaper draw our eye to the (true) relationship he sustains with his mother (Leopoldine Konstantin), brightly gowned and pouring coffee from a gleamy pot that will rest on a starched napkin. The fourth socialite is the consulting scientist Dr. Anderson (Reinhold Schunzel). Courtesy Academy of Motion Picture Arts and Sciences.*

set of technical rules. ... At Rheims, statues on the spires have arms that are too short, backs that are too long, lowered shoulders, and short legs. The demands of objective proportion were subordinated to the demands of the eye" (65–6).[2]

---

[2] In this case, as Hitchcock told Truffaut, "we wanted to show them both coming from a distance, with the camera panning from him to Bergman. Well, we couldn't have any boxes out there on the floor, so what I did was to have a plank of wood gradually rising as he walked toward the camera" (172).

As to the mother/wife,[3] in her "creepily incestuous attachment" to her adored creation Alex (Hark 299), she distrusts Alicia as, apparently, she has distrusted every woman he has befriended. Eventually, to protect the espionage operation in which she is Sebastian's true consort she must take steps to murder Alicia by poison, thus at the same time destroying her son's marriage.[4] It is with only scorn that she regards this pathetic child, and so the strange union between the two is hardly either affectionate or becharmed, even if in scene after scene Alex is the very model of both filial and husbandly propriety, tact, and politesse. This is a solid Hollywood-style representation of the dutiful European son's enslavement to an aged, tradition-bound mother,[5] but in regarding its nuances from a very close – dangerously close – vantage Alicia Americanizes the display: seeing it by virtue of her American eyes – even given her traitor father's German nationality she is an Americanized European – we read it as a portrait of what is culturally local to us. This "Oedipal marriage" between Alex and his mother thus has American resonance, for Alicia and for a whole generation of viewers in a generation born in the United States. After his gala soirée, arranged at Alicia's request, Alex comes upon Alicia

---

[3] In Ben Hecht's script she was painted with some exaggeration, because Hitchcock ordered the character "toned down" (Leff 193).
[4] Krohn notes how in a version of the ending written by Clifford Odets (and not used in the film), Mrs. Sebastian finally destroys her son altogether, shooting him in the back of the head (*Work* 98). As to the poisoning effect, it was necessary that Ingrid Bergman's appearance, as photographed in black and white, should progressively appear to decline. "Most actresses in Hollywood use make-up to make them photograph better," read a studio press release. "Ingrid Bergman uses just the opposite technique. . . . In one part of RKO Radio's 'Notorious' . . . she wears quite a lot of make-up; but it's to make her look less attractive." As she is poisoned and becomes more and more ill, this is "indicated with more and more make-up" (American Pressbook).
[5] Borrowed just a little, perhaps, from Gregory Gaye and Maria Ouspenskaya's performances in William Wyler's *Dodsworth* (1936).

with Devlin in the wine cellar, and becomes even more suspicious of their relationship than ever before (suspicious in part because he knows he hasn't really been her husband). Now, activated by that negative feeling, he sneaks downstairs himself and discovers that his bottles have been tampered with – the secret uncovered!

Early in the morning, Alex confides the horror to his "spider woman" mother (Leff 181) as she lies in bed.[6] In the words of a synopsis culled for purposes of cost estimation, "His love [for Alicia] turns to hatred *as he tells his mother* he is married to an American agent" (Martel, my emphasis). He has a deep fear that his associates will discover that he has committed the unutterable *faux pas* of marrying an American spy, yet his deeper fear is that mama will cease approving of him, and in this, for all their stiff *gemutlichkeit*, Alex and his mother are as strictly American as audiences need them to be. We can note the "*awfully personal*" theme of the doting son sitting on his mother's lap, as it were (see Fischer, "Mama's" 76). The wise mother/wife – a figure modeled here on Lady Macbeth – knows that if they eliminate Alicia silently, no one will ever be in a position to suspect anything. "We are protected," says she to Alex snidely but sagaciously, "by the enormity of your stupidity."

In *Psycho*, a film about which one is obliged to write very dexterously if not to give away the very American surprise that renders it overwhelming, we have the story of a charming boy obsessively devoted to his mother. The love of "Mom" was epidemic in America of the 1940s and 1950s, as we see in Philip Wylie's *Generation of Vipers* and Erik H. Erickson's discursion upon "momism" in *Childhood and Society*. "I cannot think offhand," wrote Wylie, "of any

---

[6] "The detail is drawn from Hitchcock's own life," writes Spoto, "his long customs, during the years he lived in Leytonstone, of reporting to his mother while standing at the foot of her bed each evening" (306).

"We are protected by the enormity of your stupidity." Digital frame enlargement.

civilization except ours in which an entire division of men has been used, during wartime ... to spell out the word 'mom' on a drill field" (184, qtd. in Fischer, "Mama's" 80). And Erickson's analysis makes us wonder what flower, bordering the roads and filling the American countryside, was ever more charming or more impressive than mom, motherliness, motherhood, maternity, eternity? He writes of the centrality of "momism" in the psychosexual development of the American character, of a centralizing formulation around "Mom," which is to say, "a stereotyped caricature of existing contradictions which have emerged from intense, rapid, and as yet unintegrated changes in American history" (291):

> "Mom" is a woman in whose life cycle remnants of infantility join advanced senility to crowd out the middle range of mature

womanhood, which thus becomes self-absorbed and stagnant. In fact, she mistrusts her own feelings as a woman and mother. Even her overconcern does not provide trust, but lasting mistrust. But let it be said that this "Mom" – or better: any woman who reminds herself and others of the stereotype Mom – is not happy; she does not like herself; she is ridden by the anxiety that her life was a waste. She knows that her children do not genuinely love her, despite Mother's Day offerings. "Mom" is a victim, not a victor. (291)

Norman Bates (Anthony Perkins) is a paragon of American boyhood. He wants, most truly, only the noblest of achievements: to have mom for himself, to adore and reshape her in his own image forever. Norman, of course, "spells out 'mom'" in a unique way, since he is not the sort for drill fields; he protects her, keeps her safe from dangerous interactions with the general public, reveres her qualities, and more than anything esteems the version of himself that is defined through the maternal gaze and fiat. Since they live together in an old house upon a hill ("In Northern California ... that type of house is very common. They're either called 'California Gothic,' or, when they're particularly awful, they're called 'California gingerbread.' ... There is no question that both the house and the motel are authentic reproductions of the real thing" [Hitchcock, qtd. in Truffaut 269]), these two are, for all intents and purposes, married. They certainly embody together a marriage of personalities, a marriage of intentions, and a marriage of memories.[7] To a

---

[7] Jessie Royce Landis wanted the role of the mother badly, even before reading a script. "JUST READ OF YOUR NEW HUSH HUSH PICTURE WITH MOTHER PART FOR [HELEN] HAYES OR [JUDITH] ANDERSON HASTEN THE THOUGHT I DON'T HAVE TO BE FUNNY LOVE TO ALMA," she wired him (Landis to Hitchcock). Hitchcock replied a week later, "I can hardly see her dressed as the elegant Royce should be dressed, and I don't think you would want to make the trip just to be a silhouette for one day. Please stay in New York and be the real fashion silhouette that you are" (Hitchcock to Seitz).

Norman Bates (Anthony Perkins). Perkins's performance in Psycho *is one of the most indelible pieces of screen acting in American history. Twenty-eight when he did this work, and the son of actor Oswald Perkins, he had already done eleven films, including* Friendly Persuasion *(1956),* Desire under the Elms *(1958),* Green Mansions, *and* On the Beach *(both 1959). Digital frame enlargement.*

motel guest who has come for the night, Marion Crane (Janet Leigh), Norman admits that "a boy's best friend is his mother," thus not only invoking a kind of unresolved Oedipal configuration but also attesting to the fidelity of the bond he keeps with the woman upstairs. If Mrs. Bates ever had a legal husband, he is long gone. Norman is all she has; and she is Norman's altarpiece.

Two other aspects of the Bates "marriage" are worth mentioning. Mrs. Bates is fiercely possessive of Norman and brings an acid challenge to any woman who dares to entertain him. While Marion does not fare well as a guest at the Bates Motel, we can have the distinct impression that many girls have preceded her there, have received the same eager hospitality from the boy whose "marriage" has been stifling and disempowering him and have suffered, similarly, the old lady's interminable wrath. The link between

Norman and his mother, then, is conventional, even traditional, in that it precludes him from having what we might see as "extra-marital" relationships. Beyond this, Norman has developed a hobby as a taxidermist, and likes to entertain his guests in a parlor chocked full of stuffed birds. "Owls," Hitchcock told Truffaut, "belong to the night world; they are watchers, and this appeals to Perkins' masochism. He knows the birds and he knows that they're watching him all the time" (282).

Norman's life in relation to his mother thus partakes of the character of three-dimensional embodiment – he is healthy, sexually active, curious, energetic, polite, modest, and articulate – and at the same time reflects the more aestheticized concerns of the boy's hobby: perfection, simulation, denaturing, sculpture, and redemption. Given Norman's deep-seated interests in the fulsome expression of his own body and in deft artistry, in charming girls while at the same time guarding his reclusive mother, Mrs. Bates is the absolutely perfect mate for him, the love that transcends all love.

Hitchcock's other American men do not show more independence: Cary Grant – as Johnny Aysgarth, as Devlin, as John Robie, as Roger Thornhill – never has children, but is invariably accompanied by a mother or a mother figure (Lina, Alicia, Mrs. Stevens, Mrs. Thornhill). For Jimmy Stewart, the boys in *Rope* are children gone bad but the housekeeper Mrs. Wilson (Edith Evanson) understands him implicitly, comes from the same class background, treats him just a little like a son. In *Vertigo* Midge (Barbara Bel Geddes) is an explicit mother figure (when he falls from her ladder, she holds him in a pietà) although Madeleine, old enough (from a certain perspective) to have mothered him many times over, is finally unreal. The insurance company nurse Stella (Thelma Ritter) mothers him in *Rear Window*, and his greatest challenge is to show proper patriarchy in *The Man Who Knew Too Much*, to bring that family back to the Savoy and show off the wife and son together to the judgmental middle-class British types. Manny Balestrero is finally saved because his mother encourages him to pray. Bruno Antony is obsessed with his mother, and Guy Haines seems like a motherless child. In *Lifeboat*, Gus adopts even the self-interested Connie Porter (Tallulah Bankhead) as a mother. And in their mutual escapades of heroism, Huntley Haverstock and Michael Armstrong evince military strength and purposiveness in the name, and for the salvation, of a mother country.

Mitch Brenner in *The Birds* has a pesky mother. Having lost a dear husband yet served by a strapping, brilliant, charming, and urbane son, she has become a little fixated, at least a little definitive in her maternity. Given that with his mother, with Melanie, and even with his young sister Mitch is stand-offish and defensive, diffident and taciturn, could he fear women as well as adore them, and might Lydia be a reincarnation of Hera, of whom Philip Slater wrote so brilliantly that from love she could easily have devoured her son?

> *The Greek male's contempt for women was not only compatible with, but also indissolubly bound to, an intense fear of them, and to an underlying suspicion of male inferiority. . . . Customs such as the rule that a woman should not be older than her husband, or of higher social status, or more educated, or paid the same as a male for the same work, or be in a position of authority – betray an assumption that males are incapable of competing with females on an equal basis; the cards must first be stacked, the male given a handicap. (8)*

Lydia is at any rate distinctly loath to part with Mitch; "The male child," Slater continues, "was . . . of vital importance to the wife – her principal source of prestige and validation" (29). She is uneasy about the women he dates, uneasy to have him far from her when his protective strength can shield her from the (perhaps enduring) agonies of the birds.

As to Mitch, he is nothing if not dutiful, staying fiercely stalwart by his mother's side and only edging her a tiny step aside as, at the film's conclusion, he marches the family in funereal dirge from the veranda to the waiting, purring car. Yet Mitch is not free from self-consciousness. Slater notes that since the mother "alternately accepts [the son] as an idealized hero and rejects his masculine pretensions, one would expect him to develop an abnormal concern about how others view him, and to have an extremely unstable self-concept" (33). Note Mitch's self-modeling for public approval in The Tides, or with Melanie on the dunes at his sister's birthday party. As to Lydia's apparently impenetrable façade, Melanie is able to crack through it only when she makes plain that she, too, suffers; that she, too, has wounds that do not show.

But Mitch remains for us as an archetype of a new American narcissism, needing to solicit approval for the self, to show off style and accomplishments, to be superhuman in the face of adversity. He is an archetype of modern society, "a mechanism which more effectively harnesses the kind of energy that narcissism makes available. The addition of a more elaborate control system – that is, the invention of chronic guilt – was successful in separating narcissistic striving from the impulsive, heroic, quixotic, self-defeating gestures one usually associates with it" (Slater 451–2). The American scene is not inherently redemptive. "In place of the mirror she would hold up to herself," writes Modleski of the woman who damages the male ego, "patriarchy holds up a distorting mirror reflecting her as a defiled, mutilated, and guilty creature" (116). Hitchcock very frequently shows that patriarchal gesture in action.

Mitch Brenner has had girlfriends (Annie Hayworth is perhaps the most recent), but his mother Lydia hasn't approved of, got along with, or been able to give a blessing to any of them. While he carries out a law practice in San Francisco during the week, his weekends are committed to his relationship with Lydia in their comfortable little home by the bay. She is the power with whom he must clear his emotional investments, while they wash the dishes together and the "girl" Melanie is sitting demurely at the dining table. As with both *Notorious* and *Psycho*, the privacy of the transgressive marriage is broken when a stranger enters the scene unbidden – Alicia with the Sebastian household, Marion with the Bateses, and the playgirl Melanie with the Brenners. Melanie's desire is to pick Mitch up. She had her eye on him at the pet shop, and her purchase of a pair of lovebirds to bring as gift for his sister is mere pretense for a journey to his weekend retreat and an invasion of his "marriage" there. Since Mitch is very stimulated by Melanie, and at the same time loyal to his widowed mother, we find once again here the theme of the loving man trapped in two weddings at once (a profoundly American theme that in his *Fool for Love* [1984] Sam Shepard would invoke explicitly).

The resolution of *The Birds* offers a conventional development for Mitch's prospects: Melanie and Lydia are able to befriend one another, largely through Melanie's "deferential" (Paglia 64) demonstration of sympathy for the older woman who, having already lost the love of her life (the husband's picture resides in the living room as a central icon; and Paglia describes Lydia sitting beneath it as being "like a priestess at the shrine" [78]), now feels she is losing a son. "Lydia is at her most confessional, and Melanie, glancing at the baby pictures on the mantelpiece, is genuinely moved by Lydia's admission of her fears and lack of her late husband's natural rapport with children. Hitchcock slows the pace, recovering the rhythms of daily life, as a lull between storms" (64). Lydia, by turn, is able to sympathize with and care for the wildly injured Melanie – "Oh, poor thing!" – who has been pecked almost to death by a pack of gulls near the film's conclusion ("the gulls and crows come storming at Melanie like a great wind, in undulations of sound.... We hear only the percussive flapping of wings, with very few bird cries and no scream whatever from Melanie" [83]). Mitch must now protect the two women equally, while also shepherding his sister and her lovebirds.

On the surface, what is interesting about Mitch Brenner's attachment to his mother is only that it represents an obstacle to be negotiated by any woman who would have a serious life commitment from him. The Mitch–Lydia connection, or "marriage," thus empowers and challenges Melanie to a certain change of attitude, an opening, a settling into vulnerability and trust, and provides a setting for the characterological transformation in her that is the motor element of the film. But beyond this, the coupling of this son with this mother is important because it so clearly and strongly reflects Hitchcock's earlier concerns with Norman Bates and Alex Sebastian in their "castrating marriages" (see Wood, *Films* 378). Infused in these "marriages" is an attitude about filial devotion that transcends the ordinary. It is America's enduring fealty to mother Europe; it is the American gender riddle writ large in culture; it is unitary freedom disciplined and shaped, finally curtailed in responsibility and social growth. The character of Thorwald in *Rear Window* is at the end of his rope by the time we meet him, as though enslaved to an invalid maternity in diabolical wedlock. Mother – that is, the past – always remains fixed on the horizon. The boy's claims upon any other person's affections – that is, the future – are always to be balanced against mother's prior claims. The "marriage" of fidelities, devotions, and desires that binds mothers and sons is never annulled, never dissipated, never transcended. Every man taking a wife is thus taking a second wife, to his credit or to his peril.

Marriage on the Battlefield: *Mr. & Mrs. Smith*

Mr. & Mrs. Smith (1941) is described by Peter Bogdanovich on the DVD commentary track as a typical screwball comedy, largely because of the dominating presence within it of the star who defined the genre, Carole Lombard (Stanley Cavell marks "the question of the heroine's identity and an emphasis taken by the cinematic medium on the physical presence, that is, the photographic presence, of the real actress playing this part" [*Pursuits* 140]). Indeed, it was as a "friendly gesture" toward Lombard that Hitchcock agreed to do the picture (Truffaut 139).[8] The film is certainly structured as a carnival ride of ups and downs, tricks, maneuvers, masquerades, and pratfalls. Because of the intensely stylistic form – carefully choreographed thrusts and parries of interaction between Lombard and Robert Montgomery, elaborate set pieces (a jam-packed nightclub, a Lake Placid resort), the centrality of tonal modulation through the actors' pitter-patter elocution – viewers might be forgiven for taking this film as little more than comedy, for failing, that is, to see Hitchcock's astutely observing sociological eye turning its focus upon the modern American marriage as crumbling institution. Even if his admission to Truffaut were true, that he "really didn't

[8] On set, they had "a kidding relationship that kept spirits high," Hitchcock chalking lines for Lombard on an "idiot board" and Lombard assuming directorial roles for Hitchcock's cameo and "gleefully driving him through repeated takes" (McGilligan 277).

understand the type of people who were portrayed in the film" and therefore set himself only "to photograph the scenes as written" (139), what he shows is fully, unrelentingly, and uncompromisingly revealing about the American bourgeois marriage. From the beginning of the film until its charmingly nutty ending there is little hope for a honey-coated entente between Ann and David (Lombard, Montgomery), but the comedic form leads us to store a bounteous supply of hope and trust, as though the perfect union were never other than a dream and by our watching we might only imagine ushering these two suffering loners into some haven of wedded bliss. For example, taking advantage of a freedom offered him at RKO to do retakes, Krohn recounts, Hitchcock had a telling inspiration, "shot the day after he had filmed a conventional close-up of Lombard looking lovingly at Robert Montgomery over breakfast ... the image he substituted of their feet under the table, with Lombard's toes inserted comfortably into Montgomery's trouser cuffs" (*Work* 34).

The premise of the film is the inherent difficulty of men and women living in marriage together, a problem that would surely manifest itself in any cultural setting where differences between gender psychologies were exemplified and magnified but that is exacerbated in America because of the pulsing thrust toward futuristic optimism, the belief in happy endings, the idealism that grounds modernity's highly technologized and fast-paced pressures for success, movement, and giddy change. David and Ann have been fighting, as many times before, and now they haven't spoken to one another for three days. They have agreed to a rule, not to leave the bedroom in the morning before apologizing for the anger of the night before, and so have been encamped for days in a space that is looking more and more like a garbage dump. They fashion a truce, but over breakfast Ann raises a provocative question to which her husband gives entirely the wrong answer: "Would you marry me again if you had the chance?" She means, of course, "Do you love me? Do you *really* love me?" but he takes her at the letter of her word and says, politely and demurely, that no, he wouldn't. He means only to suggest that –

No matter. The deed is done. He has uttered, as in fairy tales, the curse.

Soon later, in his law office, David is interrupted by a weaselly little man (Charles Halton) who offers him the information that, due to a geographical rebounding of territory in Idaho, he and Ann are not actually, not legally, thus not irrevocably married. No problem; a simple ceremony will fix everything. But Hitchcock's sleight of hand now brings this decrepit little Mr. Deever to confess himself a boyhood friend of Ann's, who has known her all her life. Taxiing uptown, he stops at her home for a quick hello and to offer best regards from his sister. But he cannot hold back from gifting Ann with the same awkward information he's shared with David downtown. The effect of this is the suspense for which Hitchcock was famous: Ann *already* knows now what David knows, but David doesn't know that she knows. As he takes her out for an evening to the little hole-in-the-wall Italian restaurant where first they courted, now sadly sunk to the darker strata of social refinement, she is waiting for him to put the cards on the table but he doesn't do it. Finally she explodes at him but it is, of course, too late for redemption.

The rest of the film is a skittering helter-skelter of Ann's conniving with David's business partner Jeff (Gene Raymond) to pretend at a love affair and of David's attempts, futile but sincere, to win her back to his heart. One little set piece shows the heights to which Ann is prepared to go. She is on a date with Jeff and he has brought her to a midway where

In Mr. & Mrs. Smith *(RKO, 1941) David (Robert Montgomery) and Ann (Carole Lombard) are dining once again at the little restaurant where it all began. Little do they know – or acknowledge – that they are putting on a show. Courtesy Academy of Motion Picture Arts and Sciences.*

they strap themselves into the parachute ride. High up in the air, however – and we are treated to several aerial shots looking down to replicate the thrilling effect – they discover that the machinery has broken and they are trapped. Worse, a pelting rainstorm has started. Soon they are soaked to the skin and must retire to his apartment in shambles. He withdraws to don a dapper tuxedo (incongruously) while – in a bizarre premonition of a scene that will follow in *Vertigo* – she combs out her golden tresses by the fire. But then she proceeds to get him hopelessly drunk, and walks out while he is in a stupor.

What is striking about Ann and David's union in this film – it begins as a marriage, is converted into a non-marriage, and at film's end is on the verge of being converted into a marriage once again – is that romance is utterly absent from it. They do not fondle one another, stimulate one another gently, tickle one another's sensibilities, nourish one another, or swoon together but devote themselves instead to constant bickering, wrestling, and struggling through the cacophonous shambles that is modern city life. What makes them seem perfectly matched – what constitutes their "chemistry" – is exactly that neither can find contentment without challenging the other in an always expanding bout of ante-raising, this formula visually apotheosized by the finale moment in which, having strapped skis onto Ann's feet, David pushes his beloved back into a chair with her legs crossed in the air, so that she cannot stand up. This "comic irony at the end of *Mr. & Mrs. Smith*," suggests Lesley Brill, "devolves from the principals' rediscovery of their suitability and need for each other" (210). The American marriage here is a relentless, unending pugilism, a face-off between eternal competitors, the source of a constant electric current and unstopping movement. Lombard, especially, adds to this effect by changing her emotional attitude and facial expression several times per minute, never settling into a position, point of view, or commitment of feeling beyond the one we at first dimly and later more desperately suspect, that she cannot stop loving David no matter what happens. It is perhaps the sense that their competition *cannot* end that leaves the "somewhat cold comforts" Stanley Cavell finds in *Mr. & Mrs. Smith* as a remarriage comedy (*Pursuits* 233). Or perhaps it was because Cary Grant dropped out of the project, leaving the less expressive Robert Montgomery in his place (McGilligan, *Darkness* 276).

Ann and David may come back together, but these two will never be happy in the conventional post-Victorian sense typified by the stodgily married Hillcrists in *The Skin Game* or, at the utopian moment to come when Rose is fully healed, by the working-class Balestreros in *The Wrong Man* (1956). They are both too smart, too fast-thinking, too streamlined ciphers of modernity. Also, their attitudes toward one another, and thus toward their world, go on and off, simulating the action of a quick-break switch – harbinger of modernity – but also the action of cinema's flicker which, Nick Yablon tells us, could be conjured through the cinematographic trick of time-lapse. He notes that early actuality filmmakers found that "by inserting a predetermined time interval between frames, they could exaggerate the speed with which a crew constructed a building" and a by-product was "exacerbation of the already jerky (or flickering) movements of traffic and pedestrians entering the frame" (281). If as characters the flickering Ann and David were less interested in other people and more blindly focused on the quality of their own movement, this would have been an early action film: in action film (notably excepting the work of Preston Sturges, where people talk to one another as they race), as characters speed through situations, they pay only nodding respect to other characters, being obsessed with purpose, fulfillment, accomplishment, and speed. Here, however, the focus is on jockeying for an ideal position from which to dominate the reconstitution of the marriage. Neither partner has patience for the constraints of social form.

Mr. & Mrs. Smith came out the same year as Sturges's *The Lady Eve* (the films "share more than their year of release" [Brill 205]). In *Pursuits of Happiness*, Cavell discusses Sturges in a way that points also to Ann: "It is not news for men to try, as Thoreau puts it, to walk in the direction of their dreams, to join the thoughts of day and night, of the public and the private, to pursue happiness. ... What is news is the acknowledgment that a woman might attempt this direction" (65). Battle as she might, Ann never has anything in mind but a pursuit of happiness. It is only that she lives in a world where so much misdirection is suffered even by those who are no longer innocent, so much appetite is piqued and unfulfilled, that happiness becomes harder and harder to recognize. Does she agree with Freud that "the husband is almost always so to speak only a substitute, never the right man" (qtd. in Cavell 149)? Cavell suggests that in comedies of remarriage, as he calls them – in general, screwball comedies – the typical absence of children tends possibly to suggest that the protagonists want to achieve childhood again themselves: perhaps Ann wants to go back to that little town in Idaho, where Deever's sister was her playmate and in which she got married before the boundaries were moved. Whatever it is she wants to do, she wants David to do it with her, knowing, one feels, that "what they do together is less important than the fact that they do whatever it is together" (Cavell 113). Even an unending war could have the merit of bringing David together with her upon the battlefield. We can be thankful that it is a shifting and confounding battlefield, no close bounds, so that their togetherness there, even – and supremely – doing battle, can go on without the ugly blot of unilateral victory.

Thorwalds and Kentleys

Virginia Wright Wexman sees in *Rear Window* "a struggle for power in a romantic relationship based on a principle of companionship. ... This power struggle must be resolved before 'the couple' can be harmoniously constituted" (14). But we must go on to see that the resolution of power struggles requires mutual knowledge, understanding, and sympathy, that is, acceptance of difference, a profoundly American challenge given that the American scene in the 1950s was frequently inharmonious, even bitterly competitive as people sought to obtain the rewards advertising was convincing everyone they deserved: love, wealth, happiness, success, glamour. As much as Americans proclaimed the noble benefits of working together, they knew more deeply that the successful self might have to be built where someone else already stood.

During the year *Rear Window* was shot, Coronet Instructional films released an eleven-minute masterpiece called *Who Are the People of America?*:

> *The narrator declares that Americans are "a mixture of the people of the world" and that "much of that which is American is of the world." A montage showing spaghetti, baseball, and a jukebox demonstrates that "these are some of the things we share as Americans. For we have become Americans through the process of sharing."* ... *"Playing together, growing together, learning together. America is a land whose people shared what they knew." (Smith 227)*

At the same time a less optimistic educational film of the same length came from Centron Corporation for Young America Films, *Health: Your Posture*: "Adrelene, an attractive young girl, is at a party where she is not having a good time. The narrator explains that Adrelene 'usually sits all alone, slumped in her chair in the corner,' and that 'for some reason, she doesn't fit into the picture'" (156). Someone, it seems, always had to *not fit* into the picture in order that others could succeed in fitting, because in the end the "picture,"

American society with its bounteous rewards, attractive and alluring to everyone, and bigger than bigness itself, wasn't big enough.

"Mental hygiene films," writes Ken Smith, "never admitted to pushing conformity" (37), but they were accomplished nuggets of propaganda that could portray America as utopian while – as we see in *Rear Window* when the little dog is killed and no one in the courtyard gives a moment's notice – it was actually a society filled with strangeness, conflict, and social disharmony. Every grouping, every incorporation, implied a rejection or ostracism. It was never hard to typify, classify, limn, and diagnose the outsider who didn't "fit." He looked at the world askance, was too critical, too self-possessed.

Distinctively not "fitting into the picture" of *Rebecca*, in her own idiosyncratic way, is Mrs. Van Hopper (Florence

Florence Bates as Mrs. Van Hopper in Rebecca *(Selznick International, 1940). Joan Fontaine is at screen left. Digital frame enlargement.*

Bates). An American abroad – an American for whom America has become uncomfortable, and something of an overgrown Daisy Miller – she is busy languishing in Monte Carlo ("Monty" to her), sapping up cultural capital for use later back home (New York and Palm Springs) by insinuating herself into the company of the magnificently eligible bachelor, Maxim de Winter (Laurence Olivier). Utterly uninterested in this phantasy "marriage," however, de Winter has his eye on the little English girl who is working as Mrs. Van Hopper's paid companion (in what Alexander Doty calls a "quasi-parent/child relationship" [486]). Is de Winter's neglect of the old lady a sly comment on a more general tendency toward English isolationism and shy withdrawal from Americans and their affectedness? Mrs. Van Hopper is certainly, as Ina Rae Hark describes her, "a monstrous embodiment of everything an Englishman might find off-putting in Americans," since she "talks too loudly and too much, is over-familiar with acquaintances, pretends to be all-knowing when she is anything but, has a *nouveau-riche* sense of entitlement, and demonstrates a basic coarseness beneath her affected mid-Atlantic accent and expensive jewelry – epitomized by the close-up of her stubbing out a cigarette in a jar of cold cream" (289).[9]

---

[9] Bates, personally tested by Hitchcock, was "a plump, middle-aged former lawyer whose previous acting experience was limited to shows at the Pasadena Playhouse" (McGilligan 245). She and Fontaine were the only American actors in the cast (Spoto 226). Preview audiences, perhaps recognizing themselves in this flagrant American intruder into high-class French society, didn't like her. They thought she did too much "dry talking" and was too "out-spoken" (Summary). Bates was not the first choice for the role, the principal possibilities having been Lucile Watson, Laura Hope Crewes, Mary Boland, Cora Witherspoon, and the popular character actor Alice Brady (Selznick to O'Shea, Schuessler, and Hitchcock), who was available for a fee of $5,000 per week with four weeks guaranteed (Schuessler to Selznick).

Shy as a mouse, beautiful as alabaster, clearly bright and impressionable and a breath of fresh air, the girl (Joan Fontaine)[10] is exactly the true, blue English tonic Maxim needs to help him recuperate from the recent death of his wife, Rebecca. And luckily for his chances, the dowager is suddenly taken to bed: too much ice cream, too many chocolates? Certainly, too much getting her way from morning until night. Encouraged to take off and have fun, the girl accepts de Winter's company, gradually, as the days wear on, becoming as attached to him as he is to her.[11] The old lady, meanwhile, has bedsheets full of chocolate wrappers and no one to whom she can direct her verbose sermons about European culture and its inferiorities. She becomes resentful, then bitter, but before vituperativeness can blossom she is called back to America for a wedding and must suddenly plan for a hasty departure. It is de Winter who takes the liberty of "divorcing" her – "Hitchcock encouraged Laurence Olivier to play Max as a boor anyway, which is how du Maurier had described him" (Krohn,

---

[10] A competitive casting competition spread through Hollywood for this role. Beyond the "somewhat frantic" Vivien Leigh (Spoto 224n; see also Behlmer for letters between Hitchcock, Leigh [née Holman], and Olivier regarding this), and the finalists, who included (Fontaine's sister) Olivia de Havilland, Margaret Sullavan, and Anne Baxter, were twenty-seven other actors including Nova Pilbeam, Loretta Young, and Anita Louise (Spoto 224n).

[11] As David O. Selznick expected it to be – since the novel from which it had been taken had sold explosively around the world (see Behlmer) – *Rebecca* was immensely and immediately popular with audiences, bringing to New York's Radio City Music Hall, for example, "the biggest opening business in its [then eight-year] history." In its first five days there, March 28 through April 1, 1940, the picture "played to more than 150,000 admissions and turned away close to 75,000 additional prospective ticket-buyers" (*Rebecca* publicity material).

Work 31)[12] – and this quite as summarily as though she were nothing but a carcass: while sitting to breakfast he beckons the dowager to his chambers and announces commandingly that he intends to marry the young companion forthwith. Here, it is the "sickness" of the widow Van Hopper that motors the plot (she was clearly suffering from nothing more than ennui), since without it the girl would have had no time for escapades. Her bond to the girl – call it a marriage of convenience – and her febrile imagination of a bond to Maxim are mocked by the marriage Maxim plans for real, one that will inspire the action of the story, even as it throws a signal in the face of the judgmental American's own sorry circumstances.

Another bedridden harridan is the wife of Lars Thorwald in *Rear Window* (Irene Winston), reminiscent of Adrelene, that exemplar of bad "social posture." If the Thorwald marriage suffers because of her alienated withdrawal from it and from her culture,[13] that culture, the containing envelope, hardly disappears but persists in the surround, the jukebox

---

[12] A boor, perhaps, but a romantic one: "He belonged to a walled city of the fifteenth century, a city of narrow, cobbled streets, and thin spires, where the inhabitants wore pointed shoes and worsted hose. His face was arresting, sensitive, medieval in some strange inexplicable way, and I was reminded of a portrait seen in a gallery, I had forgotten where, of a certain Gentleman Unknown. Could one but rob him of his English tweeds, and put him in black, with lace at his throat and wrists, he would stare down at us in our new world from a long-distant past – a past where men walked cloaked at night and stood in the shadow of old doorways, a past of narrow stairways and dim dungeons, a past of whispers in the dark, of shimmering rapier blades, of silent, exquisite courtesy" (Du Maurier 18).
[13] She has been separated from her wedding ring, which Lisa finds in the apartment on her secret foray there. "The retrieval of the wedding ring appears to confirm Jeff's suspicion that Mrs. Thorwald must have been murdered" (Street 92).

forever playing, for instance, while Miss Torso "practices her suggestive dance routines" – in the modern style – "as she goes about her daily chores" (Modleski 74). Mirror reflections of the deeply idealistic Jeff and Lisa – because, as Hitchcock said, Jeff was "in a cast, while [Lisa] can move about freely. And on the other side there is a sick woman who's confined to her bed, while the husband comes and goes" (Truffaut 216) – the Thorwalds have an execrable marriage, so much so that the husband has chosen to terminate it through a murderous butchery (that, for Robin Wood, "represents, in an extreme and hideous form, the fulfillment of Jefferies' desire" [*Films* 104]).

If we need an accounting for Thorwald's revulsion, it is provided in some early scenes of the film where we can hear the wife nagging at him from her bed. While she may be suffering, there is no evidence that anything is afflicting her beyond a kind of neurasthenic self-indulgence, a "slumping" in bed while the world is at work. Slumping near Anna Thorwald, symbolically, is that purse of hers, which "connects Lisa to the victimized woman, as does [Lisa's own expensive] negligee [that tumbles out of her Mark Cross night case], since the invalid Mrs. Thorwald was always seen wearing a nightgown; but it also, importantly, connects her to the criminal, Lars Thorwald, and so is an overdetermined image like the images in the Freudian dreamwork" (Modleski 78).

Presumably this woman's attitude has been in place for a very long time, and Thorwald has given up on the thought of his marriage delivering any interpersonal benefits. Has the woman an insatiable craving for sex, an insatiable need for comfort, an incessant disfigurement from pain? Whatever it is, Thorwald can no longer bring himself to serve her – and servility, we can see and hear, is demanded and required of him constantly.

This broken man, who has failed to achieve the freestanding liberty and power of accomplishment that the American Dream promised and is compelled, like others, to "suffer fifty weeks of the year for the sake of a two-week vacation, when all you really desire is to be outdoors, with your shirt off. And always to have to get ahead of the next fella. . . . And still . . . that's how you build a future" (Miller 14), holds down a menial job as traveling salesman,[14] trudging around to make a few dollars that must be spent on servicing the needs of a heavy anchor who gives no thanks, offers no pleasure, receives no satisfaction. Other women in the film dimly reflect Mrs. Thorwald's agonized hungers and tribulations, but more tamely. Miss Lonelyhearts (Judith Evelyn) preys upon young men and tries to entrap them into romantic bonds they are not ready for (until film's end).[15] The young newlywed (Havis Davenport) begs her strapping young husband (Rand Harper) for incessant (sexual) attention; as long as he has stamina he is eager, so she is no torment, but even the stamina of a young man has its limits. The neighbor across the way from Jeff (Sara Berner), who sleeps on the fire escape with her timid husband (Frank Cady), shrieks at the entire population of the apartment complex when her dog is dead, demanding a social approbation and concern that in a modern culture full of busy strangers she is hardly likely to receive. A sculptor (Jesslyn Fax) has made "a female torso with a large hole where the heart should be. When someone stops and asks her the name of the sculpture, she says that it's called *Hunger*" (Brand 131).

---

[14] Arthur Miller's influential and award-winning *Death of a Salesman* had premiered on Broadway on February 10, 1949, and won the Pulitzer Prize and Tony Award that year. The setting directions could have been for *Rear Window*: "We see a solid vault of apartment houses around the small, fragile-seeming home. An air of the dream clings to the place, a dream rising out of reality" (Miller 5).

[15] Robin Wood rather kindly calls this "enacting romantic situations" (*Films* 102).

But unlike Anna Thorwald, all these people get on with their lives. All the neighbors in the courtyard resist falling prey to their own deficiencies. Only Anna is locked abed as an invalid. Only Anna is "invalidated." In this condition, she becomes a "dead weight" upon her husband (for some viewers, a reflection of what Jeff is afraid Lisa will be for him if he becomes legally attached to her). But is Anna's problem only personal? Hilary Land wrote in 1975 of the socioeconomic basis for an arrangement like this; while her address is to England the figures in America were largely the same:

> In the early censuses, the idea of the individual male wage earner supporting his family was unfamiliar. It was assumed that all members of the family followed the same occupation: parents and children contributed to a family wage. In 1851, by which time married women and children had begun to be excluded from factory work, it was still assumed (as it no longer is) that wives of farmers and men with small businesses were part of the working population. ... [By 1911], nearly half a million girls under fifteen were returned in the census as neither at school nor occupied, "doubtless due to the number engaged in domestic duties at home." Today, full-time housewives and mothers are defined as "economically inactive." (352–3)

The Thorwalds are living in a postwar economy characterized by redomestication of many women and redeployment of previously fighting men into the workforce. Thus, Anna Thorwald was like many postwar women who "had lowered their expectations, came to accept their domestic role as the center of their identity. Given the limited job and career opportunities available to them, it is understandable that many would have chosen to become homemakers and to invest that role with heightened importance" (Elaine Tyler

May 87). (Dr. Ernest Dichter of New York, an admirer of and consultant to "Betty Crocker," advised removing powdered eggs from General Mills cake mixes "in order to give the housewife a sense of making a creative contribution to the process" [Marling, *Seen* 213].) Mrs. Thorwald's confinement both diegetically represents and is intended by the filmmaker to nondiegetically reference a general condition of economic withdrawal for women, a state of affairs in which, confined by domesticity (in this case, the bed is Anna Thorwald's home-within-the-home) they are obstructed from access to useful jobs in the outside world. The maintenance of the up-to-date, meticulously clean home, indeed, is redefined socially as "useful work," but work – as so many feminist theorists have skillfully shown – so hidebound to woman's "natural" identity it need not be considered work at all (and thus need not be recompensed). In a time when consumer magazines were initiated to guide people through purchasing for the home, writes Sophie Leighton, "women were told by the press that they could 'have it all. From the 1930s, paid home help rapidly became outdated. . . . Women were told they could still combine being the perfect housewife with going out to work" (29).

Anna is "sick" because she cannot be social; she is simultaneously "anti-social" because she is sick. Thorwald himself, now experiencing the pain associated with the benefits of being male in his culture, must be heroic as the breadwinner and resents his docile wife. When he confronts Jeff at the end of the film, he is as vulnerable as our hero, but for different reasons.[16] Lost, unable to negotiate his cultural status,

---

[16] "When the killer comes into Stewart's room," commented Truffaut, "he says to him, 'What do you want of me?' And Stewart doesn't answer because, in fact, his actions are unjustified; they're motivated by sheer curiosity." Hitchcock replied, "That's right, and he deserves what's happening to him!" (Truffaut 219).

terrified at the consequences of what he has done, Thorwald is one of the most pitiable villains in all of Hitchcock. And in that nocturnal scene when the dog owner calls out for sympathy, and Lisa and Jeff notice that only Thorwald, of all the tenants around, has failed to come to his window but lingers in the darkness of his cavernous apartment slowly smoking, he is again set apart, withdrawn, pulled away into his own private experience: a frequent reading of the moment is that Thorwald is arrogant, supercilious, above concern, but

Most of the cast from Rope. *From left, James Stewart as Rupert, Farley Granger as Phillip at the piano playing Poulenc (he never plays anything but Poulenc), Constance Collier as Mrs. Atwater, Joan Chandler as Janet, Cedric Hardwicke as Mr. Kentley, John Dall as Brandon, Douglas Dick as Kenneth. David Kentley is front and center, inside the chest covered over by the dinner. Courtesy Academy of Motion Picture Arts and Sciences.*

it is just as likely that he shrinks back with an abject feeling of terror and exclusion.

In *Rope* (1948), we come upon a strange little presentiment of Thorwald and his wife. Brandon and Phillip have strangled David Kentley and hidden his corpse in the tea chest around which they are choreographing their soirée.[17] The boy's father has arrived escorting his sister visiting from England and the boy's fiancée Janet (Joan Chandler) and chum Kenneth (Douglas Dick). "Is David here?" asks Mr. Kentley distractedly. "I . . . expected him to . . . come with you," demurs Brandon, looking away (and toward the camera). "He called," says Mr. Kentley, "and said that he'd meet us here." Janet now takes an interest. "Where did he call from?" As they sit, the old man recollects, "Oh, our maid spoke to him. He was at the club. Studying for his examinations. In tennis." Wearing a perfect mask of solicitousness, Janet now wonders, "How is Mrs. Kentley?" the ruffles on her scarlet gown arching up perkily at the shoulders and a tiny white lace band encircling her neck affording the look of pristine genuineness and concern, as though she is a Victorian girl dutifully performing respect for her elders (in this case, her would-be mother-in-law).

---

[17] "As one of your patrons," wrote a Staten Island viewer to Warner Bros., "I wish to state that your film 'ROPE' is about the most disgusting and disgraceful picture I have ever seen" (Walker to Warner Bros.). On January 2, 1949, the Grand Rapids Better Films Council reported that on a written ballot taken after a showing of *Rope*, "There were 45 votes cast, the result of which was that 44 voted the picture undesirable and should not be shown" (Council to Morris). There were problems as well in Seattle, Atlanta, Memphis, Birmingham, Hammond (Indiana), and "many other points which are creeping up every day" (Kalmenson to Trilling). Filmgoers in Zurich didn't like it, either: "Three-quarters of this picture with its endless talk about the superior or inferior human being, and the murder which two students commit on one of their fellow students (as crime for crime's sake) is so brutal that it almost makes your heart stop beating" (qtd. from *Weltwoche* in Westreich to Keyser).

Mr. Kentley looks down a little. "As usual. It's a cold this time. I hope David arrives soon. She wants him to call her."

Janet has looked away. "David's her only child, Mr. Kentley."

"He's my only child, too. But I'm willing to let him grow up."

In this tiny exchange, the painful irony inherent in Kentley's unknowingly hopeless comment about his son growing up is so pungent it virtually erases from our consciousness the piquant little clues the man has left about his wife. The absent – the frequently absent – Mrs. Kentley has a cold, but not really. She is a woman who stays away from social encounters, possibly (probably) in bed and claiming one ailment after another. It's a cold *this time*: she has previously claimed other afflictions in order to escape situations like this one. She is always – we can tell by the look of sighing resignation on Kentley as he gives his information – incapacitated, always unavailable, always withdrawn and degenerating. He had not hoped for such a marriage, but it has become his lot. (As she is not enslaving him with her withdrawal, he feels no need to kill her. Or does he?)

From an altogether different class than Lars Thorwald, Kentley is nevertheless suffering through the same debilitations of masculinity produced in the same relentless, patriarchal culture that relegates women to the sidelines, causes them to bury a vital part of themselves, and in doing this jeopardizes – by overpressuring – men as well:

> *What need, what part of themselves, could so many women today be repressing? In this age after Freud, sex is immediately suspect. But this new stirring in women does not seem to be sex; it is, in fact, much harder for women to talk about than sex. Could there be another need, a part of themselves they have buried as deeply as the Victorian women buried sex? (Friedan 80)*

In such a society, Judith Walkowitz informs us that Emma Brooke had written as far back as 1886, "men's labors gained a certain 'prestige,' while women's work was held in 'contempt.' . . . The nearer any industry partakes of 'femininity,' of 'life-nourishing quality,' the less it is remunerated. Motherhood itself 'remains still unrecognized and still unpaid'" (155–6). David Kentley's mother has "chosen" – or been chosen – to dote upon her son. If she will suffer soon enough when it becomes known that he is dead, the point is not this unopened bud of torment but the obsessive condition of her present doting: she is perpetually "abed" with the infant upon her breast: first he was a warm reality; now he is to be a warmer memory. The father, who has in effect placed her there (through his privileges), makes bold to complain.

Hitchcock does not offer a direct portrait of either Mrs. Thorwald or Mrs. Kentley. With the former, we must peer from a distance, catching only part of a phrase of what she says. The latter is never presented on camera. And yet even this absence of imagery speaks clearly to the "erased" status the women are forced to occupy. It is likely that they are, as Margaret Sanger wrote once to a friend, "poor, pale-faced, wretched wives. The men beat them. They cringe before their blows" (qtd. in Halberstam 284).[18] Elaine Showalter has written about the link between female malady and a trend dominating in 1940s and 1950s America, psychiatric modernism. What became rationalized by psychiatry as "schizophrenia," a condition rarely treated by psychoanalysis – and characterized, as Emil Kraepelin had stated in 1896, by "a

---

[18] In reply to those who would object that Mr. Kentley hardly looks the type to beat his wife, we might conjecture that there are many kinds of beating, some of which, institutionalized sufficiently, thoroughly fail to appear on the interpersonal stage.

peculiar and fundamental want of any *strong feeling of the impressions of life*" (qtd. in Showalter 203) – if often difficult to see and diagnose, was still broadly invoked to explain salient peculiarities in female social response. As a diagnosis, indeed, it "offers a remarkable example of the cultural conflation of femininity and insanity," writes Showalter (204); but, further, scholars and critics have recognized how very "perfect" schizophrenia was as a "literary metaphor for the female condition, expressive of women's lack of confidence, dependency on external, often masculine, definitions of the self, split between the body as sexual object and the mind as subject, and vulnerability to conflicting social messages about femininity and maturity" (213).

And when we consider that in *Notorious* the nefarious Mrs. Sebastian has about her a curious air of masculinity[19] – her posture, her clipped speech, her firm gaze, her tightly bound hair, her dictatorship – and think again of her project of slowly poisoning the flamboyantly feminine Alicia, it becomes clear that this beautiful American victim, struck into livid silence in her bed, unable to move about freely or even to articulate her symptoms, was a perfect object for murderous construction. Who could have expected of a kept woman anything but this exquisitely symptomatic passivity, this languid surrender of power? The old lady knows she can get away with murder because the ailing woman is already, and always, a victim, exactly what the world will expect to find upstairs in that over-padded bedroom. Indeed, when Devlin sneaks in to save her, his passions and empathy aroused to the full, there is not a moment in which he

---

[19] Ethel Barrymore having rejected it, "the role of the spidery, tyrannical Nazi matron" was left uncast until "the distinguished German actor-director Reinhold Schunzel" (already cast in the picture) recommended Leopoldine Konstantin, "a stronger, older presence" (Spoto 302).

expresses surprise or disorientation: Alicia is here now, as in some way she must always have been for him, a bedridden victim. Without her, Alex, his questionable mother, and his evil friends will be free to live what J. B. Priestley called "a wholly masculine way of life uncomplicated by Woman" (qtd. in Showalter 171).

Interlude: Jessie Royce Landis

Jessie Royce Landis was Hitchcock's quintessential "good mother." She was born in 1904 and by the time she was twenty-two she was onstage at the Booth Theater, New York, in *The Honor of the Family*. Thirty-two stage productions would follow on Broadway, including *Richard III* with José Ferrer, *The Winter's Tale* with Henry Daniell, and the abortive *Roar Like a Dove* with Charles Ruggles and Betsy Palmer. In film, she made *Goodbye Again* (1961) for Anatole Litvak, playing Anthony Perkins's mother; *Airport* (1970) for George Seaton; *Boys' Night Out* (1962) for Michael Gordon, as James Garner's mother; *My Man Godfrey* (1957) for Henry Koster, as June Allyson's mother; and *My Foolish Heart* (1949) for Mark Robson, as well as numerous others. Yet she was never more iconic onscreen, never more endearing, and never more unforgettable than in *To Catch a Thief* and *North by Northwest*, where she "mothered" Grace Kelly and Cary Grant, respectively.

In *Thief*, she may as well have been John Robie's (Grant) mother, since she would soon be his mother-in-law. It may as well be said that Landis (Royce, as she liked to call herself) was never anything for Hitchcock but Cary Grant's secret wife, a mother-pal one could never truly believe had given birth to him but his truest, staidest support against the crazy vicissitudes of life.

Grant was in fact eleven months her senior, but the crazy filial bond he enacted with Landis in these two films – scatterbrained and hopelessly maladept in *North by Northwest*; suave and lovably conniving in *To Catch a Thief* – became one of the centerpieces of Hitchcock's characterization. For Roger Thornhill, Landis was an East Coast matron of high distinction, wit, and impeccable savvy. For Francie Stevens she becomes coldly matter-of-fact, offering a form of advice

Jessie Royce Landis (1896–1972), at top as Mrs. Stevens in To Catch a Thief *(Paramount, 1955) and below as Mrs. Thornhill in* North by Northwest *(MGM, 1959). Digital frame enlargements.*

on courtship that is bluntly visual and blatantly direct: Robie has presented himself and is, clearly for both Mrs. Stevens and us, the epitome of gentlemen, a perfect catch. And Francie is getting older minute by minute. Ending a scene, the old lady prods the end of her cigarette into a fried egg, as though to say, "Get down to business, girl; you don't have forever." Desperate for the role of Mrs. Thornhill in *North by Northwest*, she cabled William Barns considerably in advance of production, "Tell Hitchcock will not be difficult if he gives me scene with fried egg" (Telegram to Barns, August 6, 1958). In fact, she was ninth on a list of nine for this role, behind Marion Lorne, Hermione Gingold, Ethel Barrymore, Billie Burke, and others.

These two Landis characters – they are versions of one another – are both rich and independent. Their husbands have gone – died, left: it is immaterial, since only Cary Grant will suffice as a true husband for either. They have the power to move around, the power to make decisions, and opinions about everything, but especially "young" men. That there are no traces of romantic attachment between Grant's characters and Landis's enhances rather than detracts from the "marital" bond they enjoy. Free to fritter his boyish energies on Grace Kelly and Eva Marie Saint, John/Roger can bring a serious down-to-earth stability back home to "mama," his best – that is to say, his most deeply wedded – friend.

Sons Lost and Found: *The Man Who Knew Too Much* and *Family Plot*

Jeffrey Weinstock points to "the general importance of phantoms and haunting to the constitution of the 'American imagination'" (7). Spiritualism had been a presence in American society since roughly the time of its founding, the late eighteenth century (English Shakers arrived in 1775). By the early 1840s, Andrew Jackson Davis was spreading the spiritualist word, infused with the passion to communicate across the boundary of life and death with those who had gone before and thus implying in his teachings the present coexistence of the afterworld with our own, on a different "level" but one reachable by specialized, sensitive mediums through séances and other practices. Central to spiritualist practice was a certain powerful territory, in which resided that-which-was-not-here-now, or, imagined on a more mundane and interpersonal level, those aspects of the other world not practically available to the senses yet firmly committed to in belief. Marriage, for example, could be considered a platform on which communications could be made outside the perimeter of common speech, everyday discourse, and pragmatic understanding, especially when a partner had died. Just as in séances discourse with the dead was possible through the continuation of fully credulous love, so in quotidian love relationships there existed the preconditions for a secret dialogue, aesthetic and spiritual, unbounded and profound, that could bind adherents together in denial of circumstance and history.

Writing on marriage as a type of secret social relation, Georg Simmel begins by noting how contemporary marriage differs from many historical antecedents –

> In earlier cultures particularly, marriage is not an erotic but, in principle, only a social and economic institution. The satisfaction of the desire for love is only accidentally connected with it; it is contracted . . . not only on the basis of individual attraction, but on the ground of family connections, working conditions, and descendants. In this respect, the Greeks achieved a particularly clear differentiation – according to Demosthenes: "We have hetaerae for pleasure; concubines for our daily needs; and wives to

give us legitimate children and take care of the interior of the house." In such a mechanical relationship, the psychic center is obviously put out of function. . . . There probably exists in it neither the need for any intimate, reciprocal self-revelation, nor the possibility of it. (Sociology 327)

– and proceeds to a consideration of a man's need to deposit with someone else a package of "hopes, idealizations, hidden beauties, attractions of which not even *he* is conscious." Man makes this deposit, Simmel suggests, in "the indistinct horizon of his personality, the interstitial realm, in which faith replaces knowledge." Further, "Portions even of the persons closest to us must be offered us in the form of indistinctness and unclarity, in order for their attractiveness to keep on the same high level" (329). The spirit of marriage, in other words, must not be reduced or vitiated through confinement to, or positioning within the merely conventional strictures of domesticity. As a principal character in *Family Plot* asserts, "A spirit is never at home."

If spiritualism could be enlightening and enchanting, it could also be fraudulent and performative, a matter of trickery, gulling, and exploitation. Sheri Weinstein recounts the 1848 ventriloquism of the Fox sisters, Katie and Margaret, who produced rappings (a "spiritual telegraph") using their fingers until they were investigated by the University of Buffalo medical school. While the public "remained fascinated," writes Weinstein, and Kate went on an English tour, Margaret "eventually denounced spiritualists and blamed the popular spiritualist movement for her sister's alcoholism," before making an appearance "to expose her and Kate's fraudulence" at the Boston Music Hall in 1888 (124–5). The spiritualist movement of the nineteenth century, Weinstein suggests, "was part and parcel of particularly scientific and empiricist discourses," since spiritualists, living in "an extraordinarily scientific age," still "viewed empiricism as an insufficient method of understanding the relationship between vision and experience" (126).

The chasm between sensing (seeing) and happening, a central charge to fascination, scholarship, and speculation in the modern era and one that repeatedly tickled Hitchcock, becomes the narrative center of *Family Plot*, his final film and a veritably Mozartean opera of interwoven passions, confusions, dedications, and adventures framed in terms of practical exploitation, collusive fabrication, and, ultimately, the serendipitous miracle of happenstance success.

The aging Julia Rainbird (Cathleen Nesbitt), guilty over having forced her sister to abandon him as an infant, is now searching for the Absent Presence who is her hidden nephew, in order to give him a massive inheritance. For aid in this hunt she approaches the effervescent and eccentric spiritualist medium Blanche Tyler (Barbara Harris), who sets her earnest boyfriend, actor George Lumley (Bruce Dern), to the task of gumshoeing. There is a second plot. A nefarious jeweler, Arthur Adamson (William Devane), is involved with his girlfriend, Fran (Karen Black), in a series of elite kidnappings, one of which has produced as ransom an enormous diamond while the second – heisting the Bishop of St. Anselm's – will victimize the Catholic Church itself. For their part, Blanche and George are on the trail of a living ghost, since the Rainbird child might be anyone, anywhere. But Arthur and Fran are devoted to the earthbound rewards of wealth and luxury, and operate together as a smoothly coordinated team, "moving as one, everything together, nothing held back," as Arthur very grinningly puts it: in their townhouse, they have outfitted a padded cell in the basement, tastefully decorated and furnished rather like a modest hotel room, thus itself a recursive miniature of the high-style residence they occupy; its doorway, elegantly camouflaged in a wall of false red bricks, contains an intercom system and air conditioning and lighting controls for the chamber.

The Blanche/George and Arthur/Fran plots begin to intertwine as George discovers in the country outside of town a certain mechanic named Joseph Maloney (Ed Lauter), who has some indeterminate connection to Eddie Shoebridge, adopted son of the man who was the closest friend to the former chauffeur of the Rainbird family and now ostensibly dead, along with his dear wife, from a 1950 fire. Eddie, it turns out, might have set that fire himself; and also might not really be dead. When Maloney turns up unannounced one afternoon at Adamson's posh jewelry store, we discern that indeed Adamson is Eddie reincarnated, a thoroughgoingly amoral type who once did plot the murders of his foster parents with Maloney's help. Meanwhile, in another séance with Julia Rainbird, Blanche learns that the bishop of St. Anselm's, formerly a parson, had sworn to the Rainbird chauffeur on the man's deathbed that he would always know where the Rainbird child was. George goes to the cathedral to meet with the bishop, arriving, however, just in time to witness the kidnapping that Arthur and Fran are carrying out[20] (the entire sequence between Arthur/Eddie and the bishop who might identify him is carried out while the bishop is either drugged or unable to see Arthur).

After Maloney tries and fails to murder Blanche and George, on Adamson's instructions, and dies himself in a brutal car crash, George discovers from the man's wife that Adamson is Eddie Shoebridge. He and Blanche set out to find the man in the city. Blanche locates his house, encounters him there, but also sees the bishop in Adamson's town

---

[20] The sequence was shot on location at San Francisco's Grace Cathedral (Wehmeyer to Rogers).

car. Quickly he drugs her, puts her in the cell, and proceeds to deliver the bishop in exchange for yet another sumptuous diamond. But George has followed Blanche, sneaks into the Adamson house, and manages to save her. In the finale, as Arthur and Fran try to move the "sedated" Blanche from the cell, she suddenly springs awake, rushes out calling for "George, George, George!!!" and the two innocents slam the cell door shut upon the kidnappers (Hansel and Gretel).[21]

The two will get the police reward for finding the kidnappers but how nice it would be, muses George, if they could also find the diamonds. Blanche goes into one of her trances and, as John Williams's curtain music slowly creeps up, meanders into the foyer of the house, up the stairs, until she can point in her spiritualist dream at the chandelier where a diamond is hidden. Ecstatic, George raves, "You really *are* psychic!" but when he goes to telephone the police Blanche, staring directly into Hitchcock's camera, gives us a knowing wink.

That wink (unscripted):[22] like everything in a bounded relationship between a secret pair, it cuts two ways at once. The wink is behind George's back. As he has been admonishing her throughout, she's about as psychic as a piece of salami (a cute phallic reference, one of his many): she heard, somehow, from Arthur and Fran in conversation, where the diamond is; or else she's just as smart as Arthur/Eddie, and figures easily the most obvious hiding place – as Arthur says,

---

[21] "Hitchcock didn't even give the Trader and his wife a reaction shot after Blanche and Lumley slam the door on them in the basement" (McGilligan 728).
[22] According to Krohn. "He loves the reality of the off-the-wall behavior of myself, or Blackie or Barbara Harris, because it's been a while since he had that in one of his movies – the unpredictability," said Bruce Dern (Krohn, *Work* 274).

right in the open where everyone can see (a recipe, if we think about it, for all of Blanche's chicanery as a "spiritual connection"). Or else: the wink is between Blanche and Hitchcock, since thanks to his power as medium – one that surely surpasses the artifice called "Henry" that she uses in her own constructions – she really *can* see what isn't given to the eyes. Through Hitchcock, she has, and always has had, access to a domain beyond this story, her fabrications notwithstanding. In another explicit reference to the extradiegetic world, George points out to Blanche in his taxi at one point that being an actor, not a taxi driver, he doesn't have to drive well; but even actors pretending to be taxi drivers sometimes do drive like taxi drivers – Bruce Dern is perfect evidence. In the same way, even an actor pretending to be a spiritualist might have alarming powers, powers she doesn't always trouble to use but that are there at the ready anyway (since the filmmaker and his process has gifted them to her).[23]

While *Family Plot* – a plot about a family; a story revolving around the Shoebridge gravesite and ultimately the Rainbird crypt and thus pointed toward one or another family plot – is ostensibly a treasure hunt, with Blanche trying to earn ten thousand dollars from Julia Rainbird for finding the heir and then trying to offer Adamson/Shoebridge Julia's millions once she has succeeded, what actually structures the film is a collection of marriages. Blanche and George have a marriage of true minds, not a legal one. He finds her spiritualist

---

[23] The final shot was disputed between Hitchcock, who wrote it, and the screenwriter Ernest Lehman, to whom he showed his plan. Lehman's objection was that "the medium is shown throughout as a complete fake, so to suggest at the last that maybe she has a touch of psychic power is disturbingly inconsistent," but in the end, "Hitchcock couldn't be stopped from winking at the audience" (McGilligan 728–9).

"performance" taxing but goes along with it as a colleague actor, often praising her for an expert turn. While they chew at one another, it is evident there is little between them beside genuine affection and concern, in short, friendship. George in fact speaks cooingly about "plotting strategy" while Blanche is rubbing her "beautiful" behind against his crotch, providing us with yet another meaning of the film's title, since producing children, rejecting children, adopting children, hiding children, and marshaling children are the consistent motifs – family plots – to which we return in scene after scene. Stimulating George, indeed, Blanche may be hatching a family plot of her own. The secret of this marriage inheres in Blanche's pretended spiritualism and George's willingness to abet it, thus in a performative secret (which is revealed and hidden alternately in all the sequences of her communications with the Beyond).

As for Arthur and Fran, they have a marriage of pure convenience, also connected with performance. Eddie is working in disguise as the upscale jeweler Arthur, so Arthur is entirely fake; Fran disguises herself for the kidnappings, but we never have opportunity to discover whether the person she seems to be out of costume mightn't also be a disguise. "Will you do what I tell you!" he barks at her, when she chafes at the prospect of harming Blanche, thus revealing that the deep structure of this union is hierarchical, virtually military. Arthur's (openly sexual) fantasy of them moving together and acting as one is ironically fulfilled at film's end when as a single gesticulating organism they are locked, as one, into their own (soundproof) trap. Hitchcock makes the climactic shot from close enough to the door aperture that the swinging false-brick closure moves into view from off-camera right, and very swiftly. In a sudden flash, therefore, we are staring at the flat brick wall, nondescript, pink, inviting, and as tidy as any suburban resident could wish for, with the heroic George and Blanche leaning ecstatically upon it.

Maloney and his wife (Katherine Helmond) peer anxiously out of the window of their gas station at George parked to surveil them outside.[24] He is burly, prematurely balding, uneducated, plain-speaking. She is witheringly modest and self-negating, shrinking from everyone and anything. At her husband's funeral,[25] as she minces away from the grave along the labyrinthine pathways in an attempt to avoid George, who is following a matching path to catch up with her, she is sternly dressed and fully covered, like a fundamentalist or indeed an advocate of spiritualism or Shaker Christianity. What she looks like, rather precisely, are the churchgoers at Ambrose Chapel in *The Man Who Knew Too Much*. She and Maloney have also built a marriage upon a secret, in this case who Eddie Shoebridge became and where he can be found.

The principal marriage of *Family Plot*, however, is one that never occurred, a "marriage" that made a plot, which is to say, a scandal. Julia Rainbird's sister Harriet, whom we meet only as personified through Blanche's faux vocalizations, had her child out of wedlock and was forced by Julia – who never married – to give him away. That child was raised by the Rainbird chauffeur, Shoebridge, and his wife under the name "Eddie." In a culminating irony, this story implies that if Eddie had been born in a legitimate marriage nothing of

---

[24] Shot at a vacant station in San Fernando, California (Wehmeyer to Walk).
[25] Shot at the Sierre Madre Cemetery, 422 E. Sierra Madre Blvd., Sierra Madre (Wehmeyer to Simpson). Hitchcock had been briefed while the film was being scripted as to the essential simplicity and arbitrariness of the typical Mormon funeral, and had been recommended possible graveside readings from the Book of Mormon (including from 2 Nephi, Mosiah, and Alma) (Lee to Robertson).

what we see would have come to pass. Already an inheritor, he would hardly have needed to turn to jewel thievery for his wealth. And legitimate, he would not have had to come in contact, from his earliest days, with the church as a controlling agency. The bishop he kidnaps is a man he secretly loathes – this secret even Fran does not comprehend – just as much as he denigrates the churchgoers with their too proper behavior, who flock to the cathedral but stand in silence while their bishop is kidnapped and spirited away before their eyes. The bishop is spirited away by Arthur and Fran; Arthur as Eddie was spirited away through the agency of Julia; Blanche is "spirited" away in everything she does, flighty, fanciful, desperate, both connected to and disconnected from the everyday.

Aging and ailing, Hitchcock here finally made a film – with the help of screenwriter Ernest Lehman – that openly revealed a secret to which he had become privy in his long American sojourn: that in and out of California there is a lot of "spiriting." Mostly in. "No single aspect of Southern California has attracted more attention than its fabled addiction to cults and cultists," wrote Carey McWilliams in his important book on the area (249). McWilliams moved to an explanation: "This is because its winters are mild, thus luring the pale people of thought to its sunny gates, within which man can give himself over to meditation without being compelled to interrupt himself in that interesting occupation to put on his overcoat or keep the fire going" (249–50). Hitchcock's screen is repeatedly filled here with sere mountain scenery, dried palms, resistant and dried out personalities, twisting memories, bizarre performances, charming but idiosyncratic situations, flamboyant desires, incalculable wealth, and a kind of perverse and entrenched religiosity. This is the California of heretics and visionaries, of rich men who fancy themselves kings and seekers who experiment with methods of transcending the everyday and escaping into the "memorable" and "rewarding."[26] "'I am told,' said Mrs. Charles Steward Daggett in 1895, 'that the millennium has already begun in Pasadena, and that even now there are more sanctified cranks to the acre than in any other town in America'" (249).[27]

Then, too, Hitchcock had become intensely reflective and self-referential, in a way that is deeply satisfying for the admirer who cherishes moments of recognition and reprise. Jabbed by Adamson's needle in his garage, Blanche's white blouse is stained with vivid red blood, an exact replica of Marnie's blouse when Miss Clabon's red ink spills on it to her consternation: while Marnie went hysterical for a moment, Blanche merely collapses in a heap. When George goes tiptoeing around the Adamson house in his search for Blanche, he removes his shoes so that he can move in silence (even though the place is broadloomed); he is reflecting Marnie, who pockets her shoes in order to sneak past Rita the cleaning woman after pilfering from the safe at Rutlands: one of the shoes drops and resounds when it hits the floor, but Rita isn't fazed; she's deaf. The attempted murder of

---

[26] Cathleen Nesbitt wrote to Hitchcock, "I cannot get away from L.A. without thanking you for – to quote our script – a 'most memorable *and* rewarding week.' I was, before I arrived blessing my lucky star for the luck of having you think of me for the part – but I didn't know I'd have the pleasure of listening to your conversation so long. No doubt many have written of your humour and expert's knowledge of all civilized things from food and wine to literature and pictures (both 'moving' and on canvas); but I was vastly impressed by your fantastic *memory* – from the memory of a dinner to the speech of a shop steward! I do believe that memory is the secret of good talk. Yours is like Asquith's and Haddon Chambers's (a playwright of I suspect *before* your day) who both had the same Total Recall" (Nesbitt to Hitchcock). Ed Lauter, also, was touched: "It was a real honor to appear in your film. I have never written to a director in this fashion but in your case I just had to" (Lauter to Hitchcock).

[27] For the film, the Julia Rainbird mansion was shot in Pasadena.

Blanche and George is by way of Maloney's having tampered with both the accelerator mechanism and the brake system of Blanche's car. The two are driving away from Abe and Mabel's mountain café (one of the truly perfect set renditions accomplished for Hitchcock through many films from *Rear Window* onward by Henry Bumstead) where they had hoped for a rendezvous with Maloney to get some information about Shoebridge. Now the car begins to careen down the winding mountain road, faster and faster, with oncoming traffic swiftly dodging away and Blanche trying to climb on top of George as though he were a life raft. "Hitchcock told Harris to go ahead and step on Dern's face. 'It's a twisted mouth that we are playing for'" (McGilligan, *Darkness* 728). This scene becomes an homage to the scene in Lehman's other film with Hitchcock, *North by Northwest*, where Roger careens down a Long Island clifftop road, plied with bourbon. George drives the car off the road to save them.

Soon the hapless two find themselves standing in the middle of an empty highway as Maloney shows up in his

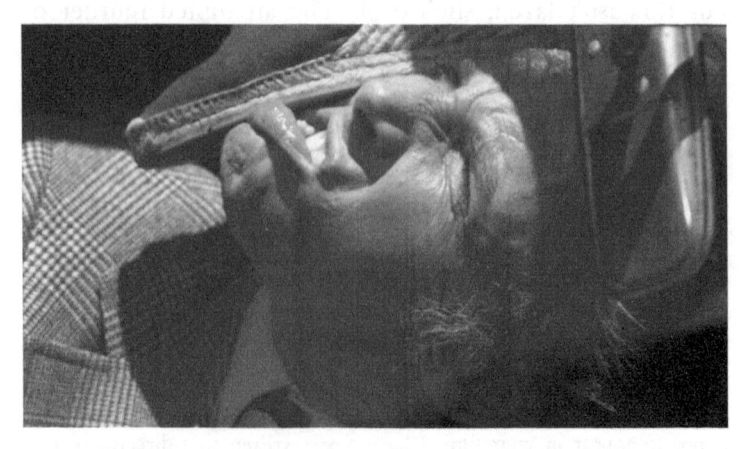

"It's a twisted mouth that we are playing for." Digital frame enlargement.

menacing green car. With "etiquette," he stops to offer them a lift. They won't get in, so he heads off, but then turns around and drives directly at them, as they run to save themselves in a double mime of Roger running from the plane in the cropduster scene. As to Blanche, her first thought in telling George of the ten thousand dollars they might possibly earn if they can find the Rainbird heir is that now they can get married. The blissful connivance etched on her face recollects Marion Crane, pushing her boyfriend Sam toward marriage at the beginning of *Psycho*. Part of what makes Blanche and George charming is their innocence of the marriage they *already* share.

To return to that garage scene where Adamson jabs Blanche with the tranquilizer: as they struggle, we see once again what we saw at a critical moment in *The Man Who Knew Too Much*, namely, an authoritative male drugging a woman who is in his power. In the earlier film, Ben McKenna had discovered a secret that as a medical practitioner he knew his wife would be unable to bear hearing, namely that their son had been kidnapped, and worse, kidnapped not by complete strangers but by a pair of British tourists they had met and confided in. Worse still, the wife had asked Jo if she would like her to look after young Hank, and in an instant of complete disattention Jo had blithely handed over the child. Sensing the incalculable magnitude of guilt his wife would bear, Ben sedates her before giving over his knowledge. This move will seem brutal, even despicable, to anyone who has not carefully been following Jo through the film this far and who therefore does not recognize the abysm of self-condemnation into which she will plunge when she learns that Lucy Drayton, of all people, has taken Hank. In fact, the dosage is an act of kindness, one that shows the true and personal complexity of emotional privacy this couple shares. Jo initially expresses anger, but this is a referral of the fear that is really moving her.

Hank McKenna, another son lost and found in a key Hitchcockian film, is a kind of happy harbinger of the Rainbird child we will meet only twenty years later, only through his disguises, and only at the finale of Hitchcock's career. Both of these boys are important in their families, both are only children, both reflect an adult struggle: Hank, the struggle of Jo for more independence in her marriage and for the second chance at mothering that her husband seems bent on denying; the Rainbird boy, the struggle between his mother and his aunt. Julia Rainbird and Ben McKenna share a strange similarity. The old lady openly admits that she comes from an ethic of intense propriety; that her sister's dark pregnancy and untellable birth would cast a stain upon the whole family if not addressed. Julia, preparing now for her own end just as Hitchcock must have been, feels guilt, therefore, at her actions and a desire to repair the damage she has done. She is "married," in effect, to her own past and the secret attached to it, and this marriage is a trap for her.

But Ben McKenna, for all his insouciance and Midwestern, plain-speaking charm, is finally subject to propriety, too. As *The Man Who Knew Too Much* concludes, it is insufficient that we should see the tormented Jo happily reunited with her son at the embassy; insufficient that Ben should have vanquished the evil Drayton; insufficient, even, that the threatened assassination should have been foiled. What must occur, what cannot be obstructed in any way, is what we see onscreen in fact: Ben brings Hank and Jo back to the Savoy Hotel where now, at last, in front of four hyper-judgmental Britons who have been pestering to see the son their famous fellow performer produced with her famous American doctor husband, the secure, unified, fully fleshed family can be put on proper display. "We just had to go over and pick up

Hank," coming out of Ben's mouth, is a proclamation of marital correctness. "We have produced a child," he as much as says; "we have cared for him. And here, now, we present him for your inspection."

By contrast, George Lumley's final act in *Family Plot* will be – as he announces – to inform Julia Rainbird of bad news: she will not have an heir to present to anyone. That desired prince, now so foully grown, has been caught in his own lustful marriage to wealth, accomplishment, and the fulfillment of narcissistic desire – a marriage, finally, like so many others in the new America. Caught, arrested, enclosed in a chamber of silence, waiting and hoping behind a locked door.

Courtesy Academy of Motion Picture Arts and Sciences.

WORKS CITED AND CONSULTED

AH = Alfred Hitchcock Collection, Margaret Herrick Library, Academy of Motion Picture Arts and Sciences, Beverly Hills
BFI = British Film Institute Library, London
HER = Margaret Herrick Library, Academy of Motion Picture Arts and Sciences, Beverly Hills
UCLA = Powell Library, University of California at Los Angeles
WB = Warner Bros. Archive, University of Southern California, Los Angeles

*

Allen, Richard. *Hitchcock's Romantic Irony*. New York: Columbia University Press, 2007.
———. "An Interview with Jay Presson Allen." *Hitchcock Annual* 2000–2001. 3–22.
American Pressbook for *Notorious*, BFI.

Ascarelli, Giulio. Wire to Peggy Robertson, regarding charges for M. Alexandre and Gwendolyn, October 23, 1963, *Marnie* file 456, AH.

Auiler, Dan. *Hitchcock's Notebooks: An Authorized and Illustrated Look Inside the Creative Mind of Alfred Hitchcock*. New York: Avon, 1999.

Barr, Charles. *Vertigo*. London: BFI, 2002.

Barrett, Linda. Personal interview. December 13, 2010.

Barton, Sabrina. "'Crisscross': Paranoia and Projection in *Strangers on a Train*." In *Out in Culture: Gay, Lesbian, and Queer Essays on Popular Culture*, ed. Corey K. Creekmur and Alexander Doty. Durham, N.C.: Duke University Press, 1995. 216–38.

Baudelaire, Charles. *The Painter of Modern Life and Other Essays*. 2nd ed. Trans. Jonathan Mayne. London: Phaidon, 1995.

Baxandall, Rosalyn, and Elizabeth Ewen. *Picture Windows: How the Suburbs Happened*. New York: Basic Books, 2000.

Behlmer, Rudy, ed. *Memo from David O. Selznick*. New York: Viking, 1972.

Belton, John. "Introduction." In *Alfred Hitchcock's Rear Window*. New York: Cambridge University Press, 2000. 1–20.

———. *Widescreen Cinema*. Cambridge, Mass.: Harvard University Press, 1992.

Benjamin, Walter. *The Arcades Project*. Cambridge, Mass.: Harvard University Press, 1999.

———. "The Paris of the Second Empire in Baudelaire." In *Charles Baudelaire: A Lyric Poet in the Era of High Capitalism*. Trans. Harry Zohn, London: Verso, 1997. 9–106.

Berger, John. *Ways of Seeing*. London: BBC/Penguin, 1972.

Berman, Marshall. *All That Is Solid Melts Into Air: The Experience of Modernity*. New York: Penguin, 1988.

———. "Too Much Is Not Enough: Metamorphoses of Times Square." In *Impossible Presence: Surface and Screen in the Photogenic Era*, ed. Terry Smith. Chicago: University of Chicago Press, 2001. 39–69.

Berwick, Ray. "Regarding Birds." Memorandum of bird possibilities to Alfred Hitchcock, *The Birds* file 104, AH.

Better Films Council of Grand Rapids and Kent County. Report to Walter Morris regarding *Rope*, January 2, 1949, *Rope* picture file, WB.

Blaetz, Robin. "Ingrid Bergman: The Face of Authenticity in the Land of Illusion." In *What Dreams Were Made Of: Movie Stars of the 1940s*, ed. Sean Griffin. New Brunswick N.J.: Rutgers University Press, 2011. 50–69.

Blumenthal, Ralph. *Stork Club: America's Most Famous Nightspot and the Lost World of Café Society*. Boston: Little, Brown, 2000.

Bolton, A. J. Letter to S(creen) A(ctors) G(uild), regarding use of doubles in Florida for *The Wrong Man*, May 26, 1956, *Wrong Man* file 1022, AH.

Borglum, Gutzon. "Mountain Sculpture." *Scientific American* 148: 1 (January 1933).

Bradley, Jim. Preview Report for *Spellbound*, based on California Theatre, Huntington Park, California, February 16, 1945, *Spellbound* file 651, AH.

Brand, Dana. "Rear-View Mirror: Hitchcock, Poe, and the Flaneur in America." In *Hitchcock's America*, ed. Jonathan Freedman and Richard Millington. New York: Oxford University Press, 1999. 123–34.

Brill, Lesley. "Redemptive Comedy in the Films of Alfred Hitchcock and Preston Sturges: 'Are Snakes Necessary?'" In *Alfred Hitchcock: Centenary Essays*, ed. Richard Allen and Sam Ishii Gonzalès. London: BFI, 1999. 205–19.

British Information Services Radio Section Release, regarding obtaining fresh water at sea from caught fish, June 22, 1943, *Lifeboat* file 355, AH.

Brock, Gustav. Letter to Alfred Hitchcock regarding hand-coloring the fire scene of *Saboteur*, March 28, 1942. *Saboteur* file 636, AH.

Brooks, Peter. *The Melodramatic Imagination: Balzac, Henry James, Melodrama, and the Mode of Excess*. New Haven, Conn.: Yale University Press, 1976.

Brown, Norman O. "Apocalypse: The Place of Mystery in the Life of the Mind." In *Apocalypse and/or Metamorphosis*. Berkeley: University of California Press, 1991. 1–7.

Browne, Porter Emerson. "The Mellowdrammer." *Everybody's 21* (September 1909).

Bumstead, Henry. Personal interview, September 27, 1995.

Burke, Kenneth. *Permanence and Change: An Anatomy of Purpose*. Indianapolis: Bobbs-Merrill, 1965.

Caffey, Frank. Inter-Office Communication to Hiller Innes, regarding sound recording, November 12, 1953, *Rear Window* files, AH.

———. Wire regarding permission for shooting *The Man Who Knew Too Much* in Morocco, *Man Who Knew Too Much* locations file, AH.

Cameron, Ian, and V. F. Perkins. "Hitchcock." In *Alfred Hitchcock Interviews*, ed. Sidney Gottlieb. Jackson: University Press of Mississippi, 2003. 44–54.

Canaday, Nicholas Jr. "Albee's *The American Dream* and the Existential Vacuum." *South Central Bulletin* 26: 4 (Winter 1966), 28–34. Reprinted in *The American Dream*, ed. Harold Bloom and Blake Hobby. New York: Bloom's Literary Criticism, 2009. 11–20.

Caro, Robert A. *The Power Broker: Robert Moses and the Fall of New York*. New York: Vintage, 1975.

Cavell, Stanley. "*North by Northwest*." In *Themes Out of School*. Chicago: University of Chicago Press, 1984. 152–72.

———. *Pursuits of Happiness: The Hollywood Comedy of Remarriage*. Cambridge, Mass.: Harvard University Press, 1981.

Chabrol, Claude. "Les Choses sérieuses." *Cahiers du cinéma* 46 (April 1955), 41–3.

Chion, Michel. "The Fourth Side." In *Alfred Hitchcock's Rear Window*, ed. John Belton. New York: Cambridge University Press, 2000. 110–17.

Cohen, Paula Marantz. "Conceptual Suspense in Hitchcock's Films." In *A Companion to Alfred Hitchcock*, ed. Thomas Leitch and Leland Poague. New York: Wiley-Blackwell, 2011. 126–37.

———. "Hitchcock's Revised American Vision: *The Wrong Man* and *Vertigo*." In *Hitchcock's America*, ed. Jonathan Freedman and Richard Millington. New York: Oxford University Press, 1999. 155–72.

Coleman, Herbert (with Judy Lanini). *The Hollywood I Knew: A Memoir: 1916–1988*. Lanham, Md.: Scarecrow, 2003.

———. Inter-Office Communication to Frank Caffey, November 11, 1953, regarding sound recording, *Rear Window* files, AH.

Corber, Robert J. "Hitchcock's Washington: Spectatorship, Ideology, and the 'Homosexual Menace' in *Strangers on a Train*." In *Hitchcock's America*, ed. Jonathan Freedman and Richard Millington. New York: Oxford University Press, 1999. 99–121.

———. *In the Name of National Security: Hitchcock, Homophobia, and the Political Construction of Gender in Postwar America*. Durham, N.C.: Duke University Press, 1993.

Curtis, Scott. "The Making of *Rear Window*." In *Alfred Hitchcock's Rear Window*, ed. John Belton. New York: Cambridge University Press, 2000. 21–56.

Davis, Mike. *City of Quartz: Excavating the Future in Los Angeles*. London: Verso, 1990.

De Segonzac, Édouard. Letter to Russell Holman for Alfred Hitchcock, regarding Moroccan shooting, *Man Who Knew Too Much* locations file, AH.

De Tocqueville, Alexis. *Democracy in America*. 2 vols. 1840. Trans. Henry Reeve. New York: Schocken, 1970.

Deutelbaum, Marshall. "Seeing in 'Saboteur.'" *Literature/ Film Quarterly* 12: 1 (1984), 58–64.

Donath, Ludwig. Letter to Alfred Hitchcock, regarding *Torn Curtain*, February 22, 1966, *Torn Curtain* files, AH.

Doty, Alexander. "Queer Hitchcock." In *A Companion to Alfred Hitchcock*, ed. Thomas Leitch and Leland Poague. New York: Wiley-Blackwell, 2011. 473–89.

Douchet, Jean. *Hitchcock*. Paris: Cahiers du cinéma, 1999.

———. *A Long Hard Look at 'Psycho.'* London: BFI: 2002.

Douglas, Ann. *Terrible Honesty: Mongrel Manhattan in the 1920s*. New York: Farrar, Straus and Giroux, 1995.

Dubreuilh, Simone, "Mais qui a tué Harry?" *Libération* (March 22, 1956), *Trouble with Harry* file 947, AH.

Du Maurier, Daphne. *Rebecca*. London: Arrow, 1992, ©1938.

Eco, Umberto. *Art and Beauty in the Middle Ages*. Trans. Hugh Bredin. New Haven, Conn.: Yale University Press, 1986.

Epstein, Edward Jay. *Between Fact and Fiction: The Problem of Journalism*. New York: Vintage, 1975.

Erickson, C. O. "Doc." Inter-Office Communication to Hugh Brown, November 5, 1953, regarding sound recording, *Rear Window* files, AH.

———. Production Note, October 14, 1954, regarding backgrounds for main titles, *Trouble with Harry* Production file, AH.

Erickson, Erik H. *Childhood and Society*. New York: W. W. Norton, 1963.

Ewen, Stuart. *Captains of Consciousness: Advertising and the Social Roots of the Consumer Culture.* New York: Basic Books, 2001.

Falconer, Haven. Letter to Herbert Coleman, September 25, 1958, regarding the Parke-Bernet Galleries, *North by Northwest* file 546, AH.

——. Wire to Lew Strohm and Ruby Rosenberg, regarding research photography assignments, July 31, 1958, *North by Northwest* file 546, AH.

Fiedler, Leslie A. *Love and Death in the American Novel.* Champaign, Ill.: Dalkey Archive, 1998.

——. "The New World Savage as Stranger; or, 'Tis New to Thee.'" In *The Stranger in Shakespeare.* New York: Stein & Day, 1973. 199–253.

——. *The Return of the Vanishing American.* New York: Stein & Day, 1969.

Fielding, Raymond. *The Technique of Special Effects Cinematography.* New York: Hastings House, 1968.

Fischer, Lucy. "Mama's Boy: Filial Hysteria in *White Heat.*" In *Screening the Male: Exploring Masculinities in Hollywood Cinema,* ed. Steven Cohan and Ina Rae Hark. New York: Routledge, 1993. 70–84.

——. "'The Shock of the New': Electrification, Illumination, Urbanization, and the Cinema." In *Cinema and Modernity*, ed. Murray Pomerance. New Brunswick, N.J.: Rutgers University Press, 2006. 19–37.

Fitzgerald, F. Scott. *The Great Gatsby.* New York: Scribner's, 1953, ©1925.

Foster, Frederick. "'Hitch' Didn't Want It Arty." *American Cinematographer* (February 1957), 84–5, 112–14.

Freedman, Jonathan. "From *Spellbound* to *Vertigo*: Alfred Hitchcock and Therapeutic Culture in America." In *Hitchcock's America*, ed. Jonathan Freedman and Richard Millington. New York: Oxford University Press, 1999. 77–98.

Fried, Debra. "Love, American Style: Hitchcock's Hollywood." In *Hitchcock's America*, ed. Jonathan Freedman and Richard Millington. New York: Oxford University Press, 1999. 15–28.

Friedan, Betty. *The Feminine Mystique*. 1963. New York: Norton, 2001.

Frye, Northrop. *The Modern Century*. New York: Oxford University Press, 1991.

Goffman, Erving. *The Presentation of Self in Everyday Life*. Garden City, N.J.: Doubleday Anchor, 1959.

Gomery, Douglas. *Shared Pleasures: A History of Movie Presentation in the United States*. Madison: University of Wisconsin Press, 1992.

Goodman, Paul. *Growing Up Absurd: Problems of Youth in the Organized Society*. New York: Random House, 1960.

———. *The Structure of Literature*. Chicago: University of Chicago Press, 1968.

Gunning, Tom. "Systematizing the Electric Message: Narrative Form, Gender, and Modernity in *The Lonedale Operator*." In *American Cinema's Transitional Era: Audiences, Institutions, Practices*, ed. Charlie Keil and Shelley Stamp. Berkeley: University of California Press, 2004. 15–50.

Halberstam, David. *The Fifties*. New York: Fawcett, 1993.

Hall, Barbara. *An Oral History with Peggy Robertson*. Beverly Hills, Calif.: Academy of Motion Picture Arts and Sciences, Oral History Program, 2002.

Hark, Ina Rae. "Hitchcock Discovers America: The Selznick-Era Films." In *A Companion to Alfred Hitchcock*, ed. Thomas Leitch and Leland Poague. New York: Wiley-Blackwell, 2011. 289–308.

Harris, Marvin. *Our Kind: Who We Are, Where We Came From, Where We Are Going*. New York: Harper Perennial, 1989.

Head, Edith, and Paddy Calistro. *Edith Head's Hollywood*. New York: E. P. Dutton, 1983.

Heckroth, Hein. Letter to Alfred Hitchcock, regarding *Francesca Da Rimini*, October 22, 1965, *Torn Curtain* files, AH.

Hemmeter, Thomas. "Hitchcock's Narrative Modernism: Ironies of Fictional Time." In *A Companion to Alfred Hitchcock*, ed. Thomas Leitch and Leland Poague. New York: Wiley-Blackwell, 2011. 67–85.

Hersey, John. *The Algiers Motel Incident*. New York: Alfred A. Knopf, 1968.

Hewitt, Rachel. *Map of a Nation: A Biography of the Ordnance Survey*. London: Granta, 2010.

Hitchcock, Alfred. Handwritten casting list for *North by Northwest*. *North by Northwest* File 526, AH.

———. Letter to Norma Varden, regarding *Psycho*, December 1, 1959, *Psycho* casting file 583, AH.

———. List of actors for possible casting in *North by Northwest*, undated, handwritten (most likely by Hitchcock), *North by Northwest* file 526, AH.

———. Memorandum to Evan Hunter, regarding local characterizations for *The Birds*, December 21, 1961, *The Birds* file 19, AH.

———. Memorandum on Set Dressing Requirements for "The Birds," January 24, 1962, *The Birds* file 111, AH.

———. Research Note regarding Bodega Bay general store, November 8, 1961, *The Birds* file 104, AH.

———. Sketch of dictation to Wolfgang Kieling, n.d., *Torn Curtain* files, AH.

———. "Some Notes about the Small Town Atmosphere." *Shadow of a Doubt* file 639, AH.

———. Telegram to Angus MacPhail regarding *Spellbound* plot, n.d., *Spellbound* file 651, AH.

———. Telegram to Mrs. J. F. R. Seitz (Jessie Royce Landis), Governor's Island, New York, January 5, 1960, regarding *Psycho*, *Psycho* casting file 583, AH.

———. Wire to Joan Fontaine, June 8, 1942, *Shadow of a Doubt* file 645, AH.

Hofstadter, Richard J. *Anti-Intellectualism in American Life*. New York: Vintage, 1963.

Jacobs, Steven. *The Wrong House: The Architecture of Alfred Hitchcock*. Rotterdam: 010 Publishers, 2007.

James, Henry. *Daisy Miller*. London: Penguin, 1986, ©1878.

Johnson, Joseph MacMillan ("Mac"). Memorandum to C. O. "Doc" Erickson, October 5, 1953, AH.

Kalmenson, Benjamin. Letter to Steve Trilling, regarding *Rope*, November 19, 1948, *Rope* file, USC.

Kerouac, Jack. *On the Road*. New York: Penguin, 1991, ©1957.

Knapp, Lucretia. "The Queer Voice in *Marnie*." In *Out in Culture: Gay, Lesbian, and Queer Essays on Popular Culture*, ed. Corey K. Creekmur and Alexander Doty. Durham, N.C.: Duke University Press, 1995. 262–81.

Knight, Arthur. "Conversation with Alfred Hitchcock." In *Alfred Hitchcock Interviews*, ed. Sidney Gottlieb. Jackson: University Press of Mississippi, 2003. 160–85.

Kraft, Jeff, and Aaron Leventhal. *Footsteps in the Fog: Alfred Hitchcock's San Francisco*. Santa Monica, Calif.: Santa Monica Press, 2002.

Krohn, Bill. *Alfred Hitchcock*. Paris: Cahiers du cinéma, 2007.

———. *Hitchcock at Work*. London: Phaidon, 2000.

———. "They Made *The Birds*: Round Table with Hitchcock's Designers Albert Whitlock, Robert Boyle, Harold Michelson, Richard Edlund." *Cahiers du cinéma* 337 (June 1982), 36–48. (A fifty-four-page English version from the original tape transcription was courteously made available to me by Bill Krohn.)

Kyvig, David E. *Daily Life in the United States, 1920–1939: Decades of Promise and Pain*. Westport, Conn.: Greenwood Press, 2002.

Land, Hilary. "The Myth of the Male Breadwinner." In *Modern Sociology: Introductory Readings*, 2nd ed., ed. Peter Worsley et al. Harmondsworth: Penguin, 1980. 352–5.

Landis, Jessie Royce (Mrs. J. F. R. Seitz). Telegram to William Barnes, August 6, 1958, regarding *North by Northwest*. *North by Northwest* File 526, AH.

———. Telegram to Alfred Hitchcock, December 28, 1959, regarding *North by Northwest*. *Psycho* casting file 583, AH.

Lauter, Ed. Letter to Alfred Hitchcock, after shooting *Family Plot*, August 1, 1975, *Family Plot* file 200, AH.

Lawrence, D. H. *Studies in Classic American Literature*. Harmondsworth, Middlesex: Penguin, 1977.

Lee, Andy. Inter-Office Communication to Peggy Robertson, regarding Mormon funerals, October 20, 1975, *Family Plot* file 220, AH.

Leff, Leonard J. *Hitchcock & Selznick: The Rich and Strange Collaboration of Alfred Hitchcock and David O. Selznick in Hollywood*. New York: Weidenfeld & Nicolson, 1987.

Lehman, David. "Alfred Hitchcock's America." *American Heritage* 58: 2 (April/May 2007), 28–36.

Lehman, Ernest. Letter to Eva Marie Saint, regarding *North by Northwest*, November 12, 1992, Eva Marie Saint Collection, HER.

Leighton, Sophie. *The 1950s Home*. Oxford: Shire, 2009.

Lemay, J. A. Leo. "Franklin's Autobiography and the American Dream." *The Renaissance Man in the Eighteenth Century*. Los Angeles: William Andrews Clark Memorial Library, 1978. Reprinted in *The American Dream*, ed. Harold Bloom and Blake Hobby. New York: Bloom's Literary Criticism, 2009. 21–36.

Lerner, Max. *America as a Civilization*. New York: Simon & Schuster, 1957.

Lesch, Paul. "L'antinazisme dans les films d'Alfred Hitchcock (1938–1944)." In Jörg Helbig, Paul Lesch, and Uli Jung, *Three Spotlights on Hitch*. Luxembourg: Ville de Luxembourg Cinémathèque Municipale, 1999. 12–53.

Lewis, Meriwether, and William Clark. *The Lewis and Clark Journals (Abridged Edition): An American Epic of Discovery*. Ed. Gary E. Moulton. Lincoln: University of Nebraska Press, 2003.

Livingston, Jay. Personal interview, September 18, 1995.

Lukas, Scott A. *Theme Park*. London: Reaktion, 2008.

Marling, Karal Ann. *As Seen on TV: The Visual Culture of Everyday Life in the 1950s*. Cambridge, Mass.: Harvard University Press, 1994.

———. *The Colossus of Roads: Myth and Symbol along the American Highway*. Minneapolis: University of Minnesota Press, 1984.

Martel, June. Synopsis of *Notorious* Estimating Script, July 25, 1945, Performing Arts Special Collections, UCLA.

May, Elaine Tyler. *Homeward Bound: American Families in the Cold War Era*. New York: Basic Books, 1988.

May, Lary. *The Big Tomorrow: Hollywood and the Politics of the American Way*. Chicago: University of Chicago Press, 2002.

McBride, Joseph, ed. *Film Makers on Film Making*, Vol. 2. Los Angeles: J. P. Tarcher, 1983.

McElhaney, Joe. "Touching the Surface: *Marnie*, Melodrama, Modernism." In *Alfred Hitchcock Centenary Essays*, ed. Richard Allen and Sam Ishii Gonzalès. London: BFI, 1999. 87–105.

McGilligan, Patrick. *Alfred Hitchcock: A Life in Darkness and Light*. New York: Regan, 2003.

———. "Hitchcock Dreams of America." *Hitchcock Annual* 2002–03. 1–31.

McWilliams, Carey. *Southern California Country: An Island on the Land*. New York: Duell, Sloan & Pearce, 1946.

Meiklejohn, William. Straight wire to Jacob Karp, April 20, 1955, regarding cable from Richard Mealand about Niall McGinnis, *Man Who Knew Too Much* casting file, AH.

Memorandum on characterizations for *Torn Curtain*, unsigned and undated, *Torn Curtain* file 881, AH.

Miller, Arthur. *Death of a Salesman*. New York: Dramatists Play Service, Inc., 1948.

Miller, Donald L. *City of the Century: The Epic of Chicago and the Making of America*. New York: Simon & Schuster, 1996.

Milliken, Carl Jr. Inter-Office Communication to Herbert Coleman, regarding possible legal censorship problems in *The Wrong Man*, *Wrong Man* file 1016, WB.

Millington, Richard H. "Hitchcock and American Character: The Comedy of Self-Construction in *North by Northwest*." In *Hitchcock's America*, ed. Jonathan Freedman and Richard Millington. New York: Oxford University Press, 1999. 135–54.

Modleski, Tania. *The Women Who Knew Too Much: Hitchcock and Feminist Theory*. New York: Routledge, 1989.

Moral, Tony Lee. *Hitchcock and the Making of Marnie*. Lanham, Md.: Scarecrow Press, 2002.

Nesbitt, Cathleen. Letter to Alfred Hitchcock, after shooting *Family Plot*, n.d., *Family Plot* file 200, AH.

Notes from telephone call, Herbert Coleman to "Doc" Erickson, 10:40 A.M. August 9, 1954, *Trouble with Harry* Production file, AH.

Nugent, Frank S. "Mr. Hitchcock Discovers Love." In *Alfred Hitchcock Interviews*, ed. Sidney Gottlieb. Jackson: University Press of Mississippi, 2003. 17–22.

Nye, David E. *Electrifying America: Social Meanings of a New Technology*. Cambridge, Mass.: MIT Press, 1992.

Orwell, George. *The Road to Wigan Pier*. London: Victor Gollancz, 1937.

Paglia, Camille. *The Birds*. London: BFI, 1998.

Païni, Dominique, and Guy Cogeval, eds. *Hitchcock and Art: Fatal Coincidences*. Montreal: Museum of Fine Arts; Milan: Mazzotta, 2000.

Perry, George. "Hitchcock on Location." *American Heritage* 58: 2 (April/May 2007), 37–41.

Peucker, Brigitte. "Aesthetic Space in Hitchcock." In *A Companion to Alfred Hitchcock*, ed. Thomas Leitch and Leland Poague. New York: Wiley-Blackwell, 2011. 201–18.

"Playing God: The Art and Artists of Matte Painting." Academy of Motion Picture Arts and Sciences exhibit at the Linwood Dunn Theater, Los Angeles, 2007–8.

Poe, Edgar Allan. "The Man of the Crowd." In *Edgar Allan Poe: Selected Tales*, ed. David Van Leer. New York: Oxford University Press, 1998. 84–91.

Points to Be Checked Out on "Wrong Man." Unsigned and undated memo, *Wrong Man* file 1037, AH.

Pomerance, Murray. "A Clean, Well-Lighted Place: Hitchcock's New York." In *City That Never Sleeps: New York and the Filmic Imagination*, ed. Murray Pomerance. New Brunswick, N.J.: Rutgers University Press, 2007. 103–17.

———. *An Eye for Hitchcock*. New Brunswick, N.J.: Rutgers University Press, 2004.

———. "Finding Release: 'Storm Clouds' and *The Man Who Knew Too Much*." In *Music and Cinema*, ed. James Buhler, Caryl Flinn, and David Neumeyer. Middletown, Conn.: Wesleyan University Press, 2000. 207–46.

———. *The Horse Who Drank the Sky: Film Experience Beyond Narrative and Theory*. New Brunswick, N.J.: Rutgers University Press, 2008.

———. *Michelangelo Red Antonioni Blue: Eight Reflections on Cinema*. Berkeley: University of California Press, 2011.

———. "Recuperation and *Rear Window*." *Senses of Cinema* 29 (November–December 2003), online at www.sensesofcinema.com.

———. "Thirteen Ways of Looking at *The Birds*." In *Hitchcock at the Source*, ed. R. Barton Palmer and David Boyd. Albany: State University of New York Press, 2011. 267–93.

Production Notes for *Strangers on a Train*, *Strangers on a Train* research file, WB.

Questions on Script Dated February 6, 1956, *Wrong Man* file 1037, AH.

Rappaport, Erika D. "'A New Era of Shopping': The Promotion of Women's Pleasure in London's West End, 1909–1914." In *Cinema and the Invention of Modern Life*, ed. Leo Charney and Vanessa R. Schwartz. Berkeley: University of California Press, 1995. 130–55.

Raubicheck, Walter. "Working with Hitchcock: A Collaborators' Forum with Patricia Hitchcock, Janet Leigh, Teresa Wright, and Eva Marie Saint." *Hitchcock Annual* 2002–03, 32–66.

Rebecca publicity material, *Rebecca* file 627, AH.

Register, Woody. *Kid of Coney Island: Fred Thompson and the Rise of American Amusements*. New York: Oxford University Press, 2001.

Rickitt, Richard. *Special Effects: The History and Technique*. New York: Billboard, 2007.

Robertson, Peggy. Inter-Office Communication to Jack Barron, regarding hair equipment, October 25, 1963, *Marnie* file 456, AH.

———. Inter-Office Communication to Paul Donnelly, regarding Virginia Darcy, October 25, 1963, *Marnie* file 456, AH.

———. Letter to Giulio Ascarelli, regarding M. Alexandre's assistant Gwendolyn, October 17, 1963, *Marnie* file 456, AH.

———. Letter to Hansjoerg [Hansjörg] Felmy, January 25, 1966, *Torn Curtain* file 879, AH.

———. Letter to Bernard Herrmann, regarding *Torn Curtain*, December 3, 1965, *Torn Curtain* files, AH.

———. Memorandum to Bob Goodfreed, March 31, 1958, regarding "Important Locations for Alfred Hitchcock's 'Vertigo.'" *Vertigo* file 994, AH.

———. Memorandum regarding cameras for theater panic scene, November 1, 1965, *Torn Curtain* files, AH.

Rohmer, Eric, and Claude Chabrol. *Hitchcock: The First Forty-Four Films*. New York: Frederick Ungar, 1979.

Rosenberg, Harold. *Artworks and Packages*. New York: Delta, 1969.

Ross, Alex. *The Rest Is Noise: Listening to the Twentieth Century*. New York: Picador, 2007.

Rothman, William. *Hitchcock: the Murderous Gaze*. Cambridge, Mass.: Harvard University Press, 1982.

———. "The Universal Hitchcock." In *A Companion to Alfred Hitchcock*, ed. Thomas Leitch and Leland Poague. New York: Wiley-Blackwell, 2011. 347–64.

———. "The Villain in Hitchcock: 'Does He Look Like a "Wrong One" to You?'" In *BAD: Infamy, Darkness, Evil, and Slime on Screen*, ed. Murray Pomerance. Albany: State University of New York Press, 2004. 213–21.

Sampson, Denis. *Brian Moore: The Chameleon Novelist*. Toronto: Doubleday Canada, 1999.

Samuels, Charles Thomas. "Alfred Hitchcock." In *Alfred Hitchcock Interviews*, ed. Sidney Gottlieb. Jackson: University Press of Mississippi, 2003. 129–55.

Schama, Simon. *Landscape and Memory*. Toronto: Vintage Canada, 1995.

Schivelbusch, Wolfgang. *The Railway Journey: The Industrialization of Time and Space in the 19th Century.* Berkeley: University of California Press, 1986.

——. *Three New Deals: Reflections on Roosevelt's America, Mussolini's Italy, and Hitler's Germany, 1933–1939.* New York: Picador, 2006.

Schuessler, Fred. Inter-Office Communication to David O. Selznick, regarding Alice Brady and Cora Witherspoon, August 21, 1939, *Rebecca* file 628, AH.

Selznick, David O. Inter-Office Communication to Daniel O'Shea, Fred Schuessler, and Alfred Hitchcock, regarding casting of Mrs. Van Hopper, July 20, 1939, *Rebecca* file 628, AH.

Showalter, Elaine. *The Female Malady: Women, Madness, and English Culture, 1830–1980.* New York: Penguin, 1987.

Simmel, Georg. "On Visual Interaction." In *Introduction to the Science of Sociology*, ed. Robert E. Park and Ernest W. Burgess. New York: Greenwood Press, 1969. 356–61.

——. *The Sociology of Georg Simmel.* Trans. and ed. Kurt H. Wolff. New York: Free Press of Glencoe, 1950.

Slater, Philip. *The Glory of Hera: Greek Mythology and the Greek Family.* Boston: Beacon Press, 1968.

Smith, Ken. *Mental Hygiene: Classroom Films 1945–1970.* New York: Blast Books, 1999.

Sodium Vapor contract with Walt Disney Studio, March 21, 1962, *The Birds* file 46, AH.

Spigel, Lynn. *Dreamhouse: Popular Media and Postwar Suburbs.* Durham, N.C.: Duke University Press, 2001.

Spoto, Donald. *The Dark Side of Genius: The Life of Alfred Hitchcock.* New York: Ballantine, 1991.

Sterritt, David. *The Films of Alfred Hitchcock.* New York: Cambridge University Press, 1993.

Stoiber, Rudolf. Letter to Michael Ludmer, Universal Story Department, October 26, 1965, regarding inaccuracies in portrayal of German types, *Torn Curtain* file 890, AH.

Strangers on a Train legal file, WB.

Street, Sarah. "The Dresses Had Told Me: Fashion and Femininity in *Rear Window*." In *Alfred Hitchcock's Rear Window*, ed. John Belton. New York: Cambridge University Press, 2000. 91–109.

Sullivan, Jack. *Hitchcock's Music*. New Haven, Conn.: Yale University Press, 2006.

Summary of 266 Preview Questionnaires for *Rebecca*, based on a preview of December 26, 1939, *Rebecca* file 627, AH.

Sweeney, Gael. "Impatient with Stupidity: Alien Imperialism in *The Day the Earth Stood Still*." In *Closely Watched Brains*, ed. Murray Pomerance and John Sakeris, 2nd ed. Boston: Pearson, 2003. 215–29.

Taylor, John Russell. *Hitch: The Life and Times of Alfred Hitchcock*. New York: DaCapo, 1996.

Thoreau, Henry David. *Walden*. New York: Penguin, 1986, ©1854.

Toles, George. "Occasions of Sin: The Forgotten Cigarette Lighter and Other Moral Accidents in *Strangers on a Train*." In *A Companion to Alfred Hitchcock*, ed. Thomas Leitch and Leland Poague. New York: Wiley-Blackwell, 2011. 529–52.

Topaz locations file 761, AH.

Toumanova, Tamara. Wire to Alfred Hitchcock, regarding her work in *Torn Curtain*, December 16, 1965, *Torn Curtain* file, AH.

The Trouble with Harry, script, July 27, 1954, *Trouble with Harry* file 945, AH.

Trow, George W. S. *My Pilgrim's Progress: Media Studies, 1950–1998*. New York: Vintage, 1999.

Truffaut, François. *Hitchcock*. Trans. Helen Scott. New York: Simon & Schuster, 1985.

Turner, George E. "*Saboteur*: Hitchcock Set Free." *American Cinematographer* (November 1993), 67–72; (December 1993), 88–92.

———. "Hitchcock's Acrophobic Vision." *American Cinematographer* (November 1996), 86–91.

Twain, Mark. *The Innocents Abroad*. New York: Dover, 2003, ©1869.

Varden, Norma. Letter to Alfred Hitchcock, regarding *North by Northwest*, August 13, 1958, *North by Northwest* file 527, AH.

———. Letter to Alfred Hitchcock, regarding *Psycho*, November 27, 1959, *Psycho* casting file 583, AH.

Vidich, Arthur J., and Joseph Bensman. *Small Town in Mass Society: Class, Power and Religion in a Rural Community*. Rev. ed. Princeton, N.J.: Princeton University Press, 1968.

Walker, J. A. Postcard to Warner Bros., regarding *Rope*, October 16, 1948, *Rope* picture file, WB.

Walkowitz, Judith R. *City of Dreadful Delight: Narratives of Sexual Danger in Late-Victorian London*. Chicago: University of Chicago Press, 1992.

Waller, Gregory A. *Main Street Amusements: Movies and Commercial Entertainment in a Southern City, 1896–1930*. Washington, D.C.: Smithsonian Institution Press, 1995.

Warhol, Andy. "Hitchcock." In *Alfred Hitchcock Interviews*, ed. Sidney Gottlieb. Jackson: University Press of Mississippi, 2003. 186–212.

Warner Bros. Research Dept. Inter-Office Communication, January 18, 1956, regarding possible names for insurance companies, *Wrong Man* file 1016, WB.

Wehmeyer, Ernest B. Letter to Canon Rogers, Grace Cathedral, regarding arrangements for shooting interiors, March 25, 1975, *Family Plot* file 204, AH.

---. Letter to Sam Simpson, regarding permission to photograph at the Sierra Madre Cemetery, March 17, 1975, *Family Plot* file 204, AH.

---. Letter to George V. Walk, regarding permission to shoot at vacant station across the highway from his property, March 17, 1975, *Family Plot* file 204, AH.

Weinstein, Sheri. "Technologies of Vision: Spiritualism and Science in Nineteenth-Century America." In *Spectral America: Phantoms and the National Imagination*, ed. Jeffrey Andrew Weinstock. Madison: University of Wisconsin Press, 2004. 124–40.

Weinstock, Jeffrey Andrew, ed. *Spectral America: Phantoms and the National Imagination*. Madison: University of Wisconsin Press, 2004.

Westreich, Joseph N. Letter to G. R. Keyser (including translation from *Weltwoche*), regarding *Rope*, December 2, 1948, *Rope* picture file, WB.

Wexman, Virginia Wright. *Creating the Couple: Love, Marriage, and Hollywood Performance*. Princeton, N.J.: Princeton University Press, 1993.

White, Susan. "A Surface Collaboration: Hitchcock and Performance." In *A Companion to Alfred Hitchcock*, ed. Thomas Leitch and Leland Poague. New York: Wiley-Blackwell, 2011. 181–97.

Wilder, Thornton. Wire to Miss Rosalie Stewart, May 13, 1942, *Shadow of a Doubt* file 642, AH.

Williams, William Carlos. "The American Background." In *Selected Essays*. New York: New Directions, 1969. 134–61.

---. "Père Sebastian Rasles." In *In the American Grain*. New York: New Directions, 1956. 105–29.

Winokur, Robert M. Letter of Agreement to Mrs. Rose Gaffney regarding use of her property for *The Birds*, October 12, 1961, *The Birds* file 57, AH.

Wood, Robin. *Hitchcock's Films Revisited*. Rev. ed. New York: Columbia University Press, 2002.

——. "The Murderous Gays: Hitchcock's Homophobia." In *Out in Culture: Gay, Lesbian, and Queer Essays on Popular Culture*, ed. Corey K. Creekmur and Alexander Doty. Durham, N.C.: Duke University Press, 1995. 197–215.

Wrong Man Publicity, *Wrong Man* publicity file, WB.

Wylie, Philip. *Generation of Vipers: A Survey of Moral Want*. New York: Rinehart, 1946.

Yablon, Nick. *Untimely Ruins: An Archaeology of American Urban Modernity, 1819–1919*. Chicago: University of Chicago Press, 2009.

Žižek, Slavoj. *Living in the End Times*. London: Verso, 2010.

INDEX

Numerals in italics indicate images or image captions

abstract expressionism, 67
Adamson, Harold, 186
Africa, 88n12
Airport (George Seaton, 1970), 268
Alexandre of Paris, *229*; assistant, Gwendolyn, *229*
Alice's Adventures in Wonderland (Lewis Carroll), reference to, 143
All Fall Down (John Frankenheimer, 1962), 195n14
Allen, Jay Presson, 112, 113, 228
Allen, Richard, 112, 140
Allyson, June, 268
Alper, Murray, 103
Amagansett, 3, 4
America, 1, 2; *see also* American: amusement park, 198; America as, 206–7; and British culture, 92, 104–5; and British speech patterns, 93; enduring fealty to Europe, 245; frontier, 24–8; Freudianism in, 167–8; and functional beauty, 162; general store in, 215n24, 216–7; as greenwood, 23; and jumping steps, 103; language, 90; mall culture, 214; modernity and, 18–19, 30–31, 201, 213, 214, 215n25; "momism" in, 237–9; and money, 105n21; obligations to Europe in wartime, 171; practical spirit in, 73; and public works before World War II, 193–4; road culture of, 190, 194, 195n14; adored by French, 195n14; social class in, 106; social mobility in, 143; spiritualism in, 269ff; suburbs in, 212; and theatricality, 34–5; as urban

America (cont.)
nation, 31; women's position in, 110; working class in, 60, 61, 103–6; and World War II, 51; yeoman life in, 29, 134, 171;
"America" (Leonard Bernstein, Stephen Sondheim), 186n4
America Firsters, 5n3
American: bicentennial, 12; character, 4; city, 1, 49, 57, 69; class relations, 8, 10; dream, 218, 259, *see also* Albee, Edward; face, 56; generosity, 100; gender riddle, 245; hero, 98, 100; hospitality, 3, 4; landscape, 30; monstrosity 121–2; narcissism, new, 243; naturalness, 78; neutrality during World War II, 5n3; opulence, 140, 219; pastoral, 18, 69, 70, 212, 213; personality, 71ff; power base, 98; president, 221; reference in Hitchcock films, *see* Hitchcock, Alfred; small town, 31, 49, 50, 52, 54, 208, 214; tourists in Europe, 98;
American Dream, The (Edward Albee, January 24, 1961), reference to, 218
American Film Institute (AFI), 193n13
American in Paris, An (Vincente Minnelli, 1951), 227
Anderson, John, 104
Anderson, Judith, 239n7
Anderson, Mary, 7
Andrews, Julie, 14, 97, 126, *128*
Andy Hardy films, 55
Angel, Heather, 7
anticipatory socialization, *see* Merton, Robert K.
Apple personal computer, 12
"Arabesque No. 1" (Claude Debussy), 77

Armstrong, Neil, moon landing of, 12
Ashcroft, Peggy, 231
Asia, 88n12
Asquith, Anthony, 279n26
Athenian civilization, 220
Auchincloss, John W., Washington residence, 219n26
Auiler, Dan, 132–3
Ayres, Lemuel, 51

Babcock, Samuel S., 3n1
Bach, Johann Sebastian, 150
Back to the Future (Robert Zemeckis, 1985), 51
Bacon, Irving, 106
Bagdasarian, Ross, 37, 104, 172
Balanchine, Georges, *128*
Balestrero, Christopher Emmanuel, 61n36, 121, 147, *147*, 150n26, *151*; family, 62n38; home, Queens, 147, 148n22; meetings with lawyer, 149n25; represented by Bernard Herrmann's music, 150; wife's decline, 149n25
Baltimore Turnpike (Highway 1), 192n11
Band-aids, 215
"Band Played On, The" (Charles B. Ward and John F. Palmer), 206
Bande à part (Jean-Luc Godard, 1964), 195n14
Bankhead, Tallulah, 6, 9, 242
Barbie doll, the, 11
Barefoot Contessa, The (Joseph L. Mankiewicz, 1954), 84n9
Barns, William, 269
Barr, Charles, 64
Barrett, James, 2
Barrett, Kate, 2
Barrett, Kay (Brown) (1905–1992), 1, 2, 4, 30n12
Barrett, Laurinda, 2, 3, 15–16

Barry, Joan, 231
Barrymore, Ethel, 266n19, 269
Basevi, James, 8
Bass, Saul, 219n29
Bassermann, Albert, 91
Bates, Charles, 53n29
Bates, Florence, 4, 219, 254–5, *254*, 255n9
Baudelaire, Charles, 13, 188
Baxter, Anne, 256n10
Bay of Pigs invasion, 11
Beatles (George Harrison, John Lennon, Paul McCartney, Ringo Starr), American visit, 12
Bel Geddes, Barbara, 241
Belton, John, 39
Bend of the River (Anthony Mann, 1952), 119n28
Bendix, William, 7, *7*, 106
Benjamin, Walter, *68*, 182
Bensman, Joseph, 54
Benton, Thomas Hart, 55
Bergdorf Goodman, 109n24
Berger, John, 162
Bergman, Ingrid, 3n1, 5, 104, 163, 164n34, *165*, 166, 167, 168, *169*, 234, 235n2, *235*, 236n4
Berlin Wall, 98
Berman, Marshall, 188
Berner, Sara, 37, 259
Beyond the High Himalayas (William O. Douglas), 163
Billingsley, Sherman, 61, 148, 148n23
"Birds, The" (Daphne du Maurier), 211n23
Black, Karen, 272, 274n22
Blackboard Jungle (Richard Brooks, 1955), rock soundtrack for, 12
Blaetz, Robin, 166
"Bluebeard" (Charles Perrault), reference to, 86
blue screen process, 76n5; *see also* Hitchcock, Alfred

Bobrinskoy, Alexei, 90
Bogart, Humphrey, death of, 12
Bogdanovich, Peter, 246
Boileau, Pierre, 46
Boland, Mary, 255n9
"Bontzye Schweig" (Isaac Leib Peretz), reference to, 149
Booth, Shirley, 192n10
Booth Theater (New York), 268
Borglum, Gutzon, 221–2
Born Yesterday (Garson Kanin, February 4, 1946), 58n33
Boston Music Hall, 271
Boyd, William, 155
Boyle, Robert, 20n2, 29, 33n16, 75n4, 76n5, 136n10, 141, 193n13
Boys' Night Out (Michael Gordon, 1962), 268
Brady, Alice, 255n9
Brainville, Yves, 89
Brayton, Margaret, 104
Breen, Joseph Ignatius, 12
Bridge Studios (Vancouver), 65n40
Brill, Lesley, 250
Britain: British family, Hitchcockian, 230; British Information Service, 227n1; British Intelligence, 5n3; isolationism, 255; judgmentalism, 242, 283; British Ministry of Information, 227n1; British Ordnance Survey, 53n29; civilization, 221; immigration to America from, 133; as origin of Hitchcockian villains, 118, 119, 262; social class in, 133; small town in, 52
Brock, Gustav, 33n16
Brooke, Emma, 265
Brown, Norman O., 129
Browne, Porter, 200
Bullitt (Peter Yates, 1968), 47n24

Bumstead, Henry, 16, *16*, 47, 51, 280
Bunyan, Paul, 219, 223
Burke, Billie, 269
Burke, Kenneth, 52
Burks, Robert, 63, 64n39, *151*, 203n20
Burr, Raymond, 37, 158, 223

Cady, Frank, 37, 259
Cagney, James, 155
California, 1, 2, 48, 56, 59n34, 98n18; *see also* Hitchcock, Alfred: gingerbread architecture, 239; Gothic, 239; Northern, 239; "spiriting" in, 278
Cameron, Ian, 71
Campbell's soup, 210
Capa, Robert, 166n35
Capri, blue grotto, 201
Carey, Macdonald, 50
Carroll, Leo G., 104, 196
Carroll, Madeleine, 231
Cartwright, Veronica, 75
Cassidy, Hopalong, *see* Boyd, William
Castle, Nick, 114
Castro, Fidel, *6*
Cavell, Stanley, 137, 232, 246, 250, 251–2
Central Intelligence Agency (CIA), 11, 12n6, 104, 127, 137
Centron Corporation for Young America Films, 253
Chabrol, Claude, 42, 43, 44, 228
Chambers, Haddon, 279n26
Chandler, Jeff, 134n8, 155
Chandler, Joan, *262*, 263
Chanel, Gabrielle Bonheur ("Coco"), 77
Chaplin, Charlie, as "Tramp," 152
Chapman, Lonny, 104
Château d'If (Marseilles), 155
Chatsworth (California), 197n16

Chekhov, Michael, 28n8, 169
Chicago, 143, 163; Lake Shore Drive, 163
Childhood and Society (Erik H. Erickson), 237–8
Chinese civilization, 221
Christie, Agatha, 52n27
Christie, June, 186
CinemaScope, 38n18
Cinémthèque Française, 126n2
Citizen Kane (Orson Welles, 1941), controversy about, 12
civil rights movement, 11
Claridge's (London), *see* Hitchcock, Alfred
Clift, Montgomery, 5
Cliquot Ginger Ale, 33
Clock, The (Vincente Minnelli, 1945), 60–1, 232
Coakley, John, *144*
Cohen, Paula Marantz, 52, 110–1
Cold War, 10, 97, 124ff, 224; 1954 armistice, 124
Coleman, Herbert, 62n38, 69n43, 109n24, 134n8, 142n20
Collier Constance, *262*
Collinge, Patricia, 53, 56n32, *57*, 108, 110, 122
Columbia Records, 84n9
Comer, Sam, 41
Communists, 221
Coney Island Steeplechase Park, 206
Connery, Sean, 188
Cool Hand Luke (Stuart Rosenberg, 1967), 130n6
Cooper, Gary, 91
Corber, Robert J., 124, 183n3, 197n15, 202
Corey, Wendell, 13, 37, 106
Cornwall, 211
Coronet Instructional Films, 253
Cotten, Joseph, 50
Count of Monte Cristo, The (Alexandre Dumas), 155
Covent Garden Choir, 84n9
Crawley, George A., 141n16

Crewes, Laura Hope, 255n9
Cronyn, Hume, 7, 54
Crowther, Bosley, 32
Cuban Missile Crisis (October 1962), 98
Cuban Revolution, 11
Cukor, George, 232
Cummings, Robert, 22, 26, 35, 197n16

Daddy Long Legs (Jean Negulesco, 1955), *159*
Daggett, Mrs. Charles Steward, 279
Daisy Miller (Henry James), references to, 73, 78, 107, 117, 118, 255
Dalí, Salvador, 168
Dall, John, *120*, 262
Daniell, Henry, 268
Dano, Royal, 68
Daphnis and Chloe (Maurice Ravel), 127n5
Darcy, Georgine, 36
Darcy, Virginia, *229*
Dassin, Jules, 232
Das Testament des Dr. Mabuse (Fritz Lang, 1933), 131n7
Date with Judy, A (Richard Thorpe, 1948), 186
Davenport, Harry, 91
Davenport, Havis, 37, 259
Davis, Andrew Jackson, 270
Davis, Mike, 20n1
Day, Doris, *16*, 84n9, *117*
Day, Laraine, 91, *95*
Death of a Salesman (Arthur Miller, February 10, 1949), 259n14
De Banzie, Brenda, 86
De Cuir, John, *28*
De Havilland, Olivia, 256n10
Delaware Turnpike (I-95), 192n12; *see also* Hitchcock, Alfred, locations
De Mille, Cecil B., 91
Demosthenes, 270

D'entre les morts (Pierre Boileau and Thomas Narcejac), 46, 64
DNA (Deoxyribosenucleic acid), 12
Dern, Bruce, *174*, 175, 272, 274n22, 275, 280, *280*
De Segonzac, Édouard, 89n13
Desire Under the Elms (Delbert Mann, 1958), *240*
De Tocqueville, Alexis, 34, 72, 131–2
Detour (Edgar G. Ulmer, 1945), 195n14
Devane, William, 121, 272
DeVol, Frank, 84n9
Deutelbaum, Marshall, 12
Dichter, Dr. Ernest, 261
Dick, Douglas, *262*, 263
Dickinson, Emily, 30
Disorderly Orderly, The (Frank Tashlin, 1964), 195n14
Dodsworth (William Wyler, 1936), 236n5
Donat, Robert, 105, 231
Donath, Ludwig, 97n15, 97, *101*, 126, 126n1
Doty, Alexander, 197n15, 255
Double Indemnity (Billy Wilder, 1944), 232
Douchet, Jean, 144, 183n3, 217
Douglas, Ann, 34, 124
Douglas, Kirk, 134n8
Douglas, Melvyn, 155
Douglas, Shirley, 192n10
Dubreuilh, Simone, 69
Du Maurier, Daphne, 211, 211n23, 256
Dunnock, Mildred, 67n42, 68
Dylan, Bob (Robert Zimmerman), 11

Earl, Harley, 194
Eastman Color, 70
Eco, Umberto, 234–5
Edouart, Farciot, *185*
Eisenhower, Dwight D., 125

Ekberg, Anita, 73n2
El Amor Brujo (Manuel de Falla), 127n5
Elephant Walk (William Dieterle, 1954), 204n21
Ellington, Edward Kennedy ("Duke"), 150n27
Elliott, Laura, 104, *198*, 199n17
Emery, John, 104, *169*
England, 1, 2, 5, 95, 104–5; as class society, 72n1
Erickson, C. O. ("Doc"), 41, 69n43
Erickson, Erik H., 237–8
Europe, 88, 88n12, 95, *95*, 96, 97, 118, 124, 137; European beauty, 161–2; classical teacher--student relationship, 131; European character types, 98n17; experience of, 89; European manners, 98n17; mother--son relationships in, 236; as Old World, 5, 106, 130, 131, 162; Soviet hegemony in, 124; European style, 143
Evans, Ray, 84n9, *85*, *117*
Evanson, Edith, 14, 104, *107*, 241
Evelyn, Judith, 37, 259
Ewen, Stuart, 134

Fairbanks, Douglas Jr., 155
Fancy Free (Leonard Bernstein and Jerome Robbins, April 18, 1944), 43, 43n22
Farrell, Tommy, 198
Faulkner, William, 224
Fax, Jesslyn, 37, 259
FDA (Federal Drug Administration), 11
Felmy, Hansjörg, 97n15, 98, 98n16, 126
Ferrer, José, 268
Ficino, Academy of, 129
Fiedler, Leslie A., 89, 227
Filene, Edward, 134

Firebird, The (Igor Stravinsky), 127n5
Fitzgerald, F. Scott, 218
Fonda, Henry, 61, 147, 150n26, *151*
Fontaine, Joan, 5, 13, 53n28, 231, *254*, 255n9, 256
Fool for Love (Sam Shepard, February 8, 1983), 244
Ford, Glenn, 134n8
Ford, John, 232
Ford, Wallace, 50
Forsythe, John, 67, *68*, 174
Fortune, 195
Fortnum & Mason (London), 11
Foster, Barry, 5
Fountain of Bakhchisarai, The (Boris Asafiev), 127n5
Fox sisters (Katie and Margaret), 271
France, 96; civilization, 221; high-class society in, 255n9
France, C. V., 230
Francesca da Rimini (Peter Ilyitch Tchaikowsky), 127, 127n5, *128*
Franey, Pierre, 190n7
Frankenheimer, John, 195n14
Frankenstein (James Whale, 1931), 24n7
Freedman, Jonathan, 168
Freud, Sigmund, 167, 252; dreamwork, 258
Fried, Debra, 93
Friendly Persuasion (William Wyler, 1956), *240*
Fuchs, Klaus, 125
Fuller, Samuel, *159*
Fulton, John, 29

Gabel, Martin, 189
Gable, Clark, 155
Gaffney ranch (Bodega Bay), 49n26
Garnelite lamp, 64n39
Garner, James, 268
Gavin, John, 144, *146*

Gayane (Aram Khatchaturian), 127n5
Gaye, Gregory, 236n5
Gélin, Daniel, 85
General Mills, 261; "Betty Crocker," 261
General Motors, 194: Cadillac, 194; Lincoln Continental, 194; Truck and Coach, 33
Generation of Vipers (Philip Wylie), 237–9
Genoa, 162
Genovese, Kitty, incident, 44n23
Gentleman Caller, The, see *Glass Menagerie, The*
Gentlemen Prefer Blondes (Howard Hawks, 1953), 204n21
German expressionism, 176n1
Germany, 97n15: history, 221; Junker class, 221; public works before World War II, 193–4; Reichsautobahnen, 193–4; *see also* Hitchcock, Alfred
Gibbons, Cedric, 51
Gillespie, A. Arnold, *185*
Gingold, Hermione, 269
Glass Menagerie, The (Tennessee Williams, March 1, 1945), 192n10
Glazer, Vaughan, 24, *26*
Goebbels, Joseph, 94
Goffman, Erving, 202n19
Goldfinger (Guy Hamilton, 1964), 195n14
Gomery, Douglas, 197–8
Gone with the Wind (Victor Fleming, 1939), 4
Goodbye Again (Anatole Litvak, 1961), 268
Goodman, Paul, 66, 82n7
Gordon, Michael, 268
Gorton, Assheton, 65n40
Gotti, Victor, 47
Gotti, Roland, 47
Graham, Fred, 104

Grand Prix (John Frankenheimer, 1966), 195n14
Grand Rapids Better Film Council, 263n17
Granger, Farley, *120*, 196, *262*
Grant, Cary (Archibald Leach), 119, 121, 122, 122n30, 133, 134n8, *139*, 155, 164, *165*, 219n29, 224, 231, 241, 250, 268, 269; residence at Plaza Hotel, 219n27; trademark scampishness, 133
Great Gatsby, The (F. Scott Fitzgerald), 218–9
Greeks: 270; male, 242
Green Mansions (Mel Ferrer, 1959), *240*
Griffies, Ethel, 49, 106
Griffin, Stephanie, 38n17
Growing Up Absurd (Paul Goodman), 82n7
Gwenn, Edmund, 68, 92

Halberstam, David, 124, 192
Hale, Jonathan, 120
Halton, Charles, 248
Hampshire (England), 71
Hamptons, The, 2
Hansel and Gretel, story of, 274
Hanson, Duane, 98
Hardwicke, Cedric, 13, 172, *262*
Hark, Ina Rae, 91–2, 255
Harper, Rand, 37, *259*
Harper's Bazaar, 163
Harris, Barbara, *174*, 175, 272, 274n22, 280
Harris, Julie, 192n10
Hartford (England), 71
Hastings, Henry, 24
Haworth, Ted, 205n22
Haye, Helen, 230, 231
Hayes, Helen, 239n7
Hayes, John Michael, 86, 157n30
Head, Edith, *16*, 77, 77n6, 156n29, *159*

Health: Your Posture (Centron Corp. for Young America Films, 1953), 253; reference to, 257
Hedren, 'Tippi,' 48, 73, 76, 78, 189, *196*, *229*
Hecht, Ben, 94, 170, 236n3
Heckroth, Hein, 127n5
Heller, Ben, 40n19
Helmond, Katharine, 277
Hemmeter, Thomas, 181
Henderson, Fletcher, 150n27
Hepburn, Katharine, 192n10
Hera, 242
Hereford (England), 71
Herrmann, Bernard, 84n9, 152n28; "Prelude" for *The Wrong Man*, 150; score for *North by Northwest*, 186n4
Highlands, Scottish, 53n29, 91
Highsmith, Patricia, 197n15
Hiroshima, 166n36
Hitchcock, Alfred (1899–1872), 1, 2, *99*, 100, *128*, 152n28, *226*
   actors, working with, 3, *99*, 106, 130, 189n6, 197n15, 204n21, 239n7, 256
   and air raids during World War II, 75, *76*
   American city in, 19
   and American marriage, 225ff
   as "Americophile," 1
   audience reaction to films of, 263n17
   and British expatriates, 5n3
   and California spiritualism, 278–9
   cameo in *Rear Window*, 172
   and Carole Lombard, 246, 246n8
   casting: *North by Northwest*, 269; *Psycho*, 204n21; *The Wrong Man*, 58n33
   Catholic Church, dramatization of, 272
   censorship of films: in Atlanta, 263n17; in Baltimore, 199n17; in Birmingham, 263n17; in Grand Rapids (Michigan), 263n17; in Hammond (Indiana), 263n17; in Massachusetts, 202n18; in Memphis, 263n17; in Milwaukee, 199n17; in Ohio, 199n17; in Ontario, 202n18; in Seattle, 263n17; in Toronto, 202n18; in Zurich, 263n17
   citizenship, 16, 155
   and classical art, 234
   as Cockney youth, 72
   comic version of final shot in *Rear Window*, 173n37
   and communism, 124
   critical of bourgeois sensibilities, 164
   and Ed Lauter, 279n26
   Edwardianism, 112
   and Ernest Lehman, 275n23
   as European filmmaker, 177
   favorite hotel in New York, 219
   favorite restaurant in New York, 219n28
   films: American content of, 5; American reference in, 4; American studio production of, 5; showing American life, 5–6
   film titles: *Birds, The* (1963), 6, 15, 48, 50, 73–81, *76*, *79–80*, 104, 106, 108, 118, 175, 207–17, 242–6: and animal rights activists, 75n4; *Blackmail* (1929), 230; *Dial M for Murder* (1953), 5; *Family Plot* (1976), 6, 118, 121, *174*, 175, 271–81, *280*, 283; *Foreign Correspondent* (1940), 4, 5, 22, 90–6, *95*, 97, 118, 227; *Frenzy* (1972), 5; *I Confess* (1953), 5; *Lady Vanishes, The* (1938), 230;

INDEX

Lifeboat (1944), 5, 6, 7, 7–10, 106, 118, 124, 125, 227, 242; *Lodger, The* (1927), 230; *Man Who Knew Too Much, The* (1956), 5–6, 16, *16*, 17, 81–90, *83*, 98n18, 114–8, 122, 125, 152n28, 157n30, 174, 178, 226, 233, 242, 277, 281–3; *Manxman, The* (1929), 48; *Marnie* (1964), 6, 14, 46, 104, *107*, 108, 111–3, *113*, 124, 158n32, 166n35, 171, 174, 188–96, *196*, 217, 228; *Mr. & Mrs. Smith* (1941), 225–6, 246–52, *249*; *North by Northwest* (1959), 6, 9n5, 12n6, 15, 19, 21, 29, 45, 46–7, 57, 58, 59, 59n34, 91, 104, 105n21, 108, 118, 124, 133–43, *142*, 179–88, 204n21, 219, 220, 224, 226, 231, 267, 268, 269, 280: opening sequence, 219n29; *Notorious* (1946), 5, 91, 108, 125, 163–7, *165*, 234–7, *235*, 244: alternate ending, 236n4, *238*, 266–7; *Paradine Case, The* (1947), 5; *Psycho* (1960), 6, 8n4, 15, 19, *20*, 46, 104, 108, 118, 121–2, 143–6, *146*, 195n14, 204n21, 217, 226, 237–41, *240*, 244, 281; *Rear Window* (1954), 5, 13, 14, 19, 36–45, 38n18, *40*, 104, 106, 108, 118, 123, 155–63, 157n30, 158n32, *159*, 165, 172, 222, 226, 241, 245, 252, 253, 254, 257–63, 259n14, 280; reflexivity in, 38, 38n17; *Rebecca* (1940), 4, 11, 22, 31, 219, 254–7, *254*, 256n10, 256n11; opening box office, 256n11; *Rich and Strange* (1931), 231; *Rope* (1948), 5, 13, 15, 36, 45, 104, *107*, 118, 119, *120*, 172, 218, 241, 262, 263–5, 263n17; *Saboteur* (1942), 5, 12, 15, 19, 20, 22–36, *26*, *28*, 30n12, 103, 106, 108, 118, 169, 171, 218, 219, 220; *Secret Agent* (1936), 103n20; *Shadow of a Doubt* (1943), 5, 15, 19, 36, 49, 50–7, 54n30, *57*, 107, 108, 110, 112, 123, 218, 226, 229–30; *Skin Game, The* (1931), 230, 251; *Spellbound* (1945), 5, 19, 28n8, 104, 106, 108, 118, 167–71, *169*, 218; *Strangers on a Train* (1951), 5, 19, 46, 104, 108, 118, 196–207, *198*, *205*, 233; *Suspicion* (1941), 231; *39 Steps, The* (1935), 31n13, 53, 91, 105, 231; *To Catch a Thief* (1955), 5, 67, *267*, 268; *Topaz* (1969), 5, *6*, 12n6, 19, 45–6, 124, 219; *Torn Curtain* (1966), 6, 14, 15, 97–103, *99*, *101*, 104, 118, 124–33, *128*, 136n9; *Trouble with Harry, The* (1955), 5, 14–15, 46, 66–70, *68*, 123, 174, 218, 225; *Under Capricorn* (1949), 5; *Vertigo* (1958), 6, 8n4, 13, 14, 22n5, 46, 47n24, 57, 64–6, 104, 106, 118, 122, 161, 165, 175, 220, 226, 241, 249: dolly-zoom shot, 66n41; *Wrong Man, The* (1956), 3, 3n1, 6, 19, 45, 57, 58, 61–4, *63*, 121, 124, 146–55, *147*, *151*, 152n28, 174, 218, 220, 251

and Filwite Productions, 83n8
and François Truffaut, 47n25, 66n41, 75, 126n4, 164n34, 168, 235n2, 241, 246, 261n16
growing up as city boy, 57, 71
and happy endings, 152
history, interest in, 64–5
and homosexuality, 121, 197n15

Hitchcock, Alfred (1899–1872) (cont.)
  and Jessie Royce Landis, 239n7, 268–9
  and Kathleen Nesbitt, 279n26
  and Laurence Olivier, 256n10
  and Leytonstone (London), 71, 237n6
  locations: Ambassador East Hotel (Chicago), 9n5, 142; Baie des Anges (Nice), 122; Bayswater (London), 87; Bickford's (Queens), 61, 218; Big Basin Redwood Forest, 22n5, 46; Bodega Bay, California, 48, 49n26, 74, 77, 78, 79, 81, 210, 211, 212, 213, 215, *216*, 244; Brocklebank, The (San Francisco), 46; Bronx (New York), 45; Brooklyn, 106; Brooklyn Navy Yard, 21, 220; Camden Town (London), *83*, 86; Casablanca-Marrakech bus, 114; Chicago, 141; C. I. T. Financial Building (New York), 140, 140n14, 180; Copenhagen, 97; Davidson's Pet Shop (San Francisco), 73, 244; Delaware Turnpike (Interstate 95), 192; E train (Eighth Avenue local, New York), 61, 148; East Berlin, 100, 126, 127; East Fifty-Third Street (New York), 61; Eighty-Eighth (Street) and Eighth (Avenue), New York, 14, 36; Empire Hotel (San Francisco), 46; England, 263; Ernie's (San Francisco), 46, 47; Fifth Avenue (New York), 61, 184, 219; Florida, 150; Fort Point (San Francisco), 46; George Washington Bridge (New York), 62, 220; Georgetown, 219; Germany, 99; Glen Cove (Long Island) Police Station, 135; Gold Coast (Chicago), 9, 9n5; Golden Gate Bridge (San Francisco), 46, 65, 65n40, 211n23, 220; Grace Cathedral (San Francisco), 273n20; Grand Army Plaza (New York), 184; Grand Central Station (New York), 58, 60, 106, 141n19; Greenwich Village (New York), 36, 39, 41, 41n21, 45; Gump's (250 Post Street, San Francisco), 218; Harlem (New York), 46; Hoover Dam (1935), 21, 220; Hotel de la Mamounia (Marrakech), 114, 233; Hotel Theresa (Seventh Avenue and 125th Street, New York), 6; Idaho, 248, 252; Indiana, 60; Jones Street (San Francisco), 46; Lake Placid (New York), 246; La Salle Street Station (Chicago), 60, 138; Leavenworth Street (San Francisco), 46; Leipzig (Germany), 97, 126, 127; Lombard Street (San Francisco), 46; London, 84, 92, 93, 94, 219; Victorian, pictured, 186; London Airport (now London Heathrow), 87, 87n11; Long Island, 45, 179; Los Angeles, 19, *20*, 20, 20n1, 36, 103; Madison Avenue (New York), 133, 179, 181, 182, 184, 219; at 60th Street, 182, 184; Manhattan: *see* Hitchcock, Alfred, locations, New York; Marrakech, 84, 85, 89, 89n13, 178; McKittrick Hotel (San Francisco), 46; Miami, 164; Middlebury (Virginia), 192; Mission

Dolores (San Francisco), 46, 47; Mission San Juan Bautista (San Juan Bautista), 46, 66; Monte Carlo, 219, 255; Mount Rushmore, 108, 136, 136n10, 138, 138n12, *139*, *142*, 143, 167, 220, 221, 222, 223; sequence, *144*, 220ff; Visitors' Center, 217; New York, 19, 21, 45, 57, 58, 62, 126, 181, 182, 183–4, 183n3, 255; Nice, 67; Nob Hill (San Francisco), 73; Oak Bar (Plaza Hotel, New York), 140, 140n15, 179, 186, 187; Old National Gallery (Berlin), 126–7; Palace of Fine Arts (San Francisco), 47; Palace of the Legion of Honor (San Francisco), 46, 47, 65; Palm Springs, 255; Philadelphia, 46, 189, 192; Phoenix, 19, *20* 46, 144, 145, 146; Plaza Hotel (New York), 58, 59, 135, 138, 141, 143, 179, 181, 184–6, 219; 59th Street entrance, 184; Podesta Baldocchi (San Francisco), 46; Queens (New York), 45, 58, 61; Rapid City (South Dakota), 142; Rio de Janeiro, 164; Roosevelt Avenue/Jackson Heights Station (Queens), 61, 148n24; Royal Albert Hall (London), 84, 116; San Fernando, 277n24; San Francisco, 46, 47, 48, 49n26, 57, 64, 54, 73, 78, *174*, 210, 244; San Juan Bautista: *see* Mission San Juan Bautista; Santa Rosa, California, 36, 50, 52, 54n30, 57, 110; Savoy Hotel (London), 87, 115, 219, 242, 282; Sierra Madre Cemetery, Sierra Madre, California, 277n25; Sixtieth Street (New York), 184; Statue of Liberty (New York), 21, *28*, 29, 171, 220; Stork Club (New York), 61, 148; Stowe, Vermont, 46; South Dakota, 125, 143; Sutter Street (San Francisco), 46; Top of the Mark (San Francisco), 65; Townsend Estate (Old Westbury, Long Island), 135, 138, 141, 141n16, 143; Triboro Bridge (New York), 141, 141n18; Twentieth Century Limited, 105n21, 141; Twin Peaks (San Francisco), 46; Union Square (San Francisco), 65; United Nations Secretariat (New York), 58, 59, 59n34, 135, 137, 141, 220; Vermont, 66, 67, 67n42, 69; Victor Moore Arcade (Queens), 61, 62; Virginia, 46, 189, 197; Washington, D.C., 192, 219, 219n26; West 52nd Street (New York), 161; West 178th Street (Bronx), 62, *63*; Westminster (London), 92

Los Angeles home, 3MacGuffin, 91, 166, 166n36

marriage, 231; bourgeois, 247; "Oedipal," 233, 236, 240; "substitute," 232ff

and modernity, 10, 50, 52, 152–4

mother, 110, 237n6

narrative strategies of, 102, 170–1

and 1920s, 124

and Norma Varden, 204n21

and picturing, 176–7

and police, 28n8

and Production Code, *165*

Hitchcock, Alfred (1899–1872) (cont.)
  and rear projection, 7, 8, *20*, 29, 29n9, 30n11, 32n14, *35*, 76n5, 94n14, 136n10, 141n19, 182, 184, *185*, 192n11, 194, 213
  and researchers, 61n35, 62n38, 148n23, 148n24, 149n25, *216*, 227n1
  Santa Cruz home, 64
  Sealyham terriors of, 73
  and self-reference, 103n20, 275
  and Selznick, 30n12, 31, 103, 225, *226*
  serving tea on set, 178, 178n2
  shoe fetish, 157n31
  and social class, 8, 10–11, 59, 64, 71, 105n21, 143
  and sound recording, 41n21
  and special effects, 76n5, *79*, 94n14, 108n23, 136n10, 142n41, 166n35, 199n17
  Surrey home, 2, 71
  suspense and, 248
  and 'Tippi' Hedren, 189n6
  tones down mother character in *Notorious*, 236n3
  and the train arrival in *Shadow of a Doubt*, 51
  use of Chevrolet, 178
  use of hand-held camera, 127n5
  and villainy, 118–22
  and Vivien Leigh, 256n10
  and Walter Wanger, 103
  women characters, 107ff, 110
  and *The Wrong Man*, 151
  yeoman life reflected in films of, 171
Hitchcock, Alma Reville (1899–1982), 1, 2, 6, 228, 239n7
Hitchcock, Patricia (b. 1928), 1, 2, 108, 203
Hitler, Adolf, 5n3
Hitler--Stalin Pact, 5n3
Hodiak, John, 6, 7, 8

Hofstadter, Richard, 140
Holden, William, 134n8
Holiday (George Cukor, 1938), 227
Holiday Inn, 193n13
Holland, 96
Holliday, Judy, 58n33
Hollywood: 5n3, 155; actresses and makeup in, 236n4; British expatriates in, 5; British government representation in, 227n1; casting competition for *Rebecca* in, 256n10; cinema and bravado, 155–6; classics, 227; and European mother-son relationships, 236; marriage in cinema of, 227; productions, 41; and the small town, 51
Hollywood 10, 1947 trial of, 12, 33, 33n15
Honor of the Family, The (Emile Fabre, December 25, 1926), 268
House of Dr. Edwardes, The (Francis Beeding), 167
Howard Johnson's, 190, 190n7, 191, 192, 193, 194, 195
Howard Winters Associates (Coral Gables, Florida), 150n26
Howitt, Barbara, 84n9
Hudson River, 141
Hudson River School, 55
Hudson, Rock, 134n8
Hull, Henry, 6, 7, 8
Hunter, Evan, 73n2
Hurricane, The (John Ford, 1937), 8
Hutchinson, Josephine, 231

In a Lonely Place (Nicholas Ray, 1950), 232
Indian civilization, 221
Indian Wells Beach, Amagansett, 3

Indianapolis, Indiana, 86
Innocents Abroad, The (Mark Twain), 95, 96, 162, 177–8
Interstate highway system, 20, 31, 189, 192; Pennsylvania Interstate, 189
Iron Curtain, the, 97, 130
Italy, public works before World War II, 193–4; renaissance, 221
"It's a Most Unusual Day" (Harold Adamson and Jimmy McHugh), 186
Ittleson, Henry, 140n14
"I've Grown Accustomed to Her Face" (Frederick Loewe and Alan Jay Lerner), 186n4

Jackson, Andrew, 140, 147
Jackson Heights (Queens, N.Y.), 148; *see also* Hitchcock, Alfred, locations
Jacobite uprising (1745), 53n29
James, Henry, 179
Japanese history, 221; Samurai class, 22
Jaws (Steven Spielberg, 1975), 12
Jefferson, Thomas, 222
Jewish civilization, 221
Job (Book of), reference to, 149
Johnson, James P., 150n27
Johnson, Joseph MacMillan ("Mac"), *40*, 41
Jolly Green Giant, 219
Jones, Henry, 13

Kagan, Vladimir, 141n17
Karloff, Boris, 5n3
Kedrova, Lila, 99, *99*, 100
Kelly, Grace, 13, 37, 108, 156, 157, *159*, 268, 269
Kendall, Henry, 231
Kennedy, Jacqueline (Bouvier), 219n26
Kennedy, John Fitzgerald (JFK), assassination of, 11–12, 191n8; presidency of, 100

Kennedy, Robert Francis ("Bobby"), assassination of, 12
Kerouac, Jack, 195–6
Kieling, Wolfgang, 14, 98, 126, 126n2
King, Martin Luther, assassination of, 12
King of Comedy, The (Martin Scorsese, 1983), 158n32
Kings Row (Sam Wood, 1942), 51
K-Mart, 214
Knight, Arthur, 211n23
Kodak Tri-X film stock, 64n39
Konstantin, Leopoldine, 234, *235*, *238*, 266n19
Korean War, 11
Koster, Henry, 268
Kraepelin, Emil, 265–6
Krohn, Bill, 29, 86, 109, 110, 114, 115, 117, 125–6, 152n28, 157n30, 166n35, 203, 205n22, 236n4, 247, 274n22
Kruger, Alma, 34, 219
Kyvig, David, 203n20

La Ciotat (France), 51
La Dolce Vita (Federico Fellini, 1961), 73n2
Lady Eve, The (Preston Sturges, 1941), 251
Ladies Man, The (Jerry Lewis, 1962), 41n20
La Gitana (Hermann Schmidt and Daniel Auber), 127n5
Lancaster, Burt, 155
Land, Hilary, 260
Landau, Martin, 121
Landis, Jessie Royce, 239n7, *267*, 268–9
Lane, Priscilla, 24, *35*, 108
Lang, Doris, 179
Lange, Jessica, 192n10
Lansing, Joy, 38n17

L'arrivé d'un train en gare de La Ciotat (Louis and Auguste Lumiere, c. 1895), 51
La Samaritaine (Paris), 214
Last Laugh, The [*Der Letzte Mann*] (Fritz Lang, 1924), 42
Latham, Louise, 111, *113*
Launder, John, 171
Laurie, John, 231
Lauter, Ed, 273, 279n26
Lawrence, D(avid) H(erbert) Richards, 72, 76
Lawrence, Gertrude, 192n10
Lee, Canada, 7, 8
Lee, Rowland V., 197n16
Legend (Ridley Scott, 1985), 65n40
Lehman, David, 12
Lehman, Ernest, 139n13, 179, 275n23, 278, 280
Leigh, Janet, 108, 143, *146*, 240
Leigh, Vivien, 256n10
Leighton, Sophie, 261
Lejeune, C. A., 176n1
Lennen, Mrs. Robert A., 34
Lerner, Max, 34, 81–2, 208, 211–2, 220–1
LeRoy, Mervyn, 232
Levitt, Helen, 40n19
Lewis, Jerry, 41n20, 158n32
Lewis, Meriwether, 23
Libération, 69
Life magazine, 32–4
Lincoln, Abraham, 222
Litvak, Anatole, 268
Livingston, Jay, 84n9, *85*, *117*
Lloyd, Norman, 29, 171
Lockheed Aircraft Corporation, 33n16
Lockwood, Margaret, 178n2, 230
Lombard, Carole, 246, 246n8, 247, *249*, 250; death of, 12
London, 96, 115, 214; police, 116
London Symphony Orchestra, 84n9
London Times, The, 11

Long Island, 4; Amityville, 59; Babylon, 59; Expressway, 58–9; Garden City, 59; Great Neck, 59; Hamptons, the, 59; Hempstead, 59; Levittown, 59; parkway system, 59; Old Westbury, 59; Patchogue, 59; Roslyn, 59
Longden, John, 230
Lorne, Marion, 121, 204, 269
Lorre, Peter Jr., 127n3
Los Angeles, 3, 4, 31, 279n26: Santa Monica Boulevard, and oil production, 33; Vermont Avenue, 33; Wilshire Boulevard, 33; *see also* Hitchcock, Alfred
Los Angeles County Court, 16
Louise, Anita, 256n10
Love Affair (Leo McCarey, 1939), 227
Love and Death in the American Novel (Leslie A. Fiedler), 227
Ludwig II (of Bavaria), 201
Lukas, Scott, 206
Lupino, Ida, 197n16

Macbeth (William Shakespeare), reference to, 237
MacGinnis, Niall, 16
Macgowan, Kenneth, 6
MacGuffin, *see* Hitchcock, Alfred
MacLaine, Shirley, 67
Macwilliams, Glen, 8
Magnificent Ambersons, The (Orson Welles, 1942), 51
Make Way for Tomorrow (Leo McCarey, 1937), 61n37
"Man of the Crowd, The" (Edgar Allan Poe), 42
March of Time, 34
Mark Cross, 258
Marseilles, 46, 65
Marshall, Herbert, 91

INDEX

Marshall Plan (European Recovery Program [ERP]), 125
Martin, Dean, 134n8
Marx, Karl, 123
Mason, James, 118, *139*, 231; and Yorkshire burr, 118
Maté, Rudolph, 61
Mathers, Jerry, 66
Matter of Life and Death, A (Stairway to Heaven) (Michael Powell and Emeric Pressburger, 1946), 52
May, Elaine Tyler, 157
May, Lary, 65
McCrea, Joel, 90, *95*, 134n8
McDonald's, 191
McElhaney, Joe, 111
McGilligan, Patrick, 1, 5n3, 132, 228
McGovern, John, 48, 207
McHugh, Jimmy, 186
McKelvey, Frank, 141n17
McWilliams, Carey, 20n1, 33, 278
Meet Me in St. Louis (Vincente Minnelli, 1944), 51, 227
Mein Kampf (Adolf Hitler), 30n12
Melton Mowbray pork pies, 11
Meredith, Burgess, 3n1
Merton, Robert K., 196
Metro-Goldwyn-Mayer (MGM), 120n29, 134n8; Properties Department, 141n17; and rear projection, *185*; Stage 27 and Mount Rushmore sequence, 136n10, *144*
Middle Ages, 221
Miles, Bernard, 86
Miles, Vera, 148
Milland, Ray, 134n8
Miller, Arthur, 259n14
Miller, Jeffrey, shot at Kent State University, 12
Milliken, Carl Jr., 62n38
Millington, Richard, 137, 138n12
Mills, Mort, 104

Minnelli, Vincente, 60, *85*, 232
Miss Marple, *see* Christie, Agatha
Mix, Tom, 155
Moby Dick (Herman Melville), 72
Modern Times (Charlie Chaplin, 1936), 152
Modleski, Tania, 243–4
Mojave National Preserve, 20
Mondrian, Piet, 220
Monroe, Marilyn (Norma Jean Baker), death of, 12
Montgomery, Robert, 246, 247, *249*, 250
Moore, Brian, 100
Moore, Victor, 61n37
Moral, Tony Lee, 189n6
Mormon: Book of, 277n25; funeral, 277n25
Morocco, 98n18; French-controlled, 88n12, 89; Glaoui of, 89, 89n13
Morris, Roland, 198
Moselle wine, 98n17
Mother's Day, *see* Wylie, Philip
Mowbray, Alan, 90
Mozart, Wolfgang Amadeus, 272
Mr. Smith Goes to Washington (Frank Capra, 1939), reference to, 87
Murrow, Edward R., *95*
Music Corporation of America (MCA), 83n8
My Fair Lady (Frederick Loewe and Alan Jay Lerner, March 15, 1956), 186n4
My Foolish Heart (Mark Robson, 1949), 268
My Man Godfrey (Gregory LaCava, 1936), 27
My Man Godfrey (Henry Koster, 1957), 268

Naked Spur, The (Anthony Mann, 1953), 119n28
Narcejac, Thomas, 46
National Organization of Women (NOW), 12

INDEX

Natwick, Mildred, 68
Naugahyde, 190
Nazism, *95*, 127, 164, 165, 166n36, 266n19
Negulesco, Jean, *159*
Nesbitt, Cathleen, 272, 279n26
New England, 69n43
Newman, Paul, 14, 97, *101*, 126, *128*, 130, 130n6, 132, 133
New Mexico, 166n36
New York, 1, 2, 44, 44n23, 45, 62n38, 97n15, 115, 143, 150n27, 239n7, 256n11, 261; addresses in: East Eighty-Sixth Street, 2; Kew Gardens (Queens), 44n23; New Yorkers, 60, 184; in *Pickup on South Street*, 158n32; Upper East Side, 184; West Fiftieth Street and Twelfth Avenue, 1
New York Times, 136, 138
New York World Telegram, 180
Nietzsche, Friedrich Wilhelm, 172
Night and the City (Jules Dassin, 1950), 232
"Nighthawks" (Edward Hopper), 61
Nixon, Richard Milhouse, 125; in China, 12; resignation of, 12
Nobel Prize, 224
Norway, 166n36
Novak, Kim, 108
Nugent, Frank, 231
Nye, David, 203

O'Connor, Frank D., 149n25
Odets, Clifford, 236n4
Oedipal relations, 232ff, 240; *see also* Hitchcock, Alfred, marriage
Olivier, Laurence, 13, 255, 256
Olsen, Christopher, *16*, *85*
Ondra, Anny, 230
On the Beach (Stanley Kramer, 1959), *240*

Opera Omnia of St. Bonaventure, 228
Our Town (Thornton Wilder, February 4, 1938), 50, 55
Ouspenskaya, Maria, 236n5

Pacific Ocean, 58
Paglia, Camille, 77, 210, 244
Paley Park (New York), 61
Palm Beach, 2
Palmer, Bertha, 163
Palmer, Betsy, 268
Palmer, John, *see House of Dr. Edwardes, The*
Palmer, John F., 206
Palmer, Potter, 9n5, 163; Gold Coast, 163
Panaieff, Michel, 127n5
Paramount, *16*, 38n18, 47, 67n42, 122n30; Paris office, 89n13; Stage 18, *40*, 41; triple-head projector, *185*
Paris, 46, 65, 96, 115, 161, 214
Parke-Bernet Galleries (New York), 142n20
Parker, Dorothy, 24n6
Pasadena: 279, 279n27; Playhouse, 255n9
Pearl Harbor (Honolulu), attack on, 30n12, 32
Peck, Gregory, 5, 134n8, 168
Pennsylvania Station (New York), 60
Pentagon, the, 11
"People, Yes, The" (Carl Sandburg), 132
Pépin, Jacques, 190n7
Perkins, Anthony, 239, *240*, 241, 268
Perkins, Oswald, 240
Perkins, V(ictor) F., 71
Perret, Nellie, 88n12
Perry, George, 11
Philadelphia, 192n12
Philadelphia Story, The (George Cukor, 1940), 232

Phipps Estate house (Old Westbury, Long Island), 141n16
Pickup on South Street (Samuel Fuller, 1953), 158n32, *159*
Pilbeam, Nova, 256n10
Pinocchio (Hamilton Luske and Ben Sharpsteen, 1940), animated camera movement in, 12
Piper, Frederick, 105
Playboy Club, 11
Pleshette, Suzanne, 48, 75
Powell, William, 27, 155
Priestley, J.B., 267
Printemps (Paris), 214
Production Code, end of, 12, *165*
Prudential Insurance Company, 62n38
Pulitzer Prize for Drama, 259n14
Pullman Company, 105n21
Pursuits of Happiness (Stanley Cavell), 251–2

Quayle, Anthony, 149n25
"Que Sera, Sera (What Will Be, Will Be)" (Jay Livingston and Ray Evans), *16*, 84, 84n9, *85*, 114, 116, *117*
Queen Mary, 1, 2
Quiet Man, The (John Ford, 1950), 232

Radio City Music Hall (New York), 31, 32n14, 256n11
Rains, Claude, 164, 164n34, 234, 235n2, *235*, *238*
RKO (Radio-Keith-Orpheum), 166n36, 236n4, 247
Ramadan, 89n13
Random Harvest (Mervyn LeRoy, 1942), 204n21, 232
Raubicheck, Walter, 109n24
Ray, Nicholas, *85*, 232
Raymond, Gene, 248

rear projection, *see* Hitchcock, Alfred
Rebecca (Daphne du Maurier), 4, 256n11, 257n12
Rebel Without a Cause (Nicholas Ray, 1955), 82
Redgrave, Michael, 230
Red Line 7000 (Howard Hawks, 1965), 195n14
Reed, Ralph, 187
Register, Woody, 200
Rheims, 235
Richard the Lionheart, 117n27
Richard III (William Shakespeare, December 9, 1953), 268
Ritter, Thelma, 37, 158, 158n32, *159*, 241
Rivas, Carlos, 6
Road films, 195n14
Road to Wigan Pier, The (George Orwell), 72n1
Roar Like a Dove (Lesley Storm, May 21, 1964), 268
Robbins, Jerome, 43n22
Robbins, Richard, 58n33, 121
Robert F. Kennedy Bridge (New York), 141, 141n18; *see also* Hitchcock, Alfred, locations, Triboro Bridge
Robertson, Peggy, 76n5, 97n15, *229*
Robinson, Edward G., 155
Robson, Mark, 268
Rohmer, Eric (Maurice Scherer), 228
Roman, Ruth, 108, 196
Roman times, 221; *see also* Capri
Romantic imagination, 57
Romm, May, 167
Roosevelt, Franklin Delano (FDR), 11
Roosevelt, Theodore ("Teddy"), 222
Ross, Alex, 150n27
Rothman, William, 56, 118–9
Rourke, Constance, 34
Ruggles, Charles, 268

Russell, Marjorie Baron, 227n1
Russia, exploding atomic device, 124

Sabrina (Billy Wilder, 1954), 232
Saint, Eva Marie, 108, 109n24, 121, 122, *139*, 139n13, 224, 269
Sandburg, Carl, 60, 218
Sanders, George, 93
Sanger, Margaret, 265
Santa Cruz Island, 79
Saratoga Springs, 2
Saunders, Hilary St. George, *see House of Dr. Edwardes, The*
Schama, Simon, 24
Scheler, Max, 9
Schivelbusch, Wolfgang, 193–4, 214–5
Schloss Linderhof, 201
Schunzel, Reinhold, *235*, 266n19
Scotland Yard (London Metropolitan Police Service), 84, 87
Scott, Randolph, 155
Scott, Ridley, 65n40
Scott, Sir Walter, 53n29
Seaton, George, 268
Secret Garden, The (Fred McLeod Wilcox, 1949), 204n21
Selfridge's (London), 214
Selznick, David O., 1, 4, 30n12, 103, 167, 225, *226*, 256n11
Selznick International, 4, 6
Sersen, Fred, 8
Seven Year Itch, The (Billy Wilder, 1955), 61n37
Seymour, Harry, 186
Shaker: Christianity, 277; English, 270
Shane (George Stevens, 1953), 215n24
Shannon Center (Iowa), 212
Shaw, Janet, 51
Shayne, Konstantin, 106
Shayne, Robert, 187
Shea's Buffalo (Buffalo, N.Y.), 17
Shepard, Sam, 244

Showalter, Elaine, 265–6
Siegel, Sol, 134n8
Simmel, Georg, 44, 270–1
Sinatra, Frank, 134n8
Slater, Philip, 242–3
Slezak, Walter, 7
Smith, H. Allen, 219n28
Smith, Jack Martin, 51
Smith, Ken, 254
sodium vapor (matte) process, 76n5
Sonoma County: Special Deputy Sheriff identification, 56; wine country, 50
Sound of Music, The (Robert Wise, 1965), 204n21
Soviet power base, 98, 125; *see also* Russia
Sportsmen's Lodge Hotel (Hollywood), *229*
Spoto, Donald, 2, 100, 113, 156n29, 176n1, 178n2, 237n6
Sputnik, 11
S. S. Normandie, 21
St. Francis, 205
St. Regis Hotel (New York), 219
Stafford, Frederick, 219
Stage Fright (1950), 5
"Star-Spangled Banner, The" (John Stafford Smith, Francis Scott Key), 94
"Star Trek" (1966), 12
Staten Island, 263n17
Steinbeck, John, 6
Sterritt, David, 150
Stewart, James, 13, 83, *83*, 83n8, *107*, 119, 119n28, *120*, 121, 122, 134n8, 156, 241, *262*; sharing in film profits, 12; 37
"Storm Clouds" Cantata (Arthur Benjamin, D. B. Wyndham-Lewis), 84n9, 116, 116n26
Stormy Weather (Tom Walls, 1935), 204n21
Strack, Gunther, 98
Stranger, The (Orson Welles, 1946), 51

Studies in Classic American Literature (D. H. Lawrence), 22
Sturges, Preston, 251
Styrofoam, 109n24
Sullavan, Margaret, 256n10
Sullivan, Francis L., 232
Sullivan, Jack, 150
"Summer Night on the River" (Frederick Delius), 26
Surrey, 2
Suspicion (1941), 5
Sweeney, Bob, 104
Sweeney, Gael, 119
Swerling, Jo, 6
Swing Time (George Stevens, 1936), 61n37

Tandy, Jessica, 49, 78, 192n10
Tashlin, Frank, 195n14
Taylor, Laurette, 192n10
Taylor, Rod, 48, 73
Tearle, Godfrey, 231
technicolor, 69; sodium process D-7 camera, 76n5
telephone, and modernity, 215n25
Tempest, The (William Shakespeare), 73, 173, 225
They Live by Night (Nicholas Ray, 1948), 195n14
Thoreau, Henry David, 24, 25–6, 77, 251–2
Three Coins in the Fountain (Jean Negulesco, 1954), 204n21
Tierney, Lawrence, 155
Tillie's Punctured Romance (Mack Sennett, 1914), 227
Tilyou, George, 206
To Kill a Mockingbird (Robert Mulligan, 1962), 51
Todd, Richard, 5
Todt, Fritz, 193–4
Toles, George, 197
"Tony" (Antoinette Perry) Award, 259n14
Toumanova, Tamara, *128*
Trafic (Jacques Tati), 195n14

Travers, Henry, 53
Trevi Fountain (Rome), 73n2
Trow, George W. S., 161n33
Truex, Philip, *68*
Truman, Harry S., 125
Truman, Ralph, 87
Tunnel of Love, 199, 200, 201, 203, 206
Twain, Mark (Samuel Langhorne Clemens), 162, 177
Twentieth Century-Fox, 6, 38n18; programming for television, 12
"21" (21 West 52 St., New York), 2, 219, 219n28
Two for the Road (Stanley Donen, 1967), 195n14

Union Station (Rudolph Maté, 1950), 61
Union Station (Los Angeles), 61
United Kingdom, 155: actors available in, 106; and social class, 4
United Nations, 6
United States of America, 99; *see also* America
UNIVAC computer, 11
Universal Studios, 32N14, 51, 76n5, 79; hair stylist, *229*
University of Buffalo, 271
U.S. Army, 33n16, 205n22
U.S. Department of the Interior, 21n3

Valéry, Paul, 54
Vancouver, 65n40
Varden, Norma, 108, 204, 204n21, *205*
Victorian: girl, 263; morality, 10, 201, 251; women, 264; *see also* London
videocassette recorder, 12
Vidich, Arthur, 54
Vienna, 167
Viertel, Peter, 22n4
Vietnam War, 11
VistaVision, 12, 38n18, 41n20, 69

Vitruvius (Marcus Vitruvius Pollio), 234
Vogue, 161

Wagner, Richard, 201
Walker, Robert, 120n29, 196, 197n15, 199n17, 203, *205*
Walkowitz, Judith, 265
Wal-Mart, 214
Walpurgis Nights (Charles Hunno), 127n5
Walt Disney Studio, 76n5
Wanger, Walter, 4, 94, 103
Ward, Charles B., 206
Warner Bros., 263n17; Research Department, 62n38
Washington, D.C., 2, 46, 196
Washington, George, 222
Wasserman, Lew, 83n8
Watergate (Hotel) break-in, 12
Waterloo Bridge (Mervyn LeRoy, 1940), 204n21
Waters, Ethel, 150n27
Watson, David, 53n29
Watson, Lucile, 255n9
Watson, Wylie, 105
Waverley (Sir Walter Scott), 53n29
Wayne, John, 134n8, 155
Weinstein, Sheri, 271
Weinstock, Jeffrey, 269
West, Vera, 34
West Chester (Pennsylvania), 192n11
West Side Story (Leonard Bernstein and Stephen Sondheim, September 26, 1957), 186n4
Wexman, Virginia Wright, 252–3
White Christmas (Michael Curtiz, 1954), 38n18
Whitlock, Albert, 79
Whitman, Walt, 30
Who Are the People of America? (Coronet Instructional Films, 1953), 253
Widmark, Richard, 158n32
Wieth, Mogens, 90

Wilcox, Frank, 186
Wilder, Billy, 232
Wilder, Thornton, 55n31
Williams, John, 274
Williams, William Carlos, 88–9
Wilson, Stanley, 127n5
Winchell, Walter, 58n33
Winchester '73 (Anthony Mann, 1950), 12
Windmill Cottage, Amagansett, 2–3, 3n1
Windsor Castle, 90
Winesburg, Ohio (Sherwood Anderson), 55
Winston, Archer, 53
Winston, Irene, 257
Winter's Tale, The (William Shakespeare, January 15, 1946), 268
Winters, Shelley, 197n16
Withers, Googie, 232
Witherspoon, Cora, 255n9
Witness for the Prosecution (Billy Wilder, 1957), 204n21
Wonacott, Edna May, 53n29, 107, 107n22
Wood, Robin, 131, 136n9, 183n3, 197n15, 213, 258, 259n15
Woodward, Joanne, 192n10
Wordsworth, Richard, *83*
World Film News, 176n1
World War I, 53, 205n22
World War II, 11, 51, 88, 88n12, 95
Wright, Frank Lloyd, 142, *142*
Wright, Teresa, 53, 53n28, 108, 121
Written on the Wind (Douglas Sirk, 1956), 195n14
Wyler, William, 236n5
Wylie, Philip, 237–9

Yablon, Nick, 251
Young, Carleton, 186
Young, Loretta, 256n10
Yuricich, Matthew, *142*, 142n41

Žižek, Slavoj, 123